Discoveries in Academic Writing

Barbara Harris Leonhard
University of Missouri–Columbia

Harcourt Brace College Publishers

Fort Worth   Philadelphia   San Diego   New York   Orlando   Austin   San Antonio
Toronto   Montreal   London   Sydney   Tokyo

Discoveries in Academic Writing

Barbara Harris Leonhard

University of Missouri–Columbia

ISBN: 0-15-507255-2

Library of Congress Catalog Card Number: 98-87749

Address for Orders: Harcourt Brace, 6277 Sea Harbor Drive, Orlando, FL 32887-6777, 1-800-782-4479

Address for Editorial Correspondence: Harcourt Brace College Publishers, ESL Editor, 301 Commerce Street, Suite 3700, Fort Worth, TX 76102

Web site address: http://www.hbcollege.com

Printed in the United States of America

8 9 0 1 2 3 4 5 6 7   066   9 8 7 6 5 4 3 2 1

Harcourt Brace & Company

Copyright and Acknowledgments

Student Essays

Marina Babenko
"The Ability to Concentrate"
"A Peer Review of 'Self-Respect'"

Kelly Boggs
"Independence in American Culture"

Abdullah Esmaeil
"Culture's Influence"

Licett Galietta
"Diligence"
"Western Influence on American Culture"
"Cultural Differences Between the U.S. and Venezuela"
"Harmful Inventions"

Yungjing Hsieh
"The House of Life"
"The Causes of the Divorce Rate in the U.S."

Jung Hee Kang
"Catch the Three Tigers"

Jeong-Seog Lee
"Benefits of TV"
"Inventions That Have Revolutionized Our Lives"

Aimée E.H. Leonhard
"The Differences Between Irish Peasant Society and
   American Society"
"A Brief History of Greek Temple Architecture"
"The European-Americans' Perceptions of the Native
American Indians and Africans"
"The Lindisfarne Gospels: A Brief Look at Their History
   and Decoration"

Kaisen Liu
"Peer Review of 'Self-Respect'"

Pattie J. Malone
"Burnout in the Healthcare Sector"
"Distillation: Simple and Fractional"

Danielle Pisani Freitas
"Statement of Purpose for the Philosophy Department"

Nancy Price
"Public Opinion and Voting Behavior in the U.S."

Milena Stanislovova
"My Ideal Husband"

Vasna Wilson
"Good Students"
"My Benchmark into Womanhood"
"The Thai Spirit"

Yunhai Yang
"One Benefit of Travel"

Photo Credits

AP/Wide World Photos, p. 140

Vasna Wilson, p. 146

Vasna Wilson, p. 147

AP/Wide World Photos, pps. 179 and 182

UPI/Corbis-Bettmann, p. 182

Miscellaneous Contributions

Susie Sullivan-Tuncan, instructor
Intensive English Program, University of Missouri–Columbia
"Suggested Time Management for the Writing Process"

Dedication

To my father, the Reverend Earle B. Harris Jr.,
and my mother, Barbara Montgomery Harris,
who fostered my love for writing

Preface

Discoveries in Academic Writing is a composition and grammar book designed for high-intermediate to advanced nonnative speakers at the pre-freshman composition level who are studying in intensive English programs or enrolled in non-credit composition courses at a college or university in the U.S. or Canada. Nonnative speakers in a high school level advanced ESL college-preparatory English class would also benefit from this book.

This book is designed for use in a 16-week semester for a class that meets five hours a week. On the average, each chapter will take eight to twelve hours to complete. For classes that meet only three hours a week, have students do the grammar review exercises on their own. If any students need to check their work, post the answers the day the work is due or meet with students individually if they have questions on grammar. In this way, the in-class work, Discovery exercises, and other writing assignments will still focus on sentence organization.

The assignments in this book are designed to allow for more flexible time management of the material by the student. Depending on the writing level of each class, some assignments may be more appropriate than others. It is important, therefore, that students have the flexibility to move on to the next chapter before actually completing an exercise from the previous chapter. In fact, due to the nature of the writing process, students will be revising drafts for an assignment in one chapter while working on new skills in the next chapter. Because writing is a dynamic process that cannot be stopped at the close of a chapter, students will continue to develop support for and refine their writing as they learn new skills.

Because the target audience is nonnative speakers, the book addresses the requirements for English academic writing from a cultural perspective. It is generally agreed that cultures vary with respect to rhetorical styles. Therefore, it cannot be assumed that all nonnative speakers will understand that there are different expectations and requirements regarding academic writing in Western culture. This book is designed to prepare nonnative speakers to develop and organize effective English academic essays. The rhetorical patterns that are covered include exemplification, classification, narration, process, comparison/contrast, and cause/effect. The book contains the following topics.

Critical-Thinking Skills

The foundation of this book is the use of critical-thinking skills. These skills are introduced in Chapter 2 to elicit student participation and collaboration in engaging activities that require thought and creativity. The concept of critical thinking is then reinforced throughout the book as students continue to refine their academic writing.

The Process and Product Approach

On the rhetorical level, the book is both process- and product-oriented. The process of writing is defined in Chapter 2 and utilized throughout the book. In Chapters 2 through 8, in fact, many of the Discovery exercises are designed to guide students through the writing process, starting with understanding the terms and the design of assignments and continuing with the major processes of writing: brainstorming, organizing, writing, peer-reviewing, revising, and proofreading/editing. Another skill crucial in the writing process is learning how to address the audience appropriately. Chapter 1 provides guidelines on choosing the correct level of diction and point of view. Students also learn how to use inclusive language and an objective tone.

The Peer Review Process

The peer review process is first addressed in Chapter 2 and is then utilized in many of the later assignments. There are 15 Peer Review Forms (see Appendix D), each tailored to the specific rhetorical method or task assigned, such as revision. The peer review activities represent an important component of academic writing for several reasons. First, the peer review process serves as a review of the requirements for each writing task. Second, it enables students to use such critical-thinking skills as analysis, problem solving, and evaluation. By peer-reviewing other students' work in relation to the models in the book and comments from the instructor, students gain more confidence in their ability to identify and solve problems with content and organization. As a result, they will be able to take a more objective approach to the revision of their own work.

In addition, peer review sessions facilitate meaningful discussions during which students can resolve differences of opinion. Those students new to the peer review process can refer to "Guidelines for Peer Review" and "Strategies for Clarification" to help them better understand and benefit from peer review activities. The peer review process is further supported with examples of first drafts, peer review comments, and revisions to illustrate the steps involved in the process of writing.

As students progress through each chapter, they study and discuss academic "products" (paragraph and essay models in the rhetorical patterns). Because nonnative speakers need to know what will be expected of them in English academic writing assignments, several chapters provide original academic papers written by native and nonnative speakers of English at the undergraduate and graduate levels. These models have been written for a variety of disciplines, including history, art, meteorology, health science, and psychology. The topics of these papers were selected to promote interesting class discussions on aspects of Western culture and cultural differences.

Most of the model compositions and essays included in this book were "A" and "B" papers. However, other models have been included to show the difference in writing abilities at this level of academic writing. In some cases, students are asked to compare or contrast essays written on the same topic to determine which essay fulfills the assignment task. The models range in length (from paragraphs to essays), and they become progressively more challenging with each chapter. Although students are taught the classic five-paragraph essay, they see that their academic papers do not have to be limited to that model. By studying these models, students not only see what actual academic essays look like, but also become more motivated as writers to compose "A" papers.

Sentence Organization

The grammar related to the rhetorical methods is also a major component of each chapter. Because the sections on sentence organization build in complexity as the book progresses, it is necessary to follow the chapters in the order presented. Early on, the book addresses surface-level problems with agreement, pronoun use, and parallelism, but the major objective is to teach students how sentence organization relates to coherence. Lack of (or inadequate) control of basic sentence organization and sequencing will affect the content of a paper. Therefore, this book systematically covers all the sentence types, problems with sentence structure (run-on sentences and sentence fragments), and rhetorical structures of exemplification, comparison/contrast, cause/effect, and definition. Students are also taught to frame essays with thesis and topic sentence patterns for each rhetorical pattern. Moreover, because control of tenses is a challenge for nonnative speakers at this level, several Discovery exercises focus on tenses, time-shifting, and using time clauses. Students are also taught how to use complex structures to link old ideas to new ones and how to avoid unnecessary repetition by using content words effectively. Finally, students learn the structures used to acknowledge sources, grammatical techniques for paraphrasing, and the rules for indirect quotation.

Study Skills and Aids

Another feature of this book is study skills. The areas covered are time management, study charts, and essay tests. In Chapter 2, students are asked to analyze their weekly schedules and their use of time in the process of writing. Suggestions are made on how to use time wisely for both in-class and out-of-class writing assignments. Another effective study skill is study charts, which students learn to write based on assigned readings. These charts can be used for summary assignments in Chapter 8. Finally, essay test skills are taught in Chapter 9. Time management and the writing process are also reviewed in this chapter. For essay test practice, students can be tested on some of the academic papers, such as the series of papers on tornadoes in Chapters 5 and 7. Finally, to aid students in their learning process, each chapter includes summary charts and a chapter summary.

Journal Entries and Writing Assignments

Each chapter contains Journal Entries, informal writing assignments that encourage students to explore their deepest beliefs and attitudes and generate ideas. Some Journal Entries are designed to help students form opinions in preparation for a Discovery exercise or analysis of a model, and some are designed as responses to those assignments. A few serve as springboards for more formal assignments that occur later in the chapter or book. The length requirement for each assignment increases with each chapter. For example, the first assignment in Chapter 1 requires 150-200 words; a typical requirement in Chapter 8 is 700-800 words. However, these are only suggested requirements and can be changed to suit the level of the class. The purpose of the suggested length is to give students a goal to work toward. The word length of the models is indicated for the same reason.

In addition to the 30 Journal Entries, the book includes several in-class/out-of-class writing assignments. Rather than using a word count as a guide, these assignments suggest a specific number of pages, usually 2 to 3. As students' writing skills progress, you will start to see their out-of-class assignments exceed the 2-to-3-page requirement.

Appendices

This book contains four appendices. Appendix A contains the format guidelines for academic papers. Appendix B is a list of common correction symbols with examples of how to correct the errors these symbols represent. Appendix C is a summary of the subject-verb agreement rules taught in the book. Appendix D contains the 15 Peer Review Forms that students use to complete the peer review activities.

Note: An Instructor's Manual written by the author is available from the publisher and is highly recommended. It contains the answer key to the Journal Entries and Discovery exercises (including the model peer reviews) and also provides pedagogical advice on how to use the material. There is also an appendix that contains a sample composition evaluation form, a course response assignment, and a student questionnaire, which helps to build individual student profiles as a means of assessing students' academic writing needs. The appendix also includes a complete set of the Peer Review Forms that appear in Appendix D of the book. Teachers will find having their own set of Peer Review Forms very useful, especially as a reference during class discussion or for duplicating extra copies for students.

To the Student

Discoveries in Academic Writing could not have been written without the input and contributions of students like you. This book will take you on a journey of discoveries about English academic writing and, more importantly, about yourself.

If you are studying in a college or university in the U.S. or Canada or are preparing to do so, you may have several questions about how to write academic papers. Because English is not your native language and because there are cultural differences in the ways writing is organized, it may be challenging for you to organize and express your ideas as well as you can in your native language.

However, do not be discouraged. This book will teach you what is expected in English academic writing and show you how to complete the writing process (brainstorming, organizing, writing, revising, and proofreading/editing) toward effective academic papers. Throughout the semester, you will grow (progress) as a writer and a critical thinker.

Your instructor will give you direction and advice, but you will need feedback (advice) from more than one reader. Your classmates (peers) will also help you find places to improve your outlines, paragraphs, and essays. This activity is called peer-reviewing. Peer-reviewing is an effective way to build your critical-thinking skills, share techniques with other writers, and improve your writing as you revise. As you learn how to peer-review other students' writing, you will also learn how to be more objective about your own writing and thereby make progress during the revision process.

This book contains Discovery exercises that will help you master your writing skills. The exercises are so named because the activities and models will help you make your own discoveries (or realizations) about the content in focus. The book is also designed to help you improve your study skills with regard to time management, text analysis, and essay tests. Moreover, the group work (peer-reviewing and brainstorming) will help you discover ways to improve the content and organization of your essays as well as build confidence in your speaking skills.

Discoveries in Academic Writing provides a broad selection of topics for you to write about. Each chapter contains formal writing assignments, which are to be completed in or out of class, and Journal Entries, which are informal compositions of varying lengths. Writing is a process of self-discovery, so the Journal Entries will help you explore your opinions about topics related to the model paragraphs and essays or other Discovery exercises. Because some of the formal writing assignments may be based on Journal Entries, do not throw the Journal Entries away. Keep them organized in a loose-leaf notebook.

This book is also designed to help you improve your sentence organization. Not only will you get a review of the basics, but you will also learn how to write complex structures to improve the coherence (the ways ideas are linked) in your writing. The sentence is the basic unit of thought, so disorganized sentences affect the message (content) of the paper. This book will help you overcome problems at the sentence level and develop a rich, complex style, which is valued in English academic writing.

The book contains four appendices, which are perforated so that you can remove the pages for photo-copying. Appendix A contains the Format Guidelines for Academic Papers in Western culture. Appendix B lists the correction symbols your instructor may use and shows how to correct the errors these symbols represent. Appendix C contains rules for subject-verb agreement. Appendix D contains the Peer Review Forms that you will use for this course.

Writing is not always easy; it just takes practice. If you complete the Discovery exercises and writing assignments carefully and revise your writings using the comments from peer reviewers and your instructor, you will be able to write effective, well-developed academic essays.

Acknowledgments

It takes a village to develop and publish a book. *Discoveries in Academic Writing* has been field tested for over a year in its various stages of development; however, the materials that went into this book have been in development for years. I extend my gratitude toward all my colleagues who have helped me in this process, especially Teresa Tuggle, who field-tested *Discoveries in Academic Writing* as a course packet. This book would not have been possible without the generous contributions of students willing to share their academic papers. I also appreciate the thoughtful comments and advice of the anonymous peer reviewers. As a new author, I am also very grateful to Joy Reid, Betty Azar, and Alison Rice for their mentoring and encouragement. Moreover, I have enjoyed working with Susan Marshall, former Acquisitions Editor at Harcourt Brace Corporation, and Debbie Slater and Dina Forbes of M.E. Aslett Corporation, who did an excellent job directing the production of this book. Last, but not least, I wish to express my deepest gratitude to my family, especially my husband, Dierik, who encouraged me to begin and to complete this project. His enthusiasm for every aspect of the development of this book sustained me.

Contents

CHAPTER 1

English Academic Writing: The "A" Paper 1

- EFFECTIVE ACADEMIC WRITING 2
- AUDIENCE AND TONE 4
- COHERENCE: POINT OF VIEW 10
- NUMBER AGREEMENT RULES 19
- PRONOUN USE AND REFERENCE 22

CHAPTER 2

Critical Thinking 31

- CRITICAL-THINKING SKILLS 32
- ACADEMIC WRITING ASSIGNMENTS 32
- THE PROCESS OF WRITING 40
- PEER REVIEW AND REVISION 1 45
- PARALLELISM 57
- PUNCTUATION: (.) (;) (,) 61
- RUN-ON SENTENCES 64

CHAPTER 3

Support in Expository Paragraphs 67

- TOPIC SENTENCES 69
- RELEVANT AND CONVINCING SUPPORT 73
- OUTLINING SKILLS 79
- CONCLUDING REMARKS 82
- SENTENCE TYPES 85
- FRAGMENTS 91

CHAPTER 4

Essay Development 95

- MANAGING YOUR MATERIAL 95
- AN OVERVIEW OF ESSAY DEVELOPMENT 97
- THE INTRODUCTION 99
- THE BODY 105
- THE CONCLUSION 111
- REVIEW OF ESSAY DEVELOPMENT 113
- PEER REVIEW AND REVISION 2 115
- EXEMPLIFICATION 118
- TIME-SHIFTING 122

CHAPTER 5

Chronological Development (Narration and Process) *131*

- NARRATION 132
- PROCESS DESCRIPTION 137
- COHERENCE: OLD IDEA–NEW IDEA 146
- TIME EXPRESSIONS AND TRANSITIONS 151

CHAPTER 6

Comparison/Contrast Analysis *161*

- STRIKING COMPARISONS/CONTRASTS 163
- METHODS OF COMPARISON/CONTRAST 166
- ANALOGIES 171
- TIME ORDER 174
- STRUCTURES OF COMPARISON 179
- STRUCTURES OF CONTRAST 182
- USE OF OLD IDEAS IN BLOCK FORM 185

CHAPTER 7

Cause/Effect Analysis *191*

- ANALYSIS OF CAUSE 191
- IDENTIFYING LOGICAL CAUSES: CRITICAL THINKING 194
- ANALYSIS OF EFFECT 202
- STRUCTURES OF CAUSE 207
- STRUCTURES OF EFFECT 210

CHAPTER 8

Using Sources *221*

- PLAGIARISM 222
- STATING ACKNOWLEDGMENTS 223
- PARAPHRASING 225
- SUMMARIZING 233
- DIRECT AND INDIRECT QUOTATION 234

CHAPTER 9

Essay Tests *241*

- WHAT IS AN ESSAY TEST? 241
- STUDYING FOR AN ESSAY TEST 242
- ADJECTIVE CLAUSES 248
- FORMAL DEFINITIONS 251
- INFORMAL DEFINITIONS 254

APPENDICES

Appendix A *Format Guidelines for Academic Writing Assignments*
Appendix B *Correction Symbols*
Appendix C *Subject-Verb Agreement*
Appendix D *Peer Review Forms*

Chapter 1

English Academic Writing: The "A" Paper

CHAPTER TOPICS

► EFFECTIVE ACADEMIC WRITING

► AUDIENCE AND TONE

► COHERENCE: POINT OF VIEW

► NUMBER AGREEMENT RULES

► PRONOUN USE AND REFERENCE

Journal ENTRY 1

Is writing hard for you?

In *Writing Fiction: A Guide to the Narrative Craft,* Janet Burroway wrote: "Remember. Writing is easy. Not writing is hard." Do you agree? Write a short organized response to this quotation by explaining two or three major reasons that writing is hard (or not hard) for you. Use details and examples to support your discussion. [150-200 words, every other line]

DISCOVERY

1.1: Sharing experiences in academic writing

Discuss the following questions as a class or in small groups.

1. What kinds of composition courses have you had up to now? Discuss the courses you have had and how they were taught.
2. Are the rules for writing essays in your native language the same as or different from those for English writing?
3. What do you hope to learn about English academic writing in this course? (Think about the writing assignments you will have to do in your academic course work.)

EFFECTIVE ACADEMIC WRITING

After discussing the previous questions, you may have discovered that approaches to writing can vary in other cultures. If the methods of writing in your culture differ from those in Western culture, you may feel uncomfortable at first learning how to complete writing assignments in English for an academic audience. Certainly, if you are currently enrolled or are preparing to enroll in a college or university in the U.S. or Canada, you want to be ready to express yourself well in your papers and your essay tests. Therefore, you will have to adapt to the Western methods of organization so that your professors can appreciate your ideas and reward you for your hard work.

The focus of this section is on English academic writing. The following essay not only explains the characteristics of effective academic writing, particularly the "A" paper, but it also demonstrates a standard typed academic essay which is ready to be submitted. (See Appendix A, "Format Guidelines for Academic Writing Assignments.")

ⒹⒾⓈⒸⓄⓋⒺⓇⓎ

1.2: Discovering the characteristics of the "A" paper

- Read the following essay.
- Then answer the Discussion Questions that follow.

Barbara H. Leonhard
ID: 123456
ELSP 003
C1D1

English Academic Writing: The "A" Paper

1   Academic writing is writing completed in a college or university setting for an academic audience consisting of professors, instructors, teaching assistants, and students. There are several features of English academic writing which make it of value for nonnative speakers to learn. Failure to master the rules for effective academic writing in this culture will affect the learner's success in a course.

5   Effective English academic writing, particularly the "A" paper, has three major characteristics. It has convincing content, clear organization, and effective use of the English language.

First, the "A" paper has convincing content. To begin with, the content is informative and thought-provoking. The purpose of academic writing is to convey knowledge and understanding of a topic in a persuasive, formal, and objective manner. Such writing is not too general. In order to

10   be convincing, academic writers in Western culture are expected to use specific and logical details, examples, facts, statistics, and case studies to support generalizations. Overly general and illogical content is not well received by professors. Second, the support is relevant. That is, the support relates directly to the thesis, which clearly presents the writer's topic, purpose, method, and opinion in an essay; and topic sentences, which do the same thing for each developmental paragraph in

15   an essay. Writers are taught not to digress by telling stories or making "by the way" statements, which are out of tone with the assignment despite attempts to be creative and entertaining. All of the sentences contain well-thought-out ideas and relevant supporting points. Third, although objective, academic writing can be creative in that the writer is able to demonstrate effective critical-thinking skills. The content, that is, has depth of thought. The writer effectively analyzes the information,

20   interprets the facts, makes judgments, draws conclusions, summarizes, and defends opinions. Shallow writing is indicative of weak critical-thinking skills, and such papers, often described as "sophomoric," receive low marks. Finally, an "A" paper has a clear purpose, which helps direct the reader, the audience. This is because the writer has clear objectives and strong control of the content. The message is clear, logical, and to the point. Indeed, papers with strong, unified support which

25   demonstrates effective critical-thinking skills are well received by professors.

---

*Kaplan, Robert B., "Cultural Thought Patterns in Intercultural Education." *Language Learning*, 16, 1966, pp. 1-20.

In addition to being convincing, effective academic writing in Western culture is well organized according to certain patterns and rules which may vary from culture to culture. The general pattern is described as linear* because of the direct relationship between generalizations and their supporting points. Academic papers generally have a deductive approach, in which the generalization is stated first and then supported by specific details, examples, and other kinds of support. Sometimes, however, academic writers use an inductive approach, in which the specific support is given before the generalizations. English academic writing is also organized on the rhetorical level. There are several classical patterns used: narration, description, definition, process, classification, comparison, cause/effect, and argumentation. The pattern chosen is the method by which the writer will convey the content. This involves learning the organizational cues for the patterns and ways to order the support with these rhetorical devices. The success of a paper depends on how well the writer handles these organizational principles.

Finally, good English academic writing demonstrates sophisticated use of the English language. First, "A" papers are clearly written at the sentence level. Organization is important not only at the rhetorical level; it is crucial at the sentence level. Disorganized sentences disrupt the flow of thought in a paper and interfere with the meaning of the passage. Frequent agreement errors, misspellings, incorrect punctuation, and other such problems also demonstrate lack of control of English and distract the reader. Second, style is important. Effective English academic writing demonstrates control over a variety of sentence types. In Western culture, complex and compound-complex sentences, which contain dependent clauses, are preferred in academic papers. Papers containing too many simple sentences and the conjunctions *for, and, nor, but, or, yet,* and *so* are considered boring and unimaginative. A wide vocabulary range is another characteristic of effective academic writing. Because information is conveyed in content words, weak (basic) vocabulary demonstrates weak thinking. Since effective sentence organization and vocabulary contribute to the content of a paper, writers who have a command of the English language are more convincing than writers who cannot articulate complex ideas.

In conclusion, nonnative speakers studying in the U.S. or Canada will benefit from learning what will be expected of them in their academic writing. If the professor's expectations are not met with regard to content, organization, and language, the papers may not be well received. Mastering the fundamentals of English academic writing will enable nonnative speakers to succeed in their academic studies. [777 words]

Discussion Questions

Use the previous essay to answer the following questions.

1. What is the writer's purpose for this essay?

   ....

   ....

2. What are the three characteristics of English academic writing? Where are they stated?

   ....

   ....

3. Briefly define the following:
   a) thesis statement:

   ....

   b) topic sentence:

   ....

c) relevant:

....

d) support:

....

e) "by the way" statements:

....

f) linear pattern:

....

g) deductive approach:

....

h) inductive approach:

....

i) classical rhetorical patterns:

....

j) sophomoric:

....

4. Is the essay convincing? Did the writer succeed in persuading you to understand the value of learning about English academic writing?

....

5. Has reading this essay changed your expectations about English academic writing?

....

6. What problems might you experience as you are getting used to the English rhetorical system and professors' expectations? Why?

....

....

AUDIENCE AND TONE

The Academic Audience

Another feature of effective academic writing is control of audience and tone, or formality. The audience is comprised of the reader(s) the writer is targeting or addressing a message to. In an academic course, the reader will be the professor and often the other students. In addition, there are other academic situations in which the assignment may directly or indirectly state who the audience will be. For example, a master's degree candidate writing comprehensive exams knows that the audience consists of a committee of professors in his or her major. Also, a student applying for a scholarship usually has to write a statement of purpose, which will be read by the committee granting the scholarships. In each of these cases, the writing should be formal (serious and objective) and contain pertinent information the committee needs to know regarding why the candidate deserves to pass the comprehensive exam or get the scholarship. On the other hand, the same students writing letters to friends should choose an informal (intimate and friendly) style to describe their daily routines, personal problems, or travel plans.

As these cases show, addressing the audience with the correct level of formality helps the writers connect with and persuade (or win) the audience. However, if the writers choose the wrong level of formality and language, they will probably alienate (or lose) their audiences. The committee members will consider the candidates disrespectful or immature (not academic material) if the language is too informal. In the same way, if the students use formal or technical language in their letters to friends, they may sound arrogant or condescending (superior to others).

When planning a paper addressed to or pertinent to a certain audience, consider the following factors.
- **Identity of Audience**
  What is the audience's age, sex, social status, level of education, special interests or needs, profession, cultural or racial background, feelings and attitudes, or relationship to you?
- **Purpose/Occasion**
  Are you writing to fulfill an academic assignment, complete an essay test in your major, share information with family or friends, get a scholarship, solve a problem, apply for a job, borrow money from your father, persuade a publisher to publish your book, or win a short-story contest? There are many other times (occasions) when you need to be convincing and persuasive in writing for different reasons (purposes).

Levels of Formality

There are different degrees of formality, but these descriptions should help you find the right level for academic writing. Academic writing can be technical, especially when the audience and situation require specialized knowledge. Formal academic writing is usually less technical because the audience and/or level of knowledge may be more general. Personal writing, however, can range from informal to colloquial, depending on the relationship the writer has with the reader and the situation. The closer the relationship between the writer and the audience, the more relaxed the language is. Therefore, the most informal discourse is colloquial (conversational).

Note: You will need this chart for Discoveries 1.3 and 1.4.

LEVELS OF FORMALITY

	THE RANGE OF FORMALITY	
	Technical → Formal → Informal → Colloquial	

	Technical/Formal (Academic)	**Informal/Colloquial (Personal)**
Audience	professors	close friends and family
Tone	formal; objective; serious	informal; intimate; friendly
Vocabulary	academic; a wide range; concise; accurate	slang; idioms; contracted forms
Style	complex (subordination); sentence variety	may contain frequent simple or compound sentences
Language	few, if any, errors	may contain fragments, run-on sentences, misspellings, punctuation errors
Content	depth of thought; unified; cogent (tight); succinct	conversational; may be repetitive
Organization	clear; coherent; well planned	may be less structured than formal writing

ⓓⓘⓢⓒⓞⓥⓔⓡⓨ

1.3: Determining appropriate levels of formality

- What level of formality should be used in each of these writing tasks? Is it technical, formal, informal, or colloquial?
- Use the chart "Levels of Formality" to help you decide.

⮑ Examples

> Your brother writes to you about his experiences as a college freshman.
>
> .... *colloquial* ....

> You need to write a note for your professor, saying you had stopped by her office and want to make an appointment.
>
> .... *formal* ....

1. You need to write a seminar report for colleagues in your major field (other educators, other engineers, other sociologists).

   ....

2. Your friend needs to write a letter to his father, who is fairly understanding and with whom he is fairly close, explaining his poor grades.

   ....

3. You need to write a letter to your sponsor, explaining your poor grades and asking for more funding.

   ....

4. It is summer vacation, and you are writing a letter to your American roommate, who has not traveled much, persuading him or her to come to visit you in your country.

   ....

5. You are writing about the history of log cabins in the U.S. for your History 101 class.

   ....

6. Your roommate is completing a term paper (a lengthy paper which usually takes several weeks and library research to complete) for a lower-level economics class.

   ....

7. You are writing comments on a peer review form for a classmate.

   ....

8. Your professor is writing an article on historical linguistics for *The TESOL Journal.*

   ....

9. You are writing about how to build a suspension bridge for an upper-level civil engineering course.

   ....

10. Your best American friend writes you a letter in which she complains about her low grades and mean professors.

    ....

DISCOVERY

1.4: Analyzing the use of audience and tone

Imagine you are teaching a composition course for native speakers. You have just finished a unit in which you studied Robert Kaplan's research on the cultural differences in writing.

- Read the following Essay Test Question and the three Essay Test Answers that follow.
- On a separate sheet of paper, analyze each Essay Test Answer for audience, tone, vocabulary, style, language, content, and organization. Use the chart "Levels of Formality" on page 5 as a guide.

↪ Example

  Audience: Other American students (we . . . us)

- Then answer the Discussion Questions that follow.

Essay Test Question

As you learned from the Kaplan article, people in different cultures have different approaches to writing. What do nonnative speakers need to know about the format rules in this culture? Write an essay in which you explain to nonnative speakers the rules for academic writing at universities in this culture. Be specific and informative.

Essay Test Answer 1

1   Professors in this culture have specific format rules. First, they want papers to be neat. This is true in other cultures too. But in our culture, we have to remember little things. Such as put the holes on the left, not the right. We also have to skip lines and leave the margin empty. Because the paper will be easy to read. Moreover, professors here want us to use only the front of the paper, not the back. We aren't supposed to flip the page over wrong. So what should be the top is used
5   as the bottom, this is confusing.

Second, a composition is supposed to be like a picture. The words are the picture and the margin is the frame. We think this is beautiful. But maybe people in other cultures think something else is beautiful. Cultures are different, nobody is right or wrong. Also, if my paper is sloppy, it looks
10   like I did it at the last minute. Professors here expect us to pay attention to details. Not just with format but with spelling, capitalization, and punctuation. For example, one of my professors gave me a C, I had too many mistakes.

Third, we have to type the right way. If a paper is typed wrong, our grade goes down. We have to double-space and leave spaces on the side. We also have to use font 12, not 15. If we use a
15   computer to write our papers and print them, we have to make sure we tear the pages apart and put them in order. Professors do not like to do that for us. I think if nonnative speakers know these rules, they will do well with format. But they need to have interesting content, too. Because a paper won't get a good grade just because it looks nice.

In conclusion, it won't be hard for nonnative speakers to learn these rules, they are easier than
20   thinking of ideas. [324 words]

Essay Test Answer 2

1   Cultural differences regarding the presentation of an academic paper may not be significant, but nonnative speakers should be aware of the format rules they will be expected to follow in academic courses.

First, effective academic writing in any culture looks polished and professional. In other words,
5   it is well presented, not sloppy or illegible. Literally, the word "paragraph" means "picture of words." The completed writing assignment is pleasing to the eye and easy to read. Good writers care as much about the paper's appearance as its message. Writing a good paper takes effort, and the "format" of the paper is the wrapping on the gift. The professor will be more willing to appreciate the

message if the presentation is pleasing to the eye. Such a paper demonstrates the writer's eye for
detail in the completion of the paper, whereas a sloppy paper indicates a slip-shod job, perhaps a
last-minute attempt. A paper that looks professional will not necessarily get an "A" in a university here,
but a carelessly assembled, messy paper will be lucky to get a "D," especially if the content is poor.

Although good academic writers in most cultures have high standards with respect to the presentation of their writing, the format rules they follow may vary in other cultures. To begin with, the
use of holes, lines, margins, and the paper space are different from culture to culture. For example,
in some cultures, writers prefer the paper holes on the right, not the left. Thus, their front page is
the back of the page in this culture. Moreover, writers in other cultures may not like to waste paper,
so they fill all the space on a page, including the margins. Professors here, however, will expect
empty margins and double spacing to allow room for comments and aid readability. Also, the
pages should be clearly numbered and in order, and the back of the paper should not be used. If
the back is used, the writing should not be upside down. The paper, therefore, should not be
flipped over from the bottom; the top of the back page should correspond to the top of the front
page, not the bottom. Finally, there are other format rules to learn regarding typed papers. Typed
papers should be double-spaced in font 12. The margins should be adequate also. Professors
expect the pages to be numbered, torn apart if printed, and handed in in the correct order.

In conclusion, nonnative speakers need to realize that, regardless of neatness, the format they
are used to may be distracting to a professor here. Learning these rules is easier than learning how
to compose a paper. [441 words]

Essay Test Answer 3

I'm going to write about the format rules for writing in school. I think good writing looks neat.
What I mean is that it is not a piece of junk. My composition teacher said my paragraphs should
be pictures. The paper is cool to look at. Easy to read if I do, I guess. I used to write yucky papers.
But now I don't. Do you? I hear that format things are different everywhere. People use lines and
stuff different all over the world. Weird. I guess people from other countries need to learn the same
things as me. If they don't, they might turn their teacher off. Even if they are neat. Writing good
papers are a pain. The "format" of the paper is a big deal. For my teachers, they will like my papers
better if they look good. I care about the little things. That's what they think. A sloppy paper makes
it look like I pulled an all-nighter. That's what I learned in my composition class. I want to write good.
So that I don't get an F. Also, I shouldn't beat around the bush. I have to say something good. I
think that's all. [199 words]

Discussion Questions

Now that you have read the above Essay Test Answers, answer the following questions.

1. Which Essay Test Answer sounds the most academic in tone? Why?

   ....

   ....

   ....

2. Which one has the most formal and sophisticated vocabulary? Why?

   ....

   ....

   ....

3. Which one has the best control of style and language? Why?

....

....

....

4. Which one has the most effective content and organization? Why?

....

....

....

The following chart provides examples of the types of expressions you should and should not use in academic writing.

COLLOQUIAL VS. FORMAL ENGLISH

In academic writing, use formal, not colloquial (spoken) language.

<u>Colloquial English</u>	<u>Formal English</u>

Contractions
   don't
   gonna
   there're
	Full Forms
	   do not
	   going to
	   there are

Slang, Idioms
   guy
   kids
   stuff, junk
   drives me nuts
	Formal Words
	   person
	   children
	   personal items, objects
	   is upsetting, upsets me

Spoken Transitions
   anyway, anyhow
	Formal Transitions
	   moreover, furthermore

Vague Expressions
   something like that
   (Any expression with *thing*)
	Specific Expressions
	   Tell *who, what, where, when, why,*
	      how much, and *how many*

Basic Vocabulary
   big
   good
   so
   but
   and
	Preferred Vocabulary
	   enormous, large, huge, immense
	   effective, suitable, beneficial
	   as a result, consequently
	   however, on the other hand
	   moreover, furthermore, in addition

ⒹⒾⓈⒸⓄⓋⒺⓇⓎ
1.5:   Translating informal language

- Review Essay Test Answers 2 and 3 (on format rules for academic writing assignments).
- Match the informal phrases based on Essay Test Answer 3 on the left with the formal translations based on Essay Test Answer 2 on the right. The first one is done for you.

Informal (Essay Test Answer 3)	**Formal (Essay Test Answer 2)**
....i.... 1. . . . writing for school looks cool . . .	a. . . . learn the same rules as I am . . .
.... 2. . . . turn their teacher off . . .	b. In conclusion, . . .
.... 3. . . . pulled an "all-nighter" . . .	c. . . . very important . . .
.... 4. . . . I want to write good . . . *	d. . . . my paper is unsatisfactory . . .
.... 5. . . . learn the same things as me . . .	e. . . . disappoint their professor . . .
.... 6. . . . my paper's a piece of junk . . .	f. . . . lines and other format rules . . .
.... 7. . . . lines and stuff . . .	g. . . . pay attention to details . . .
.... 8. . . . that's all . . .	h. I want to write well/effectively.
.... 9. . . . a big deal . . .	ⅰ. Effective writing looks presentable.
.... 10. . . . pay attention to little things . . .	j. . . . stayed up all night to complete an assignment . . .

*Note: This is grammatically incorrect.

COHERENCE: POINT OF VIEW

ⒹⒾⓈⒸⓄⓋⒺⓇⓎ
1.6:   Discovering coherence

- Read each passage aloud.
- Place a checkmark (✔) on the line if the phrase describes the passage. The first one is done for you.

	Passage A	**Passage B**
Choppy/Basic	✔	....
Fluent/Complex	....	....
Weak control of pronouns	....	....
Effective control of pronouns	....	....
Unclear audience	....	....
Clear audience	....	....
Excessive repetition	....	....
Effective repetition	....	....

One Benefit of Travel
by Yunhai Yang

Passage A

1   First of all, travel will enable people to take a break. People always have a lot of work to do. Hard work and pressure make you feel tired and uncomfortable. We are not working machines. They need time to take breaks. Travel will enable you to relax. Also, travel will energize people to work better, especially computer programmers. They use their brains a lot every day. After a long time,
5   they may become slow-witted. Under such a condition, you cannot work effectively. We need to find a place for a vacation. You need to see natural phenomena, instead of looking at computers all day. They will get energy from nature and then come back to work much more efficiently than before. I have experience with this. I have been to Buffalo. I saw a wonderful sight there. I saw Niagara Falls. I looked up at it. It seemed to fall from the sky. It was very beautiful. You could feel
10   the power coming from the falls. You were inspired to do your work. [173 words]

Passage B

1   First of all, travel will enable people to take a break. Because people always have a lot of work to do, sometimes hard work and pressure make them feel tired and uncomfortable. People are not working machines. Therefore, they need time to take breaks, and travel will enable them to relax. Also, travel will energize people to work better, especially computer programmers, who use their
5   brains a lot every day. After a long time, they may become slow-witted. Under such a condition, they cannot work effectively, so they need to find a place for a vacation where they can see natural phenomena instead of looking at computers all day. They will get energy from nature and then come back to work much more efficiently than before. For example, travel helped me overcome burnout. To relax from my stressful job as a computer programmer, I went to Buffalo, where I saw
10   a wonderful sight, Niagara Falls. When I looked up at the falls, the gushing water seemed to fall from the sky, and I could feel its power. The sight was so beautiful that I was more inspired to do my work. [191 words] (Adapted with permission, Yunhai Yang, Taiwanese)

Introduction to Coherence

Upon comparing the above two passages, you probably discovered that you preferred the second passage because it sounded smoother; that is, the ideas seemed to flow together well. The first passage has a very good progression from general to specific, yet there is only one idea in many of the sentences, causing the passage to sound choppy. Moreover, the control of point of view and pronouns is weak, causing confusion about who the audience is. The revision, however, shows more complexity in that the ideas are organized into complex and compound-complex sentences, creating a smoother flow of ideas from one sentence to another. As a result, the second passage is easier to understand at both the general and specific levels. Moreover, the relevance of the example is enhanced with improvement in vocabulary use. The control of pronouns and point of view and the repetition of key content words reinforce the writer's opinion about travel, making the example more relevant.

Several chapters in this book will provide practice with coherence devices to teach you how to make your writing sound fluent and cohesive. Learning effective coherence devices will enable you to improve your writing at both the sentence and paragraph levels.

"To cohere" means "to stick together"; "to be connected naturally or logically, by a common principle; to be consistent"; and "to become or stay united in action; to be in accord." Effective English writing is coherent; that is, the sentences follow each other smoothly and logically. In addition, the relationships between the ideas in the composition are clear to the reader. For example, the reader is able to locate the main ideas and sort out the examples. The time relationships and other forms of chronological order (steps, stages) are also clear. Old ideas link with new ideas, and pronouns are used correctly. Vocabulary, moreover, is well chosen to aid in the development of the content at every level.

COHERENCE DEVICES

Type	Description	Chapter
Point of View	The Writer's Perspective	1
Pronoun Reference	Pronoun/Antecedent Agreement (Number/Gender)	1
Content Words	Old Idea/New Idea (Repetition of Key Ideas)	5, 6, 7
Transitions	Subordinators, Phrase Markers, Connectors	4, 5, 6, 7

Point of View

Point of view is the perspective from which a paper is written. This perspective is determined by the writer's purpose and audience. If the point of view is incorrectly chosen or used inconsistently, the reader will be confused. Note that control of point of view includes control of pronouns and number agreement.

PRONOUNS FOR POINT OF VIEW

Point of View	Pronouns
First Person	*I* (singular) or *we* (plural)
Second Person	*You* (singular or plural)
Third Person	*He, she, it, one* (singular) or *they* (plural)

First Person

Use first person (*I* or *we*) in the following cases:

1. To emphasize the writer or writers

⇨ **Examples**

> In my survey, I found that . . .
> In our survey, we found that . . .

Note: *I* and *we* can be avoided:

> This survey shows that . . .

2. To give personal experience in formal writing

⇨ **Examples**

> To illustrate, when I first moved to the U.S., I could not speak English very well. I especially had trouble with . . .

> For example, travel helped me overcome burnout. To relax from my stressful job as a computer programmer, I went to Buffalo, where I saw a wonderful sight, Niagara Falls. When I looked up at the falls, the gushing water seemed to fall from the sky, and I could feel its power. The sight was so beautiful that I was more inspired to do my work.

3. To show that you (the writer) belong to a group about which you are writing (general reference)

⇨ **Examples**

> We undergraduates believe that certain changes must be made at this university.
> We teachers work hard to prepare for our classes.

Use first person with caution:
First person is more common in personal writing than in academic writing. Personal writing is informal and intimate, whereas academic writing is objective and impersonal. Therefore, avoid using first person unless you are providing a personal experience to support a generalization. In academic writing, the third person is used for generalizing.

Second Person

Use second person (*you*) to emphasize the reader.

1. To instruct (explain a process)

⇨ **Example**

> To change a flat tire, you must take a systematic approach. First, you need to . . . Then, you should . . . After . . ., it is a good idea that you . . . If you follow these steps, you shouldn't have any trouble changing a flat tire.
> (The reader wants to learn how to change a tire.)

2. To give the reader advice (make recommendations)

⇨ **Example**

> To improve your English, you can watch more TV, visit with your American friends, read more in English, and keep a journal in English. You should not just sit in your room with a book and tape because you are not getting any feedback on your use of the language.
> (The reader is a nonnative speaker.)

3. For general reference. (*You* is used impersonally to apply to people in general, not the reader specifically.)

⇨ **Example**

> When you are in trouble, you find out who your friends are.
> (This means: When people are in trouble, they find out who their friends are.)

Use second person with caution:
The use of *you* for general reference is discouraged in academic writing because it is informal (conversational) and takes the emphasis off the subject. For academic writing, third person is preferred.
Moreover, do not use *you* when writing one of your own personal experiences in your writing. Notice how strange the following examples sound; the use of *you* in these examples is inappropriate because the examples are only the writer's. If everyone felt exactly the same as the writer, *you* would be appropriate as stated. However, how likely is it that the writer's professor or the general public is new to the country or is a computer programmer who went to Niagara Falls on vacation?

⇨ **Examples**

> Speaking a foreign language can sometimes be embarrassing. To illustrate, when you first moved to the U.S., you could not speak English very well. You especially had trouble with . . .

For example, travel helped you overcome burnout. To relax from your stressful job as a computer programmer, you went to Buffalo, where you saw a wonderful sight, Niagara Falls. When you looked up at the falls, the gushing water seemed to fall from the sky, and you could feel its power. The sight was so beautiful that you were more inspired to do your work.

Third Person

Third person (*he, she, it, one, they*) is preferred in academic writing. Use it to:

1. emphasize the subject of the paper, not the reader.
2. generalize in the singular or the plural.

Note: When generalizing, make sure that pronouns agree with their antecedents and that verbs agree with their subjects. (See "Number Agreement Rules" on page 19.)

⇔ Examples

A word processor is useful because it aids in the composing process. (singular)
Word processors are useful because they aid in the composing process. (plural)

Also, be careful with other problems that can arise with sexism, inconsistency, and awkward use. These problems will be addressed next.

SUMMARY OF USE OF PRONOUNS IN POINT OF VIEW ——————

Person	Pronoun(s)	Use
First Person	*I, we*	To emphasize the writer(s) To give personal experience For general reference
Second Person	*You*	To instruct the reader To give the reader advice For general reference
Third Person	*He, she, it, they*	To emphasize the subject To generalize Preferred in academic writing

---

ⓄⒾⓈⒸⓄⓋⒺⓇⓎ
1.7: Using an objective tone

- Make the necessary changes to the following paragraph on the topic of good students so that it sounds more formal and, thus, more appropriate for academic writing. The first change is made for you.
- Use third-person plural.
- Do not merely substitute the pronouns with other pronouns. Sometimes content words will be required for clarity.

1   Second, good students are diligent. It is ~~our~~ *their* duty to prepare for class. Professors just help in the learning process; we students are the ones who really have to do all the work and put all our effort into learning. This process of learning becomes incredibly easy if we preview the topic which will be discussed in class. Generally, professors follow a schedule of classes which is given to us at the
5   beginning of the course. Using this syllabus, we can know the topics planned for each class and read ahead. If we do not understand the information given in the text, we can find more sources at the library or prepare a list of questions to ask in class. This list of questions may even help us understand the lectures better. Having previewed the daily lessons, we are also better prepared to discuss

10 the topic in class and, in fact, exchange ideas with our professors and classmates. This sharing of different perspectives is the objective of the learning process in an academic class. Such discussions are only possible if we prepare ahead of time. For this reason, reading the lessons with anticipation is essential. Those of us who are well prepared for class are good students. [207 words] (Adapted with permission from "Characteristics of Good Students," by Licett Galietta, Venezuelan)

Problems with Point of View

Sexism

The use of the singular causes problems at times because of the current concern in the U.S. and Canada that language be inclusive of both males and females. Traditionally, the masculine pronouns were acceptable for referring to a mixed-gender group (for example, "*A student* can edit *his* essays quickly with a word processor."). However, nowadays, masculine pronouns should not be used to include males and females.

Awkward Pronoun Use

Four solutions have been proposed to avoid sexism in writing. However, some of these methods create awkward expressions.

First, some writers are inclusive by stating both the masculine and feminine pronouns, as the following examples show. However, imagine trying to read an entire paper filled with such awkward usage.

↩ Example

> A *student* can write *his or her* papers quickly with a word processor. *He or she* will find that it is easier to select and move passages and proofread and edit *his or her* papers. The papers *he or she* writes will also look better and be easier for *his or her* professor to read.

Second, some writers try to solve the problem of sexism by using *one* throughout the paper. However, the use of *one* and *one's* is very formal and just as stilted as *he* and *she* and *him* and *her*. Some writers try to solve this problem by using *his* or *her* instead of *one's*, and *he* and *she* instead of *one*, but the product is still awkward.

↩ Examples

> *One* can write *one's* papers quickly with a word processor. *One* will find that it is easier to select and move passages and proofread and edit *one's* papers. The papers *one* writes will also look better and be easier for *one's* professor to read.

> *One* can write *his or her* papers quickly with a word processor. *He or she* will find that it is easier to select and move passages and proofread and edit *his or her* papers. The papers *one* writes will also look better and be easier for *his or her* professor to read.

Another proposed solution is to alternate between the use of the masculine case in one paragraph and the feminine case in another paragraph, but this is also distracting.

> *One* can write *his* papers quickly with a word processor. *He* will find that it is easier to select and move passages and proofread and edit *his* papers. The papers *he* writes will also look better and be easier for *his* professor to read.

> *One* can also benefit from a word processor by saving *her* papers on the hard drive. This way, *she* can easily recover the text for further revisions. *She* should name each file correctly, however, so that *she* will not make changes to the wrong document. In addition, due to the word processor, *she* can . . .

The best way to solve problems with sexism is to use third-person plural. The use of the plural is inclusive as well as concise.

↪ Traditional Examples

> *A student* can edit *his* essays quickly with a word processor.
> When *a student* applies to a college, *he* must fill out many forms.

↪ Inclusive Examples

> *Students* can edit *their* essays quickly with word processors.
> When *students* apply to colleges, *they* must fill out many forms.

DISCOVERY

1.8: Using inclusive language

- Read the following paragraph.
- Change the point of view from the traditional masculine point of view to the third-person plural for more inclusive usage. The first change is made for you.

>   *students have*
>
> 1   First, ~~a~~ good ~~student has~~ the ability to concentrate. Concentration in a subject means that a student realizes the goals he wants to achieve in his academic field. He is able to choose the most important courses to master his knowledge. For example, a student who is majoring in Teaching English as a Second/Foreign Language should take not only linguistics courses but also
> 5   methodology and psychology of education because he might know the language perfectly but be unable to teach it or be unable to work with a particular age group. Moreover, he should not be afraid of participating in discussions, asking and answering the questions, providing his own argumentation, and using all information available. The more questions he asks himself and his teachers, the more and deeper knowledge he gains. A student should use all the available
> 10 means of getting knowledge. For example, at the University of Missouri–Columbia, he can work with references at Ellis Library, and he may also use the Internet in the computer labs on campus. If his major is education, he can participate in classroom observations and even complete a teaching practicum as a student teacher. [191 words] (Adapted with permission from "Characteristics of Good Students," by Marina Babenko, Ukrainian)

Journal ENTRY 2

What is a good student?

   Review the paragraphs in Discoveries 1.7 and 1.8. The writers of those passages believe that good students are well focused and diligent. Write a short response [150-200 words, every other line] in which you discuss a different characteristic of good students. Include convincing examples and details.

Inconsistent Point of View

Do not change the point of view in your writing assignments. Pick one point of view and stick with it. Inconsistent point of view indicates a lack of focus and purpose.

The following paragraph demonstrates consistent point of view. The writer used third-person plural to generalize about a benefit of travel. That is, he used *people, they, their, them,* and so on consistently until he got to his personal experience, where he switched to first person, *I, me,* and *my.*

1   First of all, travel will enable people to take a break. Because people always have a lot of work to do, sometimes hard work and pressure make them feel tired and uncomfortable. People are not working machines. Therefore, they need time to take breaks, and travel will enable them to relax. Also, travel will energize people to work better, especially computer programmers, who use their
5   brains a lot every day. After a long time, they may become slow-witted. Under such a condition, they cannot work effectively, so they need to find a place for a vacation where they can see natural phenomena instead of looking at computers all day. They will get energy from nature and then come back to work much more efficiently than before. For example, travel helped me overcome burnout. To relax from my stressful job as a computer programmer, I went to Buffalo, where I saw
10   a wonderful sight, Niagara Falls. When I looked up at the falls, the gushing water seemed to fall from the sky, and I could feel its power. The sight was so beautiful that I was more inspired to do my work. [191 words]

ⓓⓘⓢⓒⓞⓥⓔⓡⓨ
1.9:   Analyzing point of view

- Compare the following two passages.
- Then answer the Discussion Questions that follow.

Independence in American Culture
by Kelly Boggs

Passage A

1   One characteristic that Americans value highly is independence. Throughout history, Americans have thought of themselves as pioneers. From settling a new country to opening the frontiers, that rugged, independent spirit has pervaded every aspect of American life. Independent people are admired as being people of strong character. The importance of independence can be clearly
5   seen in the way American children are raised. From the time that children are very small, they are encouraged to venture out on their own and try new things. For instance, playing with new toys is encouraged by parents. Parents watch proudly as children as young as two years old learn how to do things for themselves such as picking out their own clothes and deciding what they want to eat. As children grow older, they are often required to perform household tasks, like cleaning, to
10   earn their money for things they want. Over time, they are expected to continue doing things on their own, particularly earning money. Most high school students, for example, have part-time jobs to earn money for things like cars, clothes, and entertainment. This push towards independence continues until the day that children are encouraged, if not expected, to move out on their own. American adults are expected to make their own way in the world with little help from others. As you
15   can see, independence is a respected trait in American society. [239 words] (Adapted with permission, Kelly Boggs, American)

Passage B

1   One characteristic that Americans value highly is independence. Throughout history, we have thought of ourselves as pioneers. From settling a new country to opening the frontiers, that rugged, independent spirit has pervaded every aspect of American life. Independent people are admired as being people of strong character. The importance of independence can be clearly seen in the way
5   American children are raised. From the time that children are very small, you are encouraged to

venture out on your own and try new things. For instance, playing with new toys is encouraged by parents. Parents watch proudly as children as young as two years old learn how to do things for themselves such as picking out our own clothes and deciding what we want to eat. As you grow older, you are often required to perform household tasks, like cleaning, to earn their money for
10   things we want. Over time, we are expected to continue doing things on our own, particularly earning money. Most high school students, for example, have part-time jobs to earn money for things like cars, clothes, and entertainment. This push towards independence continues until the day that you are encouraged, if not expected, to move out on your own. American adults are expected to make their own way in the world with little help from others. As you can see, independence is a
15   respected trait in American society. [231 words]

Discussion Questions

Use Passages A and B to answer the following questions.

1. Which passage has consistent point of view? What is the point of view?

    ....

    ....

2. In Passage A, who is the audience? What is the writer's purpose?

    ....

    ....

What is a trait that your culture values?

   In Discovery 1.9, Kelly Boggs explains the importance of independence in American culture and shows how children are taught to be independent. Choose one trait in your culture and explain why it is important. Also, explain how children are taught to exhibit the trait. Use convincing examples and details. [150-200 words, every other line]

_____ _____

DISCOVERY
1.10:   Revising inconsistent point of view

• Read the following paragraphs from "Self-Respect."
• Correct the inconsistencies in point of view. Pay attention to number agreement and subject-verb agreement. Use inclusive and concise language. You will read the complete essay and its revision in Chapter 2.

Self-Respect
by B.A. Harris

1   If people have learned to achieve respect for themselves, they are not apt to substitute that

   respect for any feeling of inadequacy or unworthiness. We have already discovered our capabilities, set our goals, and commenced to work and achieve those goals. As each goal is achieved, whether it be studying to be on the honor roll or striving to be a better football player, people

5 reaching their goals discover an unlimited amount of satisfaction. You have no time to feel inadequate or unworthy because self-respect has given you the satisfaction of knowing that you are capable of reaching your goals and developing your worth as human beings.

As a person works to develop "self-worth" as human beings, he does so not only with respect to himself but with respect and consideration to all those he works with. In this way, we are

10 strengthening our self-respect and gaining other people's respect in return. As people strive for self-respect or seek their worth as human beings, we can improve our attitude toward people and situations to a degree that you will eventually gain the respect of others and discover your own "worth" and self-respect. [192 words] (Adapted with permission by B. A. Harris)

NUMBER AGREEMENT RULES

Number Agreement Rules

Some of your most frequent errors will be with number agreement. Having effective number agreement involves keeping track of singular and plural forms.

1. Singular countable nouns, such as "computer" and "machine," must be accompanied by one of the following:

    a) Articles: *a, an* (indefinite) or *the* (specific, limited)
    b) Singular demonstrative adjectives: *this* or *that*
    c) Quantity words: *each, every, one, another*
    d) Possessives: *my, his, Mary's*

⮑ Examples

Incorrect	Computer is amazing machine.
Correct	*A* computer is *an* amazing machine. (any computer)
	The computer is *an* amazing machine. (the class of machines called computers)
	This computer is *an* amazing machine.
	My computer is *an* amazing machine.

2. Do not use *a* and *an* with a plural noun.

⮑ Examples

Incorrect	My professor gives *a* very hard homework *assignments*.
Correct	My professor gives very hard homework *assignments*.

3. Do not use *the* when generalizing about a noncountable noun or a plural noun.

⮑ Examples

Incorrect	*The* computers are used in many fields.
	The honesty is the best policy.
Correct	Computers are used in many fields.
	Honesty is the best policy.

4. Countable nouns, such as "computer," can be singular or plural. Use articles and verbs accordingly. However, noncountable nouns, such as "information," "advice," and "equipment," are singular. For more on countable and noncountable nouns, see Appendix C, "Subject-Verb Agreement."

☞ **Examples**

> Countable   *A* computer *is an* amazing machine.
>   Computers *are* amazing machines.
>
> Noncountable   *Information is* easy to come by on the Internet.
>   *This* lab *equipment has* been repaired.

5. Pronouns and their antecedents agree in number and gender.

☞ **Examples**

> Incorrect   *A student* may fail tests if *they* do not study hard.
>   My *father* cannot walk because *she* fell and broke *her* hip.
>
> Correct   *Students* may fail tests if *they* do not study hard.
>   My *father* cannot walk because *he* fell and broke *his* hip.

6. Adjectives do not agree in number with the noun.

☞ **Examples**

> Incorrect   Computers are *amazings* machines.
>
> Correct   Computers are *amazing* machines.

SUMMARY OF NUMBER AGREEMENT RULES ──────────

1. Singular countable nouns, such as "computer" and "machine," must be accompanied by one of the following: *a, an, the;* or *this, that, one, each, every, another;* or a possessive.

2. Do not use *a* or *an* with a plural noun.

3. Do not use *the* when generalizing about a noncountable noun or a plural noun.

4. Countable nouns, such as "computer," can be singular or plural. Use articles and verbs accordingly. However, noncountable nouns, such as "information," "advice," and "equipment," are singular. For more on countable and noncountable nouns, see Appendix C, "Subject-Verb Agreement Rules."

5. Pronouns and their antecedents agree in number and gender.

6. Adjectives do not agree in number with the noun.

ⒹⒾⓈⒸⓄⓋⒺⓇⓎ
1.11:   Controlling number agreement

A. Convert the following generalizations into plural statements. Pay attention to number agreement.

☞ **Examples**

> The laser is widely used because it is so accurate.
>
> Lasers are widely used because they are so accurate.

1. The computer has helped make the world smaller due to the Internet and e-mail. It also makes calculations quickly and stores vast amounts of information.

   ....

   ....

2. A good teacher is patient with his or her students.

   ....

   ....

3. A CD provides better sound quality than a cassette tape does.

   ....

   ....

4. A good student attends class, has an efficient study plan, organizes notes and handouts well, and completes his or her work on time.

   ....

   ....

5. These days, a homeowner cannot live without his or her vacuum cleaner, washer and drier, and microwave oven.

   ....

   ....

6. The tractor has enabled the farmer to be more productive.

   ....

   ....

7. Without a car, a person could not get very much done in a day. A person needs to go to and from work, run errands, and make it to appointments on time.

   ....

   ....

8. A good research scientist makes his or her hypothesis, conducts experiments to test the hypothesis, and then draws his or her conclusions.

   ....

   ....

B. Use the following words and phrases to make sentences in both the singular and plural. Supply reasons. Pay attention to articles and number agreement.

　　↪ **Example**

　　　word processor/useful because . . .

　　　A word processor is useful because it aids in the composing process. (singular)

　　　Word processors are useful because they aid in the composing process. (plural)

1. history book/open/person's mind because . . .

   ....
   ....

2. family/important because . . .

   ....
   ....

3. laptop computer/versatile because . . .

   ....
   ....

4. library/indispensable because . . .

   ....
   ....

5. jet/make/world smaller because . . .

   ....
   ....

6. phone/convenient because . . .

   ....
   ....

7. English-English dictionary/good because . . .

   ....
   ....

8. bicycle/fun to ride because . . .

   ....
   ....

PRONOUN USE AND REFERENCE

Not only are pronouns important in determining and controlling point of view, they are necessary for coherence at the sentence level. Pronouns are used occasionally to replace content words in order to facilitate the flow of ideas and cut down on unnecessary repetition. The content words that pronouns replace are called "antecedents." "Antecedent" means "come before." A pronoun must have one antecedent to which it clearly refers. In the following example, the pronoun reference is unclear because there are two possible antecedents.

↪ Examples

Unclear Reference   *Phones* are more convenient than *letters* because *they* enable us to contact our families and friends.

Due to the content, *they* probably refers to *phones* since an advantage is stated. However, the pronoun *they* has another plural antecedent, *letters*. Therefore, a reader could get confused. The sentence could easily be restated.

Clear Reference   *Phones* are more convenient than letters because *with phones* we can contact our families and friends quicker than we can with letters.

Moreover, pronoun reference can be unclear if too many pronouns are used. In Discovery 1.9, you studied point of view in a paragraph from "Independence in American Culture" by Kelly Boggs. Note how the pronoun substitution aids readability in the following passage.

Original Passage: Correct Pronoun Use

1   One characteristic that Americans value highly is independence. Throughout history, *Americans* have thought of *themselves* as pioneers. From settling a new country to opening the frontiers, that rugged, independent spirit has pervaded every aspect of American life. Independent people are admired as being people of strong character. The importance of independence can be clearly seen in

5   the way American children are raised. From the time that *children* are very small, *they* are encouraged to venture out on *their* own and try new things. For instance, playing with new toys is encouraged by parents. Parents watch proudly as *children* as young as two years old learn how to do things for *themselves* such as picking out *their* own clothes and deciding what *they* want to eat. As *children* grow older, *they* are often required to perform household tasks, like cleaning, to earn *their* money for

10   things *they* want. Over time, *they* are expected to continue doing things on *their* own, particularly earning money. Most high school students, for example, have part-time jobs to earn money for things like cars, clothes, and entertainment. This push towards independence continues until the day that *children* are encouraged, if not expected, to move out on *their* own. American *adults* are expected to make *their* own way in the world with little help from others. As you can see,

15   independence is a respected trait in American society. [231 words]

Here is the same passage again with an overuse of pronouns. Where does the meaning change?

Adapted Passage A: Too Many Pronouns

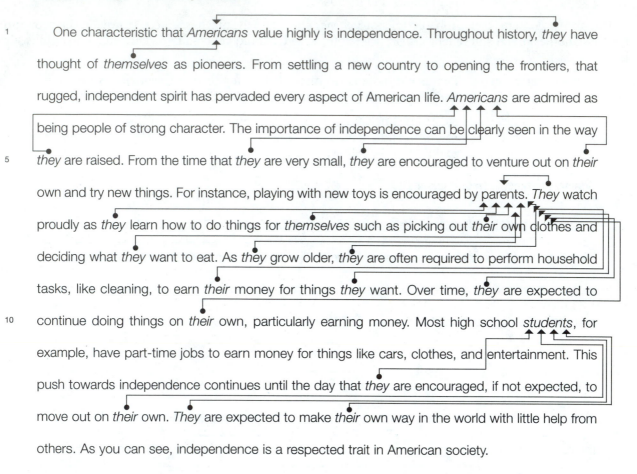

1   One characteristic that *Americans* value highly is independence. Throughout history, *they* have thought of *themselves* as pioneers. From settling a new country to opening the frontiers, that rugged, independent spirit has pervaded every aspect of American life. *Americans* are admired as being people of strong character. The importance of independence can be clearly seen in the way

5   *they* are raised. From the time that *they* are very small, *they* are encouraged to venture out on *their* own and try new things. For instance, playing with new toys is encouraged by parents. *They* watch proudly as *they* learn how to do things for *themselves* such as picking out *their* own clothes and deciding what *they* want to eat. As *they* grow older, *they* are often required to perform household tasks, like cleaning, to earn *their* money for things *they* want. Over time, *they* are expected to

10   continue doing things on *their* own, particularly earning money. Most high school *students*, for example, have part-time jobs to earn money for things like cars, clothes, and entertainment. This push towards independence continues until the day that *they* are encouraged, if not expected, to move out on *their* own. *They* are expected to make *their* own way in the world with little help from others. As you can see, independence is a respected trait in American society.

Because there are too many pronouns in the previous passage, it is not clear who watches proudly and who learns to do things for themselves. It sounds like the parents do both. Since the focus does not return to children, it is not clear who does all the rest of the things in the passage. What would happen if there were too many content words in this passage?

Adapted Passage B: Too Many Content Words

1   One characteristic that Americans value highly is independence. Throughout history, *Americans* have thought of *Americans* as pioneers. From settling a new country to opening the frontiers, that rugged, independent spirit has pervaded every aspect of American life. Independent people are admired as being people of strong character. The importance of independence can be clearly seen

5   in the way American children are raised. From the time that *children* are very small, *children* are encouraged to venture out on *children's* own and try new things. For instance, playing with new toys is encouraged by parents. Parents watch proudly as *children* as young as two years old learn how to do things for *children's selves* such as picking out *children's* own clothes and deciding what *children* want to eat. As *children* grow older, *children* are often required to perform household tasks,

10   like cleaning, to earn *children's* money for things *children* want. Over time, *children* are expected to continue doing things on *children's* own, particularly earning money. Most high school students, for example, have part-time jobs to earn money for things like cars, clothes, and entertainment. This push towards independence continues until the day that *children* are encouraged, if not expected, to move out on *children's* own. American *adults* are expected to make *adults'* own way in the world

15   with little help from others. As you can see, independence is a respected trait in American society.

The overuse of content words in this version affects readability and changes the meaning in some cases. For example, if children are deciding what children should eat, they are not necessarily deciding what they themselves want to eat. They are deciding for other children. Also, do children earn money for themselves or for other children? As you can see, you need to balance the use of pronouns and content words to aid readability. Here are a few simple rules.

RULES FOR EFFECTIVE PRONOUN USE —————————————————

1. A pronoun must have one antecedent, and pronoun reference to the antecedent should be clear.

2. The antecedent must be retained occasionally to maintain clear pronoun reference.

3. A pronoun must agree with the antecedent in number (singular or plural).

4. A pronoun must have the same gender as the antecedent (masculine and feminine).

5. A pronoun must be the correct case (subject, object, reflexive, or possessive).

DISCOVERY
1.12: Controlling pronoun reference at the sentence level

- Restate each sentence to correct the unclear pronoun reference. You may have to change the wording significantly. There is more than one way to revise the pronoun reference problem in each item.

➷ **Examples**

Unclear Reference	Dark streets are often places where unscrupulous people hide. They are dangerous.
Clear Reference	Dark streets are dangerous in that they are often places where unscrupulous people hide.
	Dark streets are often places where dangerous, unscrupulous people hide.

1. Bicycles are better for students than cars because they can get around more easily on campus.

2. English-English dictionaries are better for international students than bilingual dictionaries because they do not have enough information on words.

3. Libraries are great resources for students because they have a lot of materials.

4. Zoos are a lot of fun for children because they have many things to see and do.

5. Dogs are different from cats. Some people think they are better pets.

   ....

   ....

6. Parents should not force their children to do things because they may think they are unreasonable.

   ....

   ....

7. Some people prefer to live in cities. Some people prefer to live in small towns. They are different.

   ....

   ....

8. My teachers gave me low grades. They were unfair.

   ....

   ....

ⒹⒾⓈⒸⓄⓋⒺⓇⓎ
1.13: Controlling pronoun reference at the essay level

The following paper was written in 1971 by an American undergraduate student for a political science course.
- Supply the necessary pronouns. Use the correct gender, number, and case.
- Check your answers.
- Then answer the Discussion Questions that follow.

Public Opinion and Voting Behavior in the U.S.
by Nancy A. Price

In viewing many of the facts that we know about public opinion and voting behavior, I think that

public opinion has a great effect on popular democracy in spite of the public's voting behavior.

Most people in the United States are not in the least bit interested in politics. ....
                                                                                        (1)

do not really care about the outcome of some of the most important presidential elections. Only

about twenty-seven percent of the registered voters in this country really do care about presidential

elections and politics in general. The voting turnout during a presidential election is a testimony to

this fact. On the average, only about sixty to sixty-five percent go to the polls on election day. Many

that do go vote along party lines so that .... do not have to read through all the
                                            (2)

different offices and pick the one who looks like .... has a good name.
                                                   (3)

Since there is such a lack of interest, there is also a great lack of information. Research shows that

many people cannot even answer a question on the most basic political terms (Monsma, pp. 245-246).

Considering this lack of information, a person might wonder what makes people affiliate

.... with a certain political party. There are several different reasons, all of which are
                (4)

rather irrational. Many people simply vote as did .... parents. Without really knowing
                                                              (5)

15   why, ... associated .... to the same party as ....
                    (6)   (7)   (8)

parents' when .... were children. Others affiliate .... to a certain party
                        (9)   (10)

because of .... social status. A certain party is supposed to be good for the blue collar
                    (11)

worker, another for the corporation. In reality, if there is such a division in a political party, there are

people in each party for the blue collar workers and people for the corporations.

20   In spite of the irrationality of .... reasons, people tend to be rational in
                                                        (12)

.... voting. Once they choose a party, they stay with ....
            (13)   (14)

With all these facts, congressmen, senators, and even the president still worry about ....
                                                                                                          (15)

image in the public eye. Almost none of the constituents of congressmen and senators could tell,

or are even interested in, how .... representative voted on a particular bill. Yet these
                                            (16)

25   men still vote how .... think .... constituents would have liked
                                (17)   (18)

.... to.
            (19)

Different presidents have been said to carry copies of the different popularity polls. ....
                                                                                                              (20)

were probably worrying about the opinions on a certain issue. Most people do not even know

whether or not the president has a policy on a particular subject, much less what ....
                                                                                                  (21)

30   policy is. But these men are afraid—afraid of what public opinion can do to ....
                                                                                              (22)

if some catastrophe comes about. If this catastrophe does come about, public opinion will turn

against ...., and they probably will not be reelected.
              (23)

This fear of not being reelected is more powerful than any study on voting behavior patterns. Many

senators and congressmen could vote any way .... want, but ....
                                                                (24)   (25)

35   do not. For the most part, ... vote as .... constituents want.
                                            (26)   (27)

[506 words] (Adapted with permission, Nancy Price, American)

Discussion Questions

Use the previous essay to answer the following questions.

1. What is the writer's opinion about public opinion and voting behavior?
2. How does the writer support the opinion that most people in the U.S. are not interested in politics?
3. Why is there very little information for voters?
4. How do Americans choose their parties?
5. According to the writer, Americans vote along party lines; that is, once they pick a party, they stick to it, voting mainly for candidates in that party rather than voting on issues. Do you agree that this is rational?
6. Do politicians care what the voters think? Explain your answer.
7. Did the writer of the above essay use inclusive language? Could the use of the masculine singular and references to "men" have been avoided? (Did you use inclusive language in your answers?)

How involved in politics or government issues are people in your country?

Nancy Price describes the general lack of interest Americans show in the political process in the U.S. How involved in politics, or government issues, are people in your country? Why? Discuss one or two reasons with examples and details. [150-200 words, every other line]

What impact do U.S. presidential elections have on your country?

The U.S. has a wide scope of influence around the world. In what way, if any, does the choice of president in the U.S. affect your country? Are people in your country interested in the U.S. presidential election outcomes? Why or why not? Discuss one or two reasons with examples and details. [150-200 words, every other line]

Writing Assignment

Choose one of the following topics and write a 2-3 page composition* (handwritten, every other line).

1. People like to travel for many reasons. What are two (or three) primary benefits of travel? Discuss each benefit fully with examples, details, and personal experience (your own and/or that of others).

2. Most people want a happy life, but not everyone can be happy all of the time. What things and conditions do people need to be happy? Discuss the two (or three) most important ones. Provide specific details and examples to support the discussion. Include personal experience (your own and/or that of others).

---

*In Chapters 1–3, the term "composition" refers to one well-developed paragraph or a short essay.

CHAPTER *summary*

- Effective academic writing (the "A" paper) has convincing content, effective organization, and correct use of sophisticated grammar and vocabulary.

- The "audience" is the reader, and control of "point of view" (the perspective from which a paper is written) is closely connected to the choice of audience.

- Academic writing is addressed primarily to professors and is formal, objective, and serious in tone.

- Each point of view has a specific focus and purpose.

- In academic writing, avoid first and second person unless you are giving personal examples or instructing. Third-person plural (*people, they, them, their*) is preferred because it is inclusive of both men and women, and it is smoother than third-person singular (*a person, he or she, him or her, his or her*).

- The use of point of view (first, second, and third person) should be consistent: *students, they, them, themselves*, not *students, us, you, we, they*.

- Control of point of view also requires control of number agreement (singular and plural). Use verbs, articles, and nouns correctly. Pronouns are used to avoid unnecessary repetition. Pronouns should have one clear antecedent, agree with the antecedent in number and gender, and be in the correct case (subject, object, reflexive, or possessive).

Chapter 2

Critical Thinking

CHAPTER TOPICS

- ► CRITICAL-THINKING SKILLS
- ► ACADEMIC WRITING ASSIGNMENTS
- ► THE PROCESS OF WRITING
- ► PEER REVIEW AND REVISION 1
- ► PARALLELISM
- ► PUNCTUATION: (.) (;) (,)
- ► RUN-ON SENTENCES

Journal
ENTRY 6

How do you manage your weekly schedule?

Charting as a Means of Planning

In this journal entry, you will practice making charts as a way of planning for a composition. In a chart, information is listed in columns with the most general on the left. Each column to the right is more specific. The chart will help you see your main points and supporting points clearly. You can use charts as a way to take notes from readings also; this will help you review faster. You will practice making study charts in later chapters.

There are 168 hours in a week, and you probably have a lot to do in these few hours.

1. On a separate sheet of paper, make a list of your weekly activities and calculate approximately how many hours and what percentage of time you spend on each. In other words, how much time do you spend attending class, doing homework, socializing, exercising, sleeping, eating, doing laundry and other chores, working for pay, and the like? For example, if you spend 15 hours a week in class, divide 15 by 168 and you get 0.089. Therefore, you spend 9% of your week in class.

2. Then use the following sample to make a formal chart of your weekly activities, hours spent on each, and percentage of time each takes. Your number of hours must add up to 168 and your percentages to 100%.

My Weekly Time Management

Activity	Hours	Percentage of Time
Classes	15	9%
Study Time	....	....
Study Time	....	....
(Sum of All Other Activities)	....	....
Total:	168 Hours	100%

D I S C O V E R Y
2.1: Solving problems with time management

• In groups, compare your weekly routines. What problems, if any, do you and your partners have managing your time? How can you solve these problems?
• On a separate sheet of paper, make a chart of up to five major time-management problems and your proposed solutions.

CRITICAL-THINKING SKILLS

Critical thinking is an essential tool in both academic writing and reading. Good critical thinkers are able to do the following:

• Sort out general and specific points
• Understand the difference between facts and opinions
• Synthesize information from a variety of sources
• Summarize
• Analyze
• Evaluate
• Interpret information
• Support and defend an opinion

• Make judgments
• Make inferences
• Draw conclusions
• View a topic objectively (unbiased)
• Understand a variety of viewpoints
• Think logically
• Ask questions

In this section, you will sharpen your critical-thinking skills by:
1. learning how to follow assignments.
2. planning, organizing, writing, revising, and editing papers.
3. analyzing and evaluating the models in the text.
4. reading each other's papers and giving feedback (peer review) for revision.

ACADEMIC WRITING ASSIGNMENTS

D I S C O V E R Y
2.2: Identifying kinds of academic assignments

• With the class or in small groups, list the kinds of assignments you have had so far in your academic studies. You do not need to restrict yourself to writing assignments.
• Place a ✓ next to those which require critical thinking.

The Writing Process: A Preview

Another way you will use your critical-thinking skills in your academic course work is in writing. Completing an academic writing assignment is a thinking process which involves several activities.

THE WRITING PROCESS

Activity	*Description*
Brainstorming	Gathering/Generating/Planning ideas
Organizing	Making a formal plan (outline)
Writing	Composing the paragraph or the essay
Revising	Making major changes
Proofreading and editing	Fixing minor errors

This process of writing begins with the assignment. The assignment may be oral or written out in detail. Some assignments may be clearly delivered and offer you a great deal of direction, while others may offer too much leeway, causing you to feel lost at first. Some assignments will be extended, allowing you a few weeks to complete them (e.g., term papers, theses, lab reports). However, other assignments may be due within a week or two (e.g., short papers, journal entries). Perhaps the most intense writing assignment is the essay test, which may have a strict time limit. (See Chapter 9, "Essay Tests.")

Regardless of the various time limits, all assignments must be followed precisely. It is important for you to read the assignments carefully and understand them. If you misread an assignment, your final paper may be off focus or off topic. Such papers may fail based on content even if the organization, grammar, and presentation are excellent. It follows that you must never change an assignment to suit your interests or knowledge. For example, if you cannot answer a question on an essay test, do not rewrite the question. Answer the professor's question in the best way you can because you might be given partial credit. However, if you change the question, you might not get any credit.

Following an assignment involves understanding its wording and design. Here are some common terms used in academic writing assignments.

Analyze
An analysis is the study or examination of the parts of something or aspects of an idea. How do the parts function? What is their purpose or importance? How do the ideas relate to one another? What is your personal opinion or judgment?

Argue
Argument requires taking a position in favor of or in opposition to an issue. State your position and defend it. Explain what should be done about a problem. Be sure to indicate that you understand the opposing viewpoint(s). (Argumentation is stronger than a response.)

Classify
Classification involves arranging or organizing things into categories (kinds or types). Define each category and illustrate it.

Compare and Contrast
Comparison involves examining qualities and characteristics in order to find similarities between two or more things; contrasting requires analysis of the differences between them. The assignment should clarify whether the focus is to be on similarities, differences, or both.

Define
Defining involves giving the formal definition of a term or thing by stating the term, class (or category) to which it belongs, and the features that distinguish it from other members of that class. It may also require writing an extended definition, which would include examples, details, and explanations.

Describe/Explain/Discuss
These terms are used broadly and require complete and detailed answers to a topic. You may have to describe a place or physical structure of some kind, give a chronological (time order) explanation, enumerate or list major points, examine causes or define a process, and compare or contrast. The other vocabulary in the assignment will guide you.

Enumerate

Enumeration is a general term for listing, classifying, and recounting one by one the major points. This term is basic to almost all rhetorical methods, especially comparison/contrast, process, cause, effect, exemplification, and classification.

Evaluate

In an evaluation, you have to analyze a text or work and judge its merits or correctness as well as its short-comings. You may also need to examine advantages and disadvantages and give personal opinions on each side.

Explain

To write an effective explanation, provide support to clarify your points. Tell *how* and *why*. Anticipate the reader's questions and provide detailed answers. Look at causes and/or effects, or describe a process.

Illustrate

To write an effective illustration, supply a representative number of relevant examples. The examples can be hypothetical or specific and may include personal experience. Effective illustrations are highly valued in academic writing assignments.

Respond/Comment

Response assignments are thought papers in which you react with your personal interpretation of the text material. Agree or disagree and support your position with personal experience and/or references to assigned readings.

Summarize

In a summary, restate what the author's major points are in your own words. Do not add your own main points or opinions in a summary. Also, do not judge or evaluate the author's main points. A summary is a short report, not a critique.

Trace/Outline

When tracing or outlining the development of something, you need to provide an overview of historical events in chronological order or the major points of an issue.

ⓓⓘⓢⓒⓞⓥⓔⓡⓨ
2.3: Analyzing short writing assignments

- Circle the key words. What do the following short assignments require?
- How would you complete them?

> ⇝ **Example**
>
> In what (ways) do porpoises (differ from) dolphins?
>
> *ways: enumeration; differ from: contrast*
> I would enumerate the differences between dolphins and porpoises.

1. Explain how a caterpillar becomes a butterfly.

   ....

   ....

2. Discuss three major reasons that people who leave the security of their home cultures to move to another culture to study are heroes. Provide examples, details, and personal experience.

   ....

   ....

3. Enumerate the causes and effects of women's liberation.

   ....

   ....

4. Trace the development of satellites.

   ....

   ....

5. Define the three kinds of tornadoes. How are they classified? What are the characteristics of each?

   ....

   ....

6. Enumerate the major features of effective academic writing. Discuss them in detail.

   ....

   ....

Assignment Design

In addition to understanding the terminology in assignments, you need to learn how longer writing assignments are usually designed. Some academic assignments may be written in several sentences, and the actual assignment task is not given right away. Such assignments have two parts: the lead-in and the assignment task. Each part has a function and provides you with important cues. Your success on an assignment may depend on how well you read it. Therefore, make sure you read the entire assignment before you start.

The Lead-In

The first part of an assignment may contain a situation or some general background information to get you thinking about the topic. This part may be more than one sentence long. Do not choose these ideas as your focus because your paper will be too general. Keep reading to find the actual limited subject of the assignment.

The Assignment Task

The actual assignment, called the assignment task, usually follows the lead-in. The assignment task contains a question or a statement limiting the topic, specific instructions containing imperatives and terms for academic assignments, and directions listing the kinds of support to use.

KINDS OF SUPPORT

Type	*Description*
Examples	Specific cases/instances for illustration
Details	In-depth analysis of topic
Facts and statistics	Charts, graphs, surveys, polls
Expert opinion and/or research	Books, articles, experiments, studies
Personal experience or case studies	True stories

Instructions in Assignments

Instructions in assignments are usually given with imperatives (command forms). Moreover, you may be given limits on how many subtopics you can have. Pay attention to such expressions as "two or three," "areas," "reasons," "causes," "effects," "similarities," differences," and other rhetorical terms which signal the method of development. Also, pay close attention to the use of *and* and *or*. *And* directs you to address all of the assignment tasks, but *or* directs you to make a choice. If the assignment is to make a choice, you must do so.

Here are some examples:

Discuss two *or* three reasons for . . .
  (You have a choice of two or three reasons. Do not discuss four.)

Analyze the causes *and* effects of . . .
  (You must discuss both the causes and effects.)

Discuss the advantages *or* disadvantages of . . .
  (You must choose advantages or disadvantages. Do not discuss both.)

Define "pecking order" *and* give examples . . .
  (You must not only define the term; you need to give examples as well.)

Read the model essay *and* answer the questions that follow.
  (You must do both tasks: read the essay and answer the questions.)

⮞ Example of Assignment Analysis

Because the laser is such a powerful device, some people used to fear it. However, recently, scientists have found that the laser has a variety of applications *(lead-in)*. Discuss four important areas where lasers have been used to the benefit of society. Use specific and convincing examples and details to support your discussion *(assignment task)*.

The lead-in in the above assignment shows two opinions about the laser:
  • Some people fear the laser because it is powerful.
  • The laser is a good device which has several uses.

The assignment task limits the focus to the second opinion, the benefits of the laser to society. The essay must explore four areas of life in which the laser has helped people, not why people may fear the laser. There must also be specific and convincing examples and details.

ⒹⒾⓈⒸⓄⓋⒺⓇⓎ
2.4: Analyzing longer writer assignments

On a separate sheet of paper, analyze each of the following assignments.
• Which part is the lead-in?
• Which part is the assignment task?
• What does the assignment require?

1. Self-respect is the respect people have for themselves. People's success in life may depend on how much self-respect (self-esteem, self-regard) they have. How will having (or not having) self-respect help (or hinder) students in their academic pursuits? Discuss two or three ways self-respect (or the lack of it) can affect students' success. Provide specific support.

2. Studying in a university is challenging. Some students excel, some do an adequate job, but others fail. Why do some students do well? Discuss two or three major characteristics (qualities) of good students. Provide specific details, examples, and your own personal experience or that of someone you know.

3. In the article "A Sociological Perspective," by Donald A. Hobbs and Stuart J. Blank, the authors argue that social interaction is very important. We depend a great deal on the people around us; they influence us a lot. Think of a teacher whom you know well and who has had a good influence on your life. Describe and illustrate his or her influence in detail.

4. Languages are living as long as they are spoken. Thus, they gradually change over time. Despite the fact that the English spoken today reflects current popular usage, contemporary grammar books still prescribe formal, standard rules which do not seem to apply to current usage. What problems, if any, does this create for you as a language learner? Discuss two or three problems with specific examples and details.

🅓🅘🅢🅒🅞🅥🅔🅡🅨
2.5: Analyzing a model assignment

- Read the model assignment carefully. Label both the lead-in and the assignment task.
- Then read the student essays that follow.
- Answer the Discussion Questions that follow.

Model Assignment

Whenever two cultures come into contact, there is sharing (borrowing or adopting). The two cultures may adopt foods, customs, beliefs, and language from each other. Cultures share in many other areas as well. Think of things your culture has borrowed from another culture, such as the U.S. or Canada. Discuss two or three areas in which your culture has borrowed from the other culture. Provide specific explanations, examples, and details.

Student Essay 1

Cultures' Influence

1   Since the early ages, people have been trying to discover new places. Sometimes they succeed in that. Sometimes they don't, but if they do, they usually get to see another culture which is more likely to be different from theirs. They ponder what that other culture does. Is it right or wrong, or is it good or bad? On most occasions, they accept the differences they want, such as languages,
5   culture, and some knowledge.

Initially, we'll take the language as the way of communication between them. The language plays an important role in understanding how the other culture speaks, and how they would construct the sentences for maximum understanding. Later on, when they learn the language, they can read their knowledge and look at what level of science, art, literature and other branches of knowledge
10   that the other culture is at. In this way, they can benefit from each other to take a step forward in civilization. My culture borrowed this technique from the West and the East.

The second category is the basic structure of the culture, or how the culture is organized. Finding out how the culture is formed helps in understanding the culture, which brings some respect to the other culture's valued traits.

15   One form of the previous is understanding the religion that is predominant in the culture. The main reason for that is the people in the other culture might have high respect towards it. Anything such as little regard might be contemptible to the other country. A perfect example is the thing that foreign people who have no idea about what is good or bad. The result might be a different look at and a wrong idea about that foreign people who are from the other culture.

20   In conclusion, those categories are the most common things that my culture borrowed from Eastern and Western cultures. [310 words] (Adapted with permission, name withheld, Kuwaiti)

Student Essay 2

Western Influence on Venezuelan Culture
by Licett Galietta

1   Whenever two cultures get into contact there is a tendency for each one to adopt aspects of the other culture. The influence of one over the other is inevitable and more noticeable according to the length of time of the exposure. This influence can be appreciated in many areas such as language, customs, food, beliefs, traditions, music, art, architecture, and technology.

5   Perhaps owing to its history as a country whose population is composed mostly of immigrants from all parts of the world, Venezuela has adopted many foreign traditions and customs. In addition, Venezuelan culture has adapted those foreign traditions and customs to a point where they coexist with the native ones in perfect harmony. Venezuela's adoption of Western culture is a perfect example

of this cultural sharing. Venezuelan culture has been influenced by the Western culture, especially
5   by the United States, because of its geographical location. Two major areas of the Venezuelan culture
in which this influence can be illustrated are the language and food.

One major area of Venezuelan culture in which the influence of Western culture and specifically
American culture can be easily appreciated is language. For instance, because of the United States'
scientific and technological advances, all the new terms used in those areas are being borrowed
15 from English and used in Spanish without adaptation. The new vocabulary that has been created
recently because of the computer age is written and pronounced in English: mouse, hardware,
software, and diskette. Similarly, other terms that come from sports such as soccer and baseball
are being used not only in the sports but also in idioms. For instance, when a person is not being
honest in a relationship, it is said that he or she is playing "double play." I remember when I was a
20 child I used to play a very typical game named "eres," in which I used the term "taima," meaning
that a person was out of the play at that moment or was safe at home. A few years ago, I was
watching my brother playing the same game and using the term "time out" instead of "taima." At
that moment, I realized that the term "taima," which I thought was very Venezuelan, was really the
same "time out" from the American baseball game. Another expression, "O.K.," is also widely used
in spoken informal Spanish. It means that there is agreement or that the situation is working out. The
25 previous examples show that Spanish has been affected by the Western culture in a significant way.

Another aspect of the Venezuelan culture that has been affected is the food. Small carts in the
streets selling "perros calientes," or hot dogs, are part of the scenery of most of Venezuela's big
cities. I think that this tradition was brought to Venezuela from the first Americans who came with
30 the petroleum companies. It is important to point out that the number of American fast-food
companies in Venezuela has increased in the last fifteen years. Fast food establishments have
recently been constructed and are becoming widely accepted by Venezuelans. In fact, today fast
food is part of the daily diet of Venezuelans, particularly the working class. As a consequence, the
concept of fast food is now part of our culture.
35 In summary, the food and language in Venezuelan culture have been greatly affected by Western
culture, particularly by American culture. The influence between these cultures will continue in the
future because of the increase of the international economic relationships. Indeed, this influence will
be not only of the Western culture over Venezuela's culture, but also in the opposite way. [599 words]
(Adapted with permission, Licett Galietta, Venezuelan)

Discussion Questions

Use the assignment and the Student Essays to answer the following questions.

1. Do the essays address the assignment task? Why or why not?

   Essay 1 ....

   ....

   ....

   Essay 2 ....

   ....

   ....

2. What does each writer do well?

   Essay 1 ....

   ....

   ....

Essay 2 ....
....
....

3. What grade do you think each essay received? Why?

Essay 1 ....
....
....

Essay 2 ....
....
....

4. What does each writer need to do to improve the essay?

Essay 1 ....
....
....

Essay 2 ....
....
....

Journal ENTRY 7

In which area has your culture borrowed the most from another culture different from your own?

Has your culture been deeply influenced by another culture different from your own? Think of the most prevalent signs of influence. Pick one area, such as food or language, and discuss the influence. Provide specific examples and details. [200-250 words, every other line]

The Process of Writing

Once you understand the assignment, you are ready to start the writing process. This process includes the planning, writing, revising, and proofreading and editing of your papers. These activities are not necessarily sequential, and everyone has preferences on how to complete the process. Some people prefer brainstorming before outlining, and some may prefer listing and outlining simultaneously. Some write and revise at the same time. Critical thinking is a major part of this process, as the following outline shows.

BRAINSTORMING (Generating/Collecting/Planning ideas)

1. List possible ideas that follow the assignment focus, and make lists and clusters to "get the juices flowing."
2. Determine your focus at this point (limit your topic) if the assignment does not do so for you.
3. Consider whom you are targeting as your audience at all times.
4. Examine the ideas and choose the most convincing ones.
5. Gather and evaluate information to support the ideas. Make final selections.

ORGANIZING (Refining/Formalizing plan)

1. Determine how you will present your ideas (rhetorical method).
2. Make an outline or chart in which you clearly determine your thesis or topic statement, your subtopics (main points), and specific support.
3. Make changes; add or delete ideas.
4. Put the plan aside and take a break. New ideas will occur to you while you are doing something else.
5. Revise the plan some more.
6. Get feedback from your professor or peers (peer review).
7. Revise the plan.

WRITING (Composing in longhand or on computer)

1. Compose the first draft of the paper. Follow the plan while composing.
2. Try to write without stopping frequently to look up words or revise for fluency.
3. New ideas may occur to you. Make changes as needed to include any improvements.
4. Put the paper aside for a while and take a break so that you can look at it again with a fresh eye.
5. Get feedback from your professor or peers (peer review).

REVISING (Making major changes)

1. Return to the paper with an objective eye.
2. Be a critical thinker. Evaluate the paper. Is it effective?
3. Make major changes in the content, organization, and order of support.
4. Make the sentences more complex and smooth.

You may end up writing more than one draft to attain the final product.

PROOFREADING AND EDITING (Making minor changes to mechanics)

1. Correct grammar errors.
2. Check for errors in spelling, punctuation, and capitalization.
3. Check format (margins, use of lines, labeling, paper type).

Time Management of the Writing Process

In Journal Entry 6 and Discovery 2.1, you learned that as a college or university student, you are very busy trying to juggle all of your course work in order to get all of your assignments done on time. Writing a paper may take more time than you think it will. Due to all of the activities involved in the process of writing, you do not want to wait until the last minute to start a paper. Pulling an "all-nighter" or trying to write the paper the morning it is due may well lead to bad results. Not only is such an approach stressful, it is usually unsuccessful. The quality and appearance of the final product reveal the haste in which the paper was done, giving the professor a bad impression. Professors expect papers to be complete, well organized, and clearly presented.

It is a good idea to start the prewriting activities soon after getting an assignment; if you plan time in your daily and/or weekly schedule to complete the assignment, you will feel less stressed and more satisfied with the product. Doing a little bit every day instead of procrastinating will make you a more productive and successful student.

ⓓⓘⓢⓒⓞⓥⓔⓡⓨ
2.6: Determining time management of the writing process

In Journal Entry 6 and Discovery 2.1, you analyzed your weekly schedule, then identified and provided solutions for problems that you were having with time management. Now concentrate on the writing activities. Compare the amount of time you think each activity would take for both out-of-class and in-class writing assignments.
- By yourself, complete Chart 1 by calculating the percentage of time you would need in each activity.
- Then compare your answers to your partners'.
- Figure out the group's average in each area on Chart 2.
- Report to the class and answer the Discussion Questions that follow.

Chart 1

	Your Own Percentages	
	Out-of-Class	In-Class
Brainstorming	....	....
Organizing	....	....
Writing	....	....
Revising	....	....
Proofreading/Editing	....	....
	100%	100%

Chart 2

	Your Group's Averages	
	Out-of-Class	In-Class
Brainstorming	....	....
Organizing	....	....
Writing	....	....
Revising	....	....
Proofreading/Editing	....	....
	100%	100%

Ⓠ Discussion Questions

Discuss these questions with the class.
1. How do the percentages differ in class vs. out of class? Why?
2. Which activity do you think is the most important in each case? Why?
3. Which activities take the least amount of time? Why?
4. Turn to the chart "Suggested Time Management for Writing Process Activities" on page 44. How do your percentages compare?
5. Will you be making any changes to your approach to completing writing assignments? If so, explain.

ⒹⒾⓈⒸⓄⓋⒺⓇⓎ
2.7: Brainstorming for a writing assignment

To practice analyzing an assignment and determining the audience, do the following.
• Study the following model assignment carefully.
• Discuss the questions that follow.
• Complete the assignment by choosing one of the brainstorming methods on pages 42 through 44.

Model Assignment

The International Student Organization (ISO) at your university or college publishes a newsletter read by students, professors, and administrators. The ISO would like short articles (1 to 2 typed pages, double-spaced) written by nonnative speakers on the benefits they gain by studying in the U.S. or Canada.

Brainstorm for a few minutes alone. Make lists, clusters, and/or charts to find ideas for the article you want to write. After working alone for a few minutes, share your notes with partners. Each of you should discuss your notes and revise them (add or discard ideas) as new ideas occur to you.

Ⓠ Discussion Questions

1. Which part is the lead-in? What is the situation? Who is the audience?
2. Which part is the assignment task? How many things do you have to do? List the imperative verbs.
3. What is the topic? List the important words in the topic.
4. What level of formality (and point of view) should be used in the article?
5. How long should the article be?
6. How should the article be presented (format)?
7. Do you have to write the article yet? Why or why not?

Methods of Brainstorming

Choose one of the following brainstorming methods to generate (create) ideas for the in-class assignment.

Method 1: Listing
Listing ideas is one way to brainstorm. First, list the ideas as they occur to you.

⇨ Example

self-respect	get exercise	don't argue
care about self	eat well	be assertive
polite behavior	follow the rules	accept criticism
respect for others	attend class	like yourself
take care of appearance	arrive on time	obey the laws
avoid bad habits	do homework	self-regard

After that, organize the lists. Put related ideas together.

☞ **Example**

Self-respect	Care about self	Respect for others
1. self-regard	1. take care of appearance	1. polite behavior
2. like yourself	2. get exercise	2. follow the rules
3. confidence	3. eat well	3. obey the laws
4. self-worth	4. avoid bad habits	

Method 2: Clustering
If you are a visual learner, you might want to "cluster."

☞ **Example**

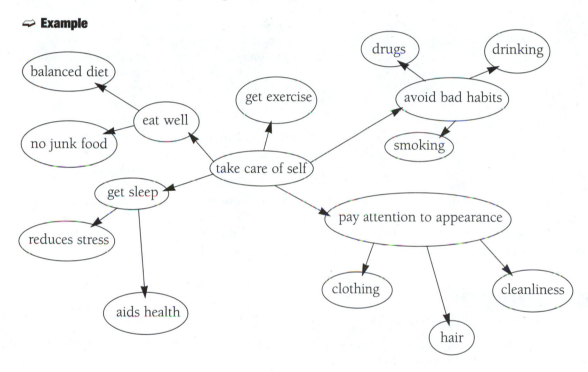

Method 3: Charting

Charts are useful if you know your main points and you want an informal way to move from general to specific.

↪ **Example**

<u>Self-Respect</u>

General	→	Less General	→	Specific	→	More Specific
Care for my well-being		Care about appearance		Cleanliness Dress appropriately		Laundry, bathing Work: formal School: informal
		Care about my health		Eat well Sleep well No bad habits		Balanced diet 6-8 hours/night No drinking, smoking, or drugs
Show others respect		Sociability		Polite behavior		Conducting daily business, making friends
		Cooperation		Follow rules/laws/customs		Driving, time commitments, work style

Be careful as you are planning the chart. Do not begin with ideas which are too general; otherwise, it will be difficult for you to find specific support. Notice that the last column (the one on the right) has specific information, such as "get eight hours of sleep a night" and "balanced diet." Finally, all of the points in the chart, even the specific ones, should be explained in the paper.

ⒹⒾⓈⒸⓄⓋⒺⓇⓎ
2.8: Writing the first draft in class

Use your brainstorming notes from the previous assignment to organize and write a short article on the benefits of studying in the U.S. or Canada.

• Choose three major benefits.
• Support your discussion with examples and details.
• Use the guidelines for in-class assignments in the following chart. Try to finish in the time given. (Calculate how many minutes to allow for each writing activity.)

Suggested Time Management for Writing Process Activities		
	<u>Out-of-Class</u>	<u>In-Class</u>
Brainstorming	25%	15% (............ minutes)
Organizing	10%	10% (............ minutes)
Writing	20%	60% (............ minutes)
Revising	35%	5% (............ minutes)
Proofreading/Editing	10%	10% (............ minutes)
Total:	100%	100% (............ minutes)

PEER REVIEW AND REVISION 1

Peer-reviewing is an integral part of the writing process. When professors write textbooks and articles, they seek out their colleagues for feedback in order to revise effectively. Likewise, when you complete writing assignments in this text, you will seek out the opinions of your peers (classmates) to improve the paper.

Peer-reviewing will help you grow as a writer and as a critical thinker. To begin with, peer-reviewing requires critical-thinking skills because you have to analyze the paper much like did you in Discovery 2.5. In your peer reviews, you will have to identify the effective areas as well as the areas which need improvement. You may wonder how qualified you are to do this. After all, you are not a teacher. Nonetheless, you are a reader, and you will be helping your classmates tremendously if you target the unclear areas in their papers. In addition, by evaluating models and your peers' papers, you will become a better writer because you will see what works and what does not, and you will have frequent practice applying the rules for effective academic writing.

Although this activity may be hard at first, you will get better at it. Your confidence will build as you make progress with both your analytical skills and writing. The final benefit is the improvement you will see in your classmates' writing as the term or semester progresses. For example, the first time you peer-review, you may notice that your partners' compositions are short and not well organized. However, at the end of the term, both you and your partners will probably be able to compose interesting and well-organized essays.

Ground Rules for Peer-Reviewing

There are different approaches to peer review, but it is usually done before the final draft is due. In general, students exchange papers, complete the peer reviews, and discuss them. Because some people may feel intimidated by peer-reviewing and discussing their papers, you should follow certain ground rules and use strategies for clarification. These guidelines for effective group dynamics will help to build trust among group members.

GROUND RULES FOR PEER-REVIEWING

1. Do not take charge or monopolize; share time with others. Help draw shy group members into the conversation. Everyone should participate.

2. Acknowledge what the writer did effectively before discussing the weak areas.

3. Defend your opinions tactfully. In other words, do not take the other students' observations and suggestions personally.

4. Be objective. Do not make fun of the writer's ideas, and do not criticize the writer for having opinions different from yours. Your task is to evaluate how well the writer defends the opinions.

5. Compromise to resolve differences of opinion. Do not let a difference of opinion hold up the group process.

6. Ask for repetition if you are unsure of what your partner said.

7. Be honest. Do not say the paper is good if there are problems. The writer wants to do a good job and deserves an honest reaction.

8. Be a good listener. Do not cut people off (interrupt).

9. Remember that you are not only giving advice, but also learning about your own writing and that of others.

Strategies for Clarification

Language in group discussions is unplanned and thus imperfect at times. People do not always have time to correct a grammar mistake or pick the best words. During a discussion, it may be difficult to understand everything that is said because of someone's speaking speed, grammar, and vocabulary choices. If you have problems communicating in your peer review groups for these reasons, use the following expressions.

If you do not understand, ask for clarification.

- Sorry?
- I'm sorry, but . . .
- Pardon me, but . . .
- I didn't catch that.
- I'm not following you.
- Could you repeat that please?
- Could you say that another way?
- Could you run that by me again?
- What did you say?
- What was that again?
- Would you mind repeating that?
- I still don't quite know what you mean. Could you put it another way?

If you want to see if someone understands, check in these ways.

- Do you see/know what I mean?
- Are you following me?
- Are you with me?

If you think someone does not understand, restate what you have just said. Use different words.

- Let me try again.
- I'll say it another way.
- Let me put it this way.
- In other words, . . . (paraphrase)

If someone is not getting a chance to talk, include the person in the discussion and use his or her name.

- What do you think, _____?
- How about you, _____?
- What about you, _____?
- What's your opinion, _____?

After a peer review session, you should study the comments your peers (and instructor) made and plan changes. The number of changes you make will depend on the number of problems your peers and instructor pointed out. This process of making changes is called *revision*. Revision involves making major changes in content and organization in order to improve the paper. Revision will be covered more extensively in Chapter 4, but it will help you now to see how two writers benefited from peer review.

DISCOVERY
2.9:   Studying a model peer review of a first draft

- Read the following model assignment and model composition on "The Thai Spirit" by Vasna Wilson.
- Study the peer review that follows. (The composition has not been edited for grammar or mechanics. You will see a revision later.)
- Answer the Discussion Questions that follow.

Model Assignment

You analyzed a short reading in which Kelly Boggs explained the importance of independence in American culture. Choose two or three traits in your culture and explain why they are important. Pay close attention to formality, point of view, pronouns, and number agreement.

The Thai Spirit
by Vasna Wilson

1   Every morning, as dawn greets the sun over the Mekong River, in my hometown, Ubon, Thailand, I wake to the delicious smells and clicking noises of my mother cooking. From my earliest memory, my mother and sisters have risen before the sun rises to prepare food for the family and set aside a portion of our meal to make an offering to the monks. It is a Thai tradition for monks to

5   accept people's offerings as part of their existence. We Thai people believe in working as a unit and our spirituality weave all our lives together. My family's daily ritual: preparing food together and offering a portion of our meal to monks illustrates two principles that govern the heart of the Thai spirit: collectiveness and spirituality.

     A whole is the sum of its parts. This is the foundation of Thai collectiveness. In Thai culture, we

10   believe in working together as a unit, and this unit is what makes us strong. I will never forget a folk tale my mother told me when I was a child. She said that if you take one bamboo stick, you can easily break it, but if you try to break a bundle of bamboo sticks, it is very hard to do. We Thai think of the family as a tightly knit unit and that the collective spirit is in the heart of every Thai person. The importance of collectiveness can be clearly seen in how my family cooks together. In

15   our family, my mother is the first to get up to start the rice, which takes the longest to cook. She then wakes up my two sisters to help cook the meat and vegetables. My grandparents are the last to come in, and they help set the table. My brother and I are responsible for cleaning up. My family usually cooks four or five dishes per meal, and with all of us working together, we get all of our cooking done in an hour. Imagine, if it were just one person making all the food preparations, it

20   would take hours. Members of the Thai family do not do things just to satisfy individual needs. We each take an active role to help one another to get things done efficiently. Collectiveness is an important trait in Thai culture.

     At the center of every culture, there is a religion that holds the spirit of the people together. Ninety-nine percent of Thai people are Buddhist, and the Buddha is the center of the Thai spirit. Buddhism

25   teaches compassion and kindness to others, especially to those who have less. My family and I believe in this teaching. We embrace it by going to the temple, and we practice the teaching of Buddha in our daily life. For example, every morning, the monks walk the neighborhoods to accept public offering. The monks are poor and must depend on others to feed them. The monks, have given up worldly needs, such as earning an income, to concentrate on meditation and the

30   teachings of the Buddha. The monk role is very important to Buddhism because their efforts show that anyone who desires enlightenment through meditation can do so. They are also a symbol of compassion. This allows people to learn how to show compassion, not only with the monks but also with others. A good example of this was when our neighbor's father was hurt in a car accident. Our family gave him a helping hand on his farm until he was well again. The simple act of feeding

35   the monks is the basis of the Buddha's teaching of compassion that reveals Thai spirituality and enables us to help others.

     In conclusion, the two traits that Thai culture values highly are collectiveness and spirituality. These two principles have governed my life and how I view the world. I believe that Thai collectiveness and Thai compassion are the foundations of my life, and have made me what I am today.

40   [659 words] (Adapted with permission, Vasna Wilson, Thai)

The following peer review is a model for you to study and learn from. The purpose of this model is two-fold: to show you how to peer-review and to teach you what is expected in academic writing.

Peer Review of "The Thai Spirit"

1. Does the composition follow the assignment?
   Yes.

2. Is the topic of the composition clearly introduced? Is it effectively focused?
   Yes. The composition is focused correctly.

3. Are the main points clearly stated?
   Yes. The first two sentences in both paragraphs two and three work together to state the topic and focus of each paragraph.

4. Is the content informative and convincing? Why or why not?
   Yes. The writer is able to describe in vivid detail how these traits are demonstrated in Thai culture. The reader can "picture" the writer's family cooking together and "see" how everyone helps the monks. Examples of specific instances are given as well.

5. Is the composition clear?
   Yes. The composition is well written and clear.

6. Is the composition unified (no irrelevant support)?
   Yes. All of the points and examples are relevant.

7. Is the composition well organized?
   Yes. The thesis, topic sentences, and conclusion all tie together well. The transitions are well chosen, so the reader is guided well. The only problem may be the last sentence in paragraph three. It follows the support about feeding the monks but does not address the other act of compassion with the injured neighbor.

8. Is the tone formal and objective?
   Yes. The tone is appropriate for academic writing.

9. Is the use of language effective?
   Yes, fairly effective. The writer does not rely on basic words. In fact, the use of language contributes to the dramatic descriptions. There are some problems. Although the writer uses a variety of sophisticated structures (subordinate clauses), there are a number of simple sentences which could be combined in paragraph three. Also, the point of view is a little inconsistent because sometimes she writes about the Thai people in third person and sometimes she does so in first person. Finally, there are punctuation errors which affect the content in the thesis and in paragraph three.

10. Is the conclusion logical?
    Yes. The conclusion restates the thesis, summarizes the main points, and has a final comment.

11. What does the writer do especially well?
    She organizes well and is able to use specific details.

12. Make three suggestions to the writer.
    1) Fix the punctuation problems and combine some of the simple sentences.
    2) Improve the point of view (<u>the</u> Thai = <u>we</u> Thai).
    3) Revise the last sentence in paragraph three so that it ties in the example of the injured neighbor's father.

Discussion Questions

Use the model composition and peer review to answer these questions.

1. What was your general impression of "The Thai Spirit" when you read it?

    ....

    ....

2. What does the previous peer reviewer appreciate in the composition?

    ....

    ....

3. What does the peer reviewer think needs improvement in the composition?

    ....

    ....

4. Do you agree with the peer reviewer?

    ....

    ....

DISCOVERY
2.10: Studying a model peer review of a revision

- Study the following revision of "The Thai Spirit." Is it better than the original one?
- Read the comments on the Model Peer Review Form for Revision and answer the Discussion Questions that follow.

The Thai Spirit
by Vasna Wilson

1   Every morning, as dawn greets the sun over the Mekong River in my hometown, Ubon, Thailand, I wake to the delicious smells and clicking noises of my mother cooking. From my earliest memory, my mother and sisters have risen before the sun rises to prepare food for the family and set aside a portion of our meal to make an offering to the monks. It is a Thai tradition for monks to

5   accept people's offerings as part of their existence. We Thai people believe that by working as a unit and by living by our spiritual principles, all our lives are woven together. My family's daily ritual, preparing food together and offering a portion of our meal to monks, illustrates two principles that govern the heart of the Thai spirit: collectiveness and spirituality.

   A whole is the sum of its parts. This is the foundation of Thai collectiveness. In Thai culture, we

10   believe in working together as a unit, and this unit is what makes us strong. I will never forget a folk tale my mother told me when I was a child. She said that if you take one bamboo stick, you can easily break it, but if you try to break a bundle of bamboo sticks, it is very hard to do. We Thai think of the family as a tightly knit unit and that the collective spirit is in the heart of every Thai person. The importance of collectiveness can be clearly seen in how my family cooks together. In our family,

15   my mother is the first to get up to start the rice, which takes the longest to cook. She then wakes up my two sisters to help cook the meat and vegetables. My grandparents are the last to come in, and they help set the table. My brother and I are responsible for cleaning up. My family usually cooks four or five dishes per meal, and with all of us working together, we get all of our cooking done in an hour. Imagine if it were just one person making all the food preparations; it would take

20   hours. Members of the Thai family do not do things just to satisfy individual needs. We each take

an active role to help one another to get things done efficiently. Collectiveness is an important trait in Thai culture.

At the center of every culture, there is a religion that holds the spirit of the people together. Ninety-nine percent of Thai people are Buddhist, and the Buddha is the center of the Thai spirit.
25 Buddhism teaches compassion and kindness to others, especially to those who have less. My family and I believe in this teaching. We embrace it by going to the temple, and we practice the teaching of Buddha in our daily life. For example, every morning, the monks, who are poor and must depend on others to feed them, walk the neighborhoods to accept public offering. The monks have given up worldly needs, such as earning an income, to concentrate on meditation and
30 the teachings of the Buddha. The monks' role is very important to Buddhism because their efforts show that anyone who desires enlightenment through meditation can do so. They are also a symbol of compassion. The monks' teaching allows people to learn how to show compassion, not only with the monks but also with others. A good example of this was when our neighbor's father was hurt in a car accident. Our family helped him on his farm until he was well again. The simple act of
35 feeding the monks is the basis of the Buddha's teaching of compassion that reveals Thai spirituality and enables us to help others.

In conclusion, the two traits that Thai culture values highly are collectiveness and spirituality. These two principles have governed my life and how I view the world. I believe that Thai collectiveness and Thai compassion are the foundations of my life, and they have made me what I am today.
40 [664 words] (Adapted with permission, Vasna Wilson, Thai)

Model Peer Review Form for Revision

Study the peer reviewer's answers to the questions.

1. Did the writer successfully follow your suggestions in your original peer review? What did the writer do especially well in the revision?

    Yes, she followed the comments fairly well. She . . .
    1) Improved the punctuation
    2) Improved the style in places
    3) Tied in the examples in paragraph three—The relevance of the example of the injured neighbor's father is clearer.

2. How and where did the writer make the content more convincing?

    The content is clearer due to the changes, but there are no new examples. I also think more details are needed to express "helpfulness."

3. What new things did you learn about the topic assigned?

    The content was already convincing. Since the writer used personal experience, I could visualize her family life and see how it tied into the Thai cultural values.

4. How and where did the organization improve?

    The organization is basically the same. There were no major problems in this area.

5. How and where did the language (grammar and vocabulary) improve?

    The language was strong to begin with. I think her use of vivid vocabulary and complex grammar were effective. I felt like I was cooking in the kitchen with her family! Nevertheless, she made progress with punctuation in the thesis, and she combined some of the sentences in the body. The point of view, however, is still informal (we Thai, not the Thai).

6. What did you learn from this writer about writing? What changes will you make in how you revise in the future?

    I think I can learn to use words and sentences better. I can try to make my examples more dramatic by paying attention to the details in the stories and by using words effectively.

Q Discussion Questions

Answer the following questions on the peer review of "The Thai Spirit."

1. Is the revision of "The Thai Spirit" effective? Why or why not?

   ....

   ....

   ....

2. Do you agree with the peer reviewer's comments? Why or why not?

   ....

   ....

   ....

3. Are there any other suggestions you have for the writer?

   ....

   ....

   ....

Journal ENTRY 8

What is self-respect?

Before analyzing the following model on "Self-Respect," write a composition [200-250 words every other line] explaining what you think self-respect is. Use the following questions as a guide.

1. What is self-respect, in your opinion?
2. How do you know if someone has self-respect? Give examples.
3. How do you know if someone does not have self-respect? Give examples.

DISCOVERY

2.11: Peer-reviewing a model composition

- Read the following thought paper (personal opinion composition) titled "Self-Respect," which was written by an American student. The paper is presented here with the original wording; it has not been edited for punctuation or spelling. (You will see the revisions later).
- Then use Peer Review Form 1 from Appendix D to evaluate the model composition. Report to the class.

Model Assignment

Self-respect is the respect people have for themselves. People's success in life may depend on how much self-respect (self-esteem, self-regard) they have. How will having (or not having) self-respect help (or hinder) students in their academic pursuits? Discuss two or three ways self-respect (or the lack of it) can affect students' success. Provide specific support.

Self-Respect
by B. A. Harris

1   Self-respect is ones realization of his worth as a human being. When one realizes his worth, he realizes who he is and what he is able to accomplish in his life. He learns to respect his own ideals, principles, and beliefs as well as the principles and the beliefs of others. His consideration for his friends, and teachers, will help him gain their respect.

5   When one speaks of the worth of the human being, it is hard not to think of self-respect, because if a person is very disrespectful, he normally doesn't consider himself "worthy" of anything. Perhaps his attempts to achieve self-respect failed because he could not develop worthy principles or accomplish a mutual respect with his peers and colleagues as well as some of his friends could. Finally, because he was beginning to feel inadequate and becoming jealous of his friends who had

10   succeeded in gaining self-respect, he substitutes the ungained self-respect for a feeling of disrespect, a feeling of unworthiness, and a feeling of hate for respect. His disrespect and feeling of unworthiness is easily reflected in his "I-could-care-less" attitude toward morals, school work, appearance, teachers, and friends. Since he has gained no self-respect, his "worth" as a human being decreases, and he is promptly labeled as "problem child."

15   One can see a similar degrading of attitude in the bored English student who, after a few vain attempts to master his grammar, becomes jealous of those who have the talents and tools to achieve success with the language. In order to make up for his inadequacy, the student substitutes in place of his ungained success with grammar, an actual "hate" for English, which eventually causes the quality of his work to become worse. The student then becomes notoriously known for terrible

20   spelling and awkward sentences.

     If one has learned to achieve a respect for himself, he is not apt to substitute that respect for any feeling of inadequacy or unworthiness. For, he has already discovered his capabilities, set his goals, and commenced to work and achieve those goals. As each goal is achieved, whether it be studying to be on the honor roll, or striving to be a better football player, the person reaching his goal discovers

25   an unlimited amount of satisfaction. He has no time to feel inadequate or unworthy, because self-respect has given him the satisfaction of knowing that he is capable of reaching his goals and developing his worth as a human being.

     As each person works to develop his "worth" as a human being, he does so not only with respect to himself but with respect and consideration to all those he works with. In this way, he is

30   strengthening his self-respect and gaining anothers respect in return. If the "problem child" had possibly worked harder to develop his own self-respect, and had been more considerate to others, he would have eventually gained the respect of the other people. the same is true of the English student; if he had put a little more effert forward, he would have eventually mastered the grammar and begin to improve his grade. So as one strives for self-respect or seeks his worth as a human

35   being, he can improve his attitude toward people and situations to a degree that he will eventually gain their respect and discover his own "worth" and self-respect. [556 words] (Adapted with permission, B. A. Harris, American)

Synthesis

Synthesis is an important critical-thinking skill that involves gathering pieces of information and finding how they are related. When you do research on a topic, you will have to collect books and articles on the topic, read everything, take notes, and then bring all of the information together as a coherent discussion in your paper. Likewise, when you receive peer reviews, you will have to read all of them, sort through the positive and negative comments, and make decisions on how to revise each draft. Sometimes the reviewers may disagree, but you should consider each comment, especially the constructive ones. You will also consider all of the instructor's comments as you plan your revisions. Only by improving on the weak areas will you improve in your writing.

ⓓⓘⓢⓒⓞⓥⓔⓡⓨ
2.12: Comparing peer reviews

The draft of the composition you read earlier titled "Self-Respect" received the following peer reviews. The readers from the U.S., Taiwan, and Ukraine had different reactions to the composition.
- Read the reviews carefully and compare them.
- Answer the Discussion Questions that follow.

Peer Review by a Native Speaker

1. The introduction gives a definition of self-respect. The topic of this composition is not direct and clear. It does not repeat the words in the assignment. However, the writer does discuss the consideration of friends and teachers.

2. The main points are stated indirectly, which may cause problems.

3. The writer did a fairly good job with the support. The composition could be more detailed and have specific cases.

4. The abstract ideas are harder to understand than the examples, but overall the composition is clear.

5. The composition is fairly unified. The contents follow the title.

6. The composition is fairly well organized. There is a train of thought. The writer does a fairly good job contrasting people who lack self-respect with those who have self-respect. However, the organizational cues are not strong and direct.

7. The tone is formal and objective, but the writer did not use inclusive language.

8. The language is not effective in some places. There are misspelled words ("develop" and "effort"), and the verb tense is incorrect in one place ("begin" is used instead of "begun"). Again, the point of view should be third person plural (*Students, . . . they, . . . their, . . . them*). Also, there are long sentences which need dividing (the first sentence in paragraph two).

9. The last paragraph is long. However, it is analytical, effectively showing how the examples are relevant.

Peer Review by a Taiwanese Reader

1. The topic of the composition is not clearly stated, which makes the reader confused.

2. The main points are not clearly stated, so the writer cannot use the support well enough to follow the topic.

3. The composition is not really informative and convincing. The writer did not use enough examples and did not go into detail deeply, either. The readers are not able to receive the information for the composition and will not be convinced.

4. The composition is not clearly stated. It makes the readers confused because it is hard to find the main point of the composition.

5. The composition is fairly well unified; there are still some irrelevant points in the paragraphs.

6. The composition is not well organized, so the readers cannot distinguish the introduction, the topic, the main points, support, and conclusion clearly.

7. The tone is fairly formal, not as formal as that in "English Academic Writing: The 'A' Paper" and other academic writing.

8. The use of language in the composition is not effective. The writer just used general and ordinary vocabulary, which does not convey the writer's ideas well.

9. The conclusion for me is not logical. It lacks support for the topic and the statements in the composition are too simple for readers to be persuaded.

Peer Review by a Ukrainian Reader

1. To my mind, the topic of the composition is rather clear because the main points and the subject are outlined.

2. The main points are not clearly stated, but each paragraph supports one idea.

3. The composition is quite informative and includes several examples as support to the main idea. At the same time, the support given needs to be more specific.

4. The composition is clear enough, and its contents enable the reader to understand the author's main points.

5. The composition is unified and devoted mainly to the topic outlined.

6. In my opinion, the composition is quite well-organized because it provides a main idea (subject) and support, and the conclusion is clear. At the same time, some main ideas are absent.

7. The tone is objective, but not very formal. The use of vocabulary is rather wide. Sometimes the composition sounds too passionate.

8. The use of grammar is not very effective as there are many spelling and grammar mistakes. However, the sentences are complex and derived, which means the writer can put ideas on paper quite successfully.

9. The conclusion is rather logical and is connected with the main subject of the composition, but it is a bit too long and not direct enough.

Discussion Questions

Answer these questions about the three peer reviews.

1. Which peer review most closely matches your own? Why?
2. Which areas need improvement according to the native speaker? Why?
3. Which areas need improvement according to the reader from Taiwan? Why?
4. Which areas need improvement according to the reader from Ukraine? Why?
5. List five to seven specific suggestions you think these peer reviewers want the writer to do to improve the essay.

DISCOVERY
2.13: Peer-reviewing and revising a first draft

• Use Peer Review Form 1 from Appendix D to evaluate the first draft that you wrote for Discovery 2.8.
• Revise the first draft.

DISCOVERY
2.14: Studying a revision of a composition

The writer of "Self-Respect" actually used the previous peer reviews to revise the composition.
• Compare the following revision to the original draft.
• Use Peer Review Form 2 from Appendix D to evaluate the revision.
• Compare your reviews to those of your classmates.

Self-Respect
by B. A. Harris

1.   Self-respect is the realization of one's worth as a human being. When people recognize their worth, they realize who they are and what they are able to accomplish in life. They learn to respect their own ideals, principles, and beliefs as well as the principles and the beliefs of others. Students are at a point in life when they may or may not develop self-respect and gain respect from others.

5   Students reveal self-respect or lack of it in how they feel about themselves and act at school. How well students succeed at school may depend on whether or not they have self-respect.

Take disrespectful students, for instance. When one speaks of self-respect, it is hard not to think of self-worth because if students are very disrespectful, they normally do not consider themselves "worthy" of anything. Perhaps their attempts to achieve self-respect fail because they cannot
10   develop worthy principles or accomplish mutual respect with their classmates and teachers as well as some of their other classmates can. Finally, because these disrespectful students begin to feel inadequate and become jealous of others who have succeeded in gaining self-respect, they substitute the lack of self-respect for a feeling of disrespect, a feeling of unworthiness, and a feeling of hate for respect. This disrespect and feeling of unworthiness is easily reflected in an "I-could-care-less"
15   attitude toward schoolwork, teachers, and classmates. Since these students lack self-respect, their "worth" as human beings decreases, and they may be labeled as "problems" in school. Because these students have bad reputations, their self-esteem suffers, and they begin to feel like they cannot do anything right. This negative attitude ultimately affects their academic performance and, thus, their future.

20   Once, I saw a similar degrading of attitude in a bored student in an English class. After a few vain attempts to master the grammar rules and use interesting vocabulary, "Tammy" became jealous of those of us in class who had the talents and tools to achieve success with the language. In order to make up for her feelings of inadequacy, Tammy substituted in place of her success with grammar, an actual "hate" for English, which eventually caused the quality of her work to become worse rather
25   than better. Our professor and her peer reviewers told her that her papers had lack of support, frequent misspellings, and sentence-level problems. We were surprised to hear that Tammy thought the professor and peer reviewers were just picking on her. She did not trust anyone to help her with her writing. In fact, she complained openly about the peer reviews and said they did not help her, even when the professor gave the same advice. Instead of striving to do better, Tammy started to
30   skip class. Because she was not keeping up with the assignments, she failed the class. This story shows how a lack of self-respect can lead to disrespect and eventually failure.

On the other hand, students who have learned to achieve respect for themselves feel and behave differently from students who lack self-respect. Students with self-respect are not apt to substitute their self-respect for any feeling of inadequacy or unworthiness because they have already discovered
35   their capabilities, set their goals, and commenced to work hard to achieve those goals. As each goal is achieved, whether it be studying to be on the honor roll or striving to be better soccer players, the students reaching their goals discover an unlimited amount of satisfaction. They have no time to feel inadequate or unworthy, because self-respect has given them the satisfaction of knowing that they are capable of reaching their goals and developing their worth as a human being.

40   For example, in the same English class mentioned earlier, there was a student named "Steve." He was not a strong student at the beginning of the semester, but he attended all of the classes and did all of the work. Whenever he made a mistake, he learned from it and did not repeat the error. Furthermore, he did not feel picked on when the professor explained where his problems were because he realized from the professors and peer reviewers that he was doing well in some
45   areas. He decided that he could do better than "C" work, so he set a goal to increase his scores one half a grade with each draft. Because he applied himself, he saw his scores increase with each assignment, and he eventually made an "A" on the last paper. Steve respected himself enough to have faith in his ability to make progress with his writing and celebrate his "A."

Steve's story shows us that as students work to develop self-worth, they do so not only with
50   respect to themselves but with respect and consideration to all those they work with: not just their professors but also classmates. In this way, they are strengthening their own self-respect and gaining others' respect in return. If Tammy had possibly worked as hard as Steve had to develop her own self-respect and had been more considerate to others, she would have eventually gained our respect. More importantly, if she had put a little more effort forward, she would have eventually
55   mastered the composition skills and begun to improve her grades like Steve had.

In conclusion, the lack of self-respect can lead to failure. However, if students have a positive attitude about their studies and develop good relationships with people, they will eventually gain others' respect and realize their own "worth" and self-respect. This discovery will enable them to succeed in their academic studies. [919 words] (Adapted with permission, B. A. Harris, American)

DISCOVERY
2.15: Peer-reviewing a revision

• Use Peer Review Form 2 from Appendix D to evaluate the revision of the article you wrote for Discovery 2.8.

Out-of-Class Writing Assignment

1. Choose one of the following topics and determine an audience and purpose.
2. On a separate sheet of paper, write a well-organized 2-3 page composition. Complete the activities in the writing process.
3. For all drafts that you submit, follow the format rules given in Appendix A.
4. Use Peer Review Form 1 in Appendix D to evaluate the first draft.

Here are some possible audience choices. Choose a logical one for your topic.
• the student newspaper on your campus
• your sociology class
• native speakers who are unfamiliar with problems that nonnative speakers have coping with their host culture

1. Whenever two cultures come into contact, there is sharing (borrowing or adopting). The two cultures may adopt foods, customs, beliefs, and language from each other. Cultures share in many other areas as well. Think of things your culture has borrowed from another culture that is different from your own. Discuss two or three areas of influence. Provide specific explanations, examples and details.

   Audience: ....

   Purpose: ....

   ....

2. Studying in a university is challenging. Some students excel, some do an adequate job, but others fail. Why do some students do well? Discuss two or three major characteristics (qualities) of good students. Provide specific details, examples, and your own personal experience or that of someone you know.

   Audience: ....

   Purpose: ....

   ....

3. In the article "A Sociological Perspective," by Donald A. Hobbs and Stuart J. Blank, the authors argue that social interaction is very important. We depend a great deal on the people around us; they influence us a lot. Think of a teacher whom you know well and who has had a good influence on your life. Describe and illustrate two or three ways the teacher influenced you. Provide specific details, examples, and your own personal experience.

   Audience: ....

   Purpose: ....

   ....

4. Time Management was a big theme in this chapter. Using your chart from Journal Entry 6 and Discovery 2.1, write a report of how you will use your time to get everything done this semester. The report should take into consideration any problems you foresee with the schedule and how you will solve them. Also, be specific, accurate, and logical about the number of hours and percentages of time.

   Audience: ....

   Purpose: ....

   ....

5. You analyzed a short reading in which Kelly Boggs explained the importance of independence in American culture. Choose two or three valued traits in your culture and explain why they are important. Provide specific explanations, examples, and details.

   Audience: ....

   Purpose: ....

   ....

PARALLELISM

In academic writing, it is important to express main points clearly and smoothly in both the outline and written drafts. An effective way to do this is with parallel structure. Parallel structure is the repetition of the same grammatical form: words, phrases, and clauses. With parallel structure, you can combine ideas into concise lists. Such lists are common in thesis statements.

Writing is more effective when words, phrases, or clauses linked by coordinating conjunctions are parallel.

Coordinating conjunctions:	for	and	nor	but	or	yet	so

➷ Examples

Nonparallel: English academic writing has good content, effective language, and is clearly organized.

Parallel: English academic writing has good content, effective language, and clear organization. (parallel noun phrases)

Nonparallel: In conclusion, the two traits that Thai culture values highly are collectiveness and being spiritual.

Parallel: In conclusion, the two traits that Thai culture values highly are collectiveness and spirituality. (parallel nouns)

Nonparallel: Most of the company's employees work at home or are commuters.

Parallel: Most of the company's employees work at home or commute to the office. (parallel verb forms)

Using parallelism with correlative conjunctions is more difficult but just as important. The word, phrase, or clause that follows the first correlative conjunction of the pair should be parallel with the word, phrase, or clause that follows the second conjunction.

Correlative conjunctions
both . . . and   not only . . . but also   neither . . . nor   either . . . or

⇨ **Examples**

Nonparallel: Both relaxation and exercising can help reduce stress.

Parallel: Both relaxation and exercise can help reduce stress. (parallel nouns)

Nonparallel: On our vacation in Beijing, we can either visit the Great Wall of China or Tiananmen Square.

Parallel: On our vacation in Beijing, we can either visit the Great Wall of China or see Tiananmen Square. (parallel verb phrases) *or* Visitors to Beijing can visit either the Great Wall of China or Tiananmen Square. (parallel noun phrases)

Nonparallel: The restaurant's menu not only offers standard fare but exotic dishes as well.

Parallel: The restaurant's menu offers not only standard fare but exotic dishes as well. (parallel noun phrases)

ⓓⓘⓢⓒⓞⓥⓔⓡⓨ
2.16:   Identifying parallel structure

• Underline the conjunctions.
• Identify the grammatical structures in the parallel lists. The parallel items are correct.

⇨ **Example**

A video CD-ROM, seeds, <u>and</u> letters are things that the time capsule can preserve.

parallel noun phrases: a video CD-ROM, seeds, letters

1. Travelers eat native foods, see local sights, and experience native life.

   ....

   ....

2. It is exciting to get more new information about other customs, languages, and religions.

   ....

   ....

3. Some of the benefits can be illustrated by having time to share with the family, relaxing with loved ones, and learning about history and geography.

   ....

   ....

4. People sometimes feel both bored and fatigued in daily life.

   ....

   ....

5. In conclusion, relaxing the body, experiencing novel things, and enriching life experience are benefits of travel.

....

....

....

6. In the time capsule, I would like to keep not only records of our lives but also a message to the future generations.

....

....

ⓓⓘⓢⓒⓞⓥⓔⓡⓨ
2.17: Revising sentences lacking parallelism

Some of the items in the following sentences are not parallel.

- Read each sentence and decide whether or not the items are parallel.
- If the items in the sentence are parallel, write "correct" in the space provided.
- If the items are not parallel, rewrite the sentence correctly.

☞ **Example**

Visitors to Philadelphia can see interesting places, historical landmarks, and get a taste of culture.

Visitors to Philadelphia can see interesting places, visit historical landmarks, and get a taste of culture.

1. I will put a few items in the time capsule that are interesting, important, and characterize the time.

....

....

2. People escape the cities which have traffic jams, huge concrete buildings, and are polluted.

....

....

3. I could hardly sleep the day before I made the presentation because of nervousness and being unprepared.

....

....

4. On a vacation, you can forget about not only work, but have a good time as well.

....

....

5. They should enjoy the natural wonders, the regional food, and experience the freedom of travel.

....

....

6. The experience and knowledge gained from traveling enable people to broaden their horizons and take an interest in other cultures.

....

....

7. Because society is becoming industrialized and complicated, people are under more stress.

....

....

8. Other advantages of traveling include eating regional food, enjoying free time, and appreciation of another culture.

....

....

ⓓⓘⓢⓒⓞⓥⓔⓡⓨ
2.18: Composing parallel items

- Complete each sentence logically with a word, phrase, or clause.
- Make sure the items in each completed sentence are parallel.

⮕ Example

Going to school gives students an opportunity to increase their .... knowledge .... ,

.... imagination ...., and .... experience ....

1. The more educated people a country has, the more .... and

.... the country is.

2. TV gives us information about ...., ..., and

....

3. Living in this country has made me more .... ,

...., and ....

4. Before I came to the U.S., I ...., ..., and

....

5. In my country, it is impolite to .... and ....

6. Some of the students in the dorm are ...., ...,

and ....

7. Women in my country today are .... , ... , and

....

8. When I .... or .... , I become very unhappy.

PUNCTUATION: (.) (;) (,)

Punctuation includes all those annoying dots, squiggles, and dashes that are hard to remember to use because they are so small and seem so unimportant. However, several punctuation marks such as the period (.), semicolon (;) and comma (,) are closely related to sentence organization. If you learn how to use these marks correctly, your sentences will be well organized and readable, giving you more credibility as a writer. That is, punctuation is grammar related, so following the rules enables you to demonstrate your control of the English language at the sentence level.

Where does punctuation come from? In general, punctuation marks are written symbols for the pauses in spoken English. Have you ever tried to speak without breathing? It is not possible to continue speaking without taking a breath. Therefore, speakers have to make logical pauses to catch their breath and give the listener time to comprehend what was just said. Likewise, it is not easy for a reader to keep reading without logical pauses which indicate units of meaning. The key phrase here is "units of meaning." Punctuation helps organize words into meaningful phrases and clauses just as pauses in spoken language help group such "thought groups." Good listeners and good readers are able to comprehend the meaning of a message via these groups of phrases and clauses. Pauses signal the end of one group and the beginning of another. If pauses are missing or misplaced, the message is affected: it may become unclear or inaccurate.

For example, imagine that you have one brother, and he lives with you here. If you say, "My brother (no spoken pause) who lives with me (no spoken pause) is graduating soon," it means, "I have more than one brother, and the one who lives with me is going to graduate soon." In writing, no commas are used; this signifies that it is the brother who is living with you, not the one who is living with your parents, who will be graduating soon.

However, because you have only one brother, you need spoken pauses around the adjective clause to signify that fact. Thus, if you say, "My brother (spoken pause) who lives with me (spoken pause) is graduating soon," it means, "I have only one brother. He lives with me, and he is graduating soon." In writing, commas are used to signify these spoken pauses.

⇨ Example

My brother who is living with me is graduating soon.
(I have more than one brother.)

My brother, who is living with me, is graduating soon.
(I have one brother.)

This is just one small example of how the simple omission of commas (pauses) creates a completely different message. Let's take a longer example. Read each passage out loud (in an audible voice). Which passage makes sense? Why?

Passage 1

A physical change never changes the composition of a pure substance in a sample of matter, the shape or size may differ after the change, but the composition does not, if you break a piece of chalk into two pieces, the shape and size of the chalk change, but the substance is still chalk chemical changes, however, always change the composition of pure substances because the substances are converted into new ones with a different composition and color, when white sugar is heated, for example, it changes to caramel, which is a brownish color, this is a chemical change.

Passage 2

A physical change never changes. The composition of a pure substance in a sample of matter, the shape or size may differ after the change. But the composition does not if you break a piece of chalk into two pieces. The shape and size of the chalk change, but the substance is still chalk chemical changes, however, always change the composition of pure substances. Because the substances are converted into new ones with a different composition and color when white sugar is heated. For example, it changes to caramel. Which is a brownish color? This is a chemical change.

Passage 3

A physical change never changes the composition of a pure substance in a sample of matter. The shape or size may differ after the change, but the composition does not. If you break a piece of chalk into two pieces, the shape and size of the chalk change, but the substance is still chalk. Chemical changes, however, always change the composition of pure substances because the substances are converted into new ones with a different composition and color. When white sugar is heated, for example, it changes to caramel, which is a brownish color. This is a chemical change.

Passage 4

A physical change never changes the composition of a pure substance in a sample of matter, the shape or size may differ after the change, but the composition does not; if you break a piece of chalk into two pieces, the shape and size of the chalk change, but the substance is still chalk. Chemical changes, however, always change the composition of pure substances because the substances are converted into new ones with a different composition and color; when white sugar is heated, for example, it changes to caramel. Which is a brownish color; this is a chemical change.

Answer

Passage 1 shows an overuse of commas; Passages 2 and 4 have punctuation, but it either is used in illogical places or includes too many semicolons. Passage 3 is the easiest to understand because the thought groups are logically organized. Every comma and period has a purpose. The periods signify the ends of sentences, and the commas help organize the information inside of each sentence.

Following is Passage 3 with its thought groups identified for you. Note that the commas follow introductory clauses and phrases, set off connectors and nonessential phrases and clauses, and join other independent clauses to make compound or compound-complex sentences.

Passage 3

A physical change never changes the composition of a pure substance in a sample of matter. The shape or size may differ after the change, but the composition does not. *If you break a piece of chalk into two pieces* (*Introductory Clause*), the shape and size of the chalk change, *but the substance is still chalk* (*Part of a Compound-complex Sentence*). Chemical changes, *however* (*Connector*), always change the composition of pure substances because the substances are converted into new ones with a different composition and color. *When white sugar is heated* (*Introductory Clause*), *for example* (*Connector*), it changes to caramel, *which is a brownish color* (*Nonessential Clause*). This is a chemical change.

ANALOGY*

The previous passages illustrate the relationship between grammar and meaning. Learning to use punctuation to sort out meaningful units is like learning to drive. Imagine that you are approaching a four-way stop. What is the law? You must come to a complete stop (period). A period is a complete stop at the end of a sentence, the longest pause in both spoken and written English. After stopping, you are supposed to yield to any oncoming drivers (give the reader or listener a chance to think). Then you may proceed through the intersection. Now imagine that you are in a hurry to get to this class. You approach the intersection, but you do not have time to stop. Since there are no other cars or police around, you do a rolling stop (semicolon). That is, you do not come to a full stop; instead, you stop briefly and then proceed slowly into the intersection. A semicolon is weaker than a period, but it can be used between two complete sentences that are so closely related that a rolling stop rather than a complete stop seems appropriate. The shorter pause creates rhythm and balance.

Read these pairs of sentences out loud. Pause longer for the period (.) than for the semicolon (;).

Set 1

> A physical change never changes the composition of a pure substance. A chemical change does.

> A physical change never changes the composition of a pure substance; a chemical change does.

Set 2

> Breaking chalk into two pieces is a physical change. There is no change in the composition of the chalk.

> Breaking chalk into two pieces is a physical change; there is no change in the composition of the chalk.

Using too many semicolons is confusing (see Passage 4). Therefore, do not overuse the semicolon. Save it for emphasis. Returning to the analogy of the traffic intersection, what if you do not stop at all? Let's say you slow down only a little bit. In fact, since there are no other cars, you quickly run through the intersection. Such a short pause is like a comma (,) the shortest pause in English. However, using too many commas instead of periods is confusing (see Passage 1).

Here is a simple chart showing the strength of each punctuation mark.

THE POWER OF THE (.), (;), AND (,) ──────────────

(.) _____   The strongest—Use at the ends of sentences.
(Full Stop)

(;) _____   The next strongest—Use between two closely related sentences.
(Rolling Stop)

(,) ____   The weakest—Use to organize phrases and clauses inside sentences.
(Pause)

---

*An analogy is a comparison of a concrete (or familiar) object to an abstract (or unfamiliar) idea. In this analogy, the ways to use the different punctuation marks (unfamiliar) are compared to the ways people stop at an intersection (a familiar idea). Each punctuation mark is similar to a way people stop (or do not stop) at intersections. If you understand the familiar ideas, you can understand the unfamiliar ideas better. This textbook contains many analogies to help you understand new ideas. See "Analogies" in Chapter 6.

RUN-ON SENTENCES

In English, the period is usually used to mark the end of a statement, but the comma never is. The use of a comma instead of a period is a comma splice. Also, every sentence must have an end mark (period, semicolon, question mark, or exclamation point). If it does not, this is a problem with fusion. Comma splices and fused sentences are both examples of run-on sentences.

⇔ Examples

> A physical change never changes the composition of a pure substance, a chemical change does. (comma splice)

> Breaking chalk into two pieces is a physical change there is no change in the composition of the chalk. (fusion)

Rules for Correcting Run-On Sentences

To correct run-on sentences, do the following.

1. Put a period at the end of the first sentence and capitalize the first word of the next word.

> Breaking chalk into two pieces is a physical change. There is no change in the composition of the chalk. (simple sentences)

2. Combine the sentences with a coordinating conjunction (*for, and, nor, but, or, yet,* or *so*) or a semicolon (;) to make a compound sentence. Punctuate and capitalize correctly.

> Breaking chalk into two pieces is a physical change; there is no change in the composition of the chalk. (compound sentence)

> A physical change never changes the composition of a pure substance, but a chemical change does. (compound sentence)

3. Combine the sentences with a subordinator such as *because* or *although* to make a complex sentence. (Commas follow introductory phrases and clauses.) Read these examples out loud so that you can hear the difference.

> Although a physical change never changes the composition of a pure substance, a chemical change does. (complex sentence)

> Breaking chalk into two pieces is a physical change because there is no change in the composition of the chalk. (complex sentence)

ⓓⓘⓢⓒⓞⓥⓔⓡⓨ
2.19: Using commas correctly

- Insert commas as needed in the following sentences.
- If no commas are needed, write "correct" in the space provided.

⇔ Example

> The Paralympics* are the second largest sporting event in scope, number of competitors, and number of events.

1. Although the Paralympics outrank the World Series the Super Bowl and the World Cup they are smaller than the Olympics.

---

*The Paralympics are similar to the Olympics, except that the competitors in the Paralympics are physically disabled. These Discoveries will tell you more about the Paralympics.

2. When the Paralympics began in Rome in 1960, only people with spinal cord injuries could compete but now blind people amputees paraplegics quadriplegics dwarfs and people with cerebral palsy compete.

3. In 1960, 400 athletes from 23 countries competed in the Paralympics but in 1996, 4,000 athletes from 100 countries participated in 700 events in the Atlanta Games.

4. The Paralympics are governed by the International Paralympic Committee (IPC) and recognized by the International Olympic Committee (IOC).

⬤⬤⬤⬤⬤⬤⬤⬤⬤
2.20: Revising sentences containing run-on sentences

Some of the following sentences contain run-on sentences (comma splices and fused sentences).
* Correct each run-on sentence by using commas and semicolons correctly.
* If the item is correct, write "correct" in the space provided.

➯ Examples

In the Paralympics, the football teams are composed of seven athletes with cerebral palsy. They play on a slightly smaller field, and they follow modified FIFA rules for football.

Correct

The lawnbowling event is open to wheelchair athletes, amputees, and the visually impaired; in this event, the playing area is larger than that of the lawnbowling event in the Olympics.

1. In racquetball, the rules are slightly modified, minor changes to the equipment or crew are made for the yachting event.

2. There were seventeen sports in the 1996 Paralympics fourteen of them were actual Olympic sports.

3. The theme of the 1996 Paralympics was "Triumph of the Human Spirit," this motto represented the combination of the Paralympic athletes and the struggle of humanity the disabled are equal physically, mentally, and spiritually to the nondisabled, in other words.

4. Some people think the Paralympics are like the Special Olympics, but this is not true, the Special Olympics are for the mentally disabled, not the physically disabled.

5. The Paralympians are competitors, not participants. It is very difficult to qualify for the Paralympics one must be a world-class athlete to compete.

6. Some people think that because Paralympians have disabilities, they do not attempt Olympic sports. However, 14 out of 17 of the Paralympic sports are Olympic sports, too.

Journal ENTRY 9

Do you know of anyone who overcame a physical or mental disability to accomplish great things?

As you can see from reading Discoveries 2.19 and 2.20, people with physical disabilities are not helpless. History is full of examples of people with physical or mental disabilities who have accomplished great things. For example, although Beethoven was deaf and suffered from a serious mental illness, he was a gifted composer. Do you personally know anyone who overcame a physical or mental disability to accomplish great things? Choose someone you actually know. Describe the nature of the person's disability and show how he or she overcame it. [200-250 words, every other line]

CHAPTER *summary*

- Effective time management of both weekly activities and the writing process is crucial to academic success.

- Academic assignments require effective critical-thinking skills.

- Academic assignments include a number of terms which direct the student.

- Academic assignments may have both a lead-in and an assignment task. It is important to read and understand the entire assignment to write correctly focused papers.

- The writing process involves five major activities: brainstorming, organizing, writing, revising, and proofreading/editing. Revision is the most important activity because it involves taking a second look at the content and organization and making major improvements.

- There are three methods of brainstorming: listing, clustering, and charting.

- Peer-reviewing is an essential aspect of the revision process.

- Effective sentence organization contributes to the content in a paragraph. Sentence problems (run-on sentences and ineffective parallelism) cause problems for the reader.

The following sources were used for Discoveries 2.19 and 2.20.

1. Tammy Leigh Cook, "Top 10 Myths of the Paralympics," [http://www.ajc.com/oly/gzztop10.html], July 1996.

2. "History of the Paralympics," [http://www.flexfoot.com/atlanta/history.html], July 1996.

3. "Paralympic Fact Sheet August 15-25, 1996 Atlanta, Georgia, U.S.A.," [http://www.uscpaa.org/cppara.html], July 1996.

Chapter 3

Support in Expository Paragraphs

CHAPTER TOPICS

▶ TOPIC SENTENCES

▶ RELEVANT AND CONVINCING SUPPORT

▶ OUTLINING SKILLS

▶ CONCLUDING REMARKS

▶ SENTENCE TYPES

▶ FRAGMENTS

Journal ENTRY 10

What is good writing?

On a separate sheet of paper, answer the following questions in complete sentences. This activity will help you summarize what you have learned in Chapters 1 and 2. [250-300 words, every other line]

1. In your opinion, what is interesting writing? What characteristics does it have?
2. What are the characteristics of uninteresting writing?
3. What can you do to make your writing interesting and meaningful?

In Journal Entry 10, you may have described good writing as informative and interesting. Writers are able to make their writing interesting by digging deeply into the topics. In other words, good writing has depth of thought. "Depth" is the noun for "deep," which is the opposite of "shallow." If a professor comments that a paper is shallow, it means that the writer did not dig deeply into the topic. The ideas are very general, and the support is lacking. In effect, shallow writing might be thought of as uninteresting because of weak critical-thinking skills. The following analogy presents a more vivid analogy of "depth of thought."

ⓓⓘⓢⓒⓞⓥⓔⓡⓨ
3.1: Discovering depth of thought

The following analogy illustrates how writers draw pictures with words to define abstract ideas. These pictures are analogies, which will be discussed in Chapter 6, "Comparison/Contrast."
* Read the analogy.
* Answer the Discussion Questions that follow.

ANALOGY

Depth of Thought

1   A good writer is like a scuba diver. Imagine that you are in the Florida Keys on spring break doing some scuba diving, and you want to see the coral reefs. What can you see of the coral reefs from the beach? Sometimes they are visible from the surface, but they are not as vivid and clear from here. As a writer, you would be too distant from the topic at this point. You need to get closer. If you want

5   to see the coral reefs more closely, you need to get in the water and start wading. Deeper and deeper you go, and the water is up to your knees, your waist, and your neck. Although you are closer to your goal, either the water is too shallow or you are too far away from the reef. As a writer, you cannot discuss your topic in detail yet because the ideas are too shallow; although you can see some details, you are still too far away, too general. Finally, you plunge into the water, and deeper and

10   deeper you swim until you are next to the coral reefs. As a writer, it is at this point you are able to become specific and vivid. You can paint this picture with words for the reader. It is here that the colors, shapes, and size of the reef are revealed. You can see all the plants and animals living on and around the reef. You can feel the water around you; it is cool and clear. Fish swim past you and possibly nibble on you. You are awed and possibly transformed by this miracle of nature before you.

15   As a writer, you have to invest yourself in the writing and reveal part of yourself in your opinions, reactions, personal experiences, and understanding of the world. If you love your topic, your reader will too.

Ⓠ Discussion Questions

1. What is the meaning of "depth of thought"?
2. How do writers show they are thinking deeply? What do they use in their compositions?
3. How does this writer explain depth of thought?
4. Is the explanation effective? Why or why not?
5. Is there another way to "draw a picture" of deep thinking?

The previous analogy illustrates that every detail in a composition is informative. The more details, the more informative and descriptive the content is because it shows "depth of thought." Perhaps the description of the coral reefs is vivid enough to persuade the reader to want to see the coral reefs up close, too. The fewer the details, however, the less persuasive the content is because it is "shallow." That is, the writer did not dive in close enough to the reefs, and such distance from the heart of the topic is uninspiring.

Effective academic writing, therefore, is "expository." The verb "to expose" means "to reveal or show, exhibit, or make known." In other words, effective expository writing is informative. Writers reveal or show, exhibit, or make known by using vivid and substantial details and examples. Good writers are able to draw pictures with words, enabling the reader to visualize the ideas. Every sentence, moreover, carries the reader deeper into the topic because the level of support is so specific. The stronger the support, the more persuasive (convincing) the writing. Such writing is not difficult; it just takes time and thought (as the description of the process of writing in Chapter 2 showed). Good writers are good critical thinkers who understand the value of digging deeply into their minds, life experiences, and other resources (research, libraries, the Internet) to design effective papers which reveal the facts and exhibit them in a persuasive manner. This chapter will teach you techniques to help you compose unified and organized thought-provoking papers.

TOPIC SENTENCES

The papers you write for your classes may be short (one paragraph, such as a summary) or long (many pages, such as a term paper). A paragraph is an organized unit of thought, or group of words, on one topic, and it is the fundamental building block for longer papers. Thus, if you are able to design and develop one paragraph, it is likely that you will be able to construct longer papers. Also, if you are attempting to write essays (compositions of more than one paragraph) at this point, you need to learn how to make each paragraph in the body of the essay convincing.

A well-written paragraph is like a pleasurable trip planned by the writer for the reader. What makes the trip a well-directed journey is the topic sentence. The topic sentence explains to the readers why they are taking the trip (purpose), where they will be going on this trip (focus), and how the trip will proceed (method). If the paragraph contains information that is not immediately relevant to the trip, the paragraph will lack unity, and the readers will get lost.

In order to control the content of the paragraph (details about the trip) and not lose the readers, you need a strong topic sentence, one which is not too general or too specific. The topic sentence should contain any important words that introduce the topic, show how you are limiting (focusing) the topic, and reveal your method (reasons, effects, similarities, differences, process, and so on).

Rules for Composing Effective Topic Sentences

1. Topic sentences must be limited and correctly focused on the topic assigned.

↪ **Examples**

Assignment:
Computers are used in almost every area of life, such as business, science, and the home. Choose one area in which computers are used and discuss the benefits.

Problem: Off Topic	Pursuing a degree in business is beneficial for several reasons. (This sentence should introduce one area in which computers are used, not one area in which it is beneficial to get a degree.)
Problem: Off Focus	It is easy to learn how to use a computer. (This sentence is about computers, but the assignment is not to explain how to operate a computer.)
Correct Focus	Computers have become essential in the home these days for three major reasons. (This sentence is about one area in which computers are used these days, so it follows the assignment.)

2. Each topic sentence must be about one topic.

↪ **Examples**

Ineffective	San Francisco has many tourist attractions and is a cosmopolitan city.
Effective	San Francisco has many tourist attractions that families enjoy seeing. (Enumeration of Places/Description)

3. Topic sentences must be arguable (express an opinion) and include signals which indicate the method of development and writer's purpose.

↪ **Examples**

Effective	Dolphins and porpoises differ in several major ways. (Contrast) Operating a word processor is an easy procedure if you follow these steps. (Process)

4. Topic sentences must be concise and complete sentences in statement form.

⇨ **Examples**

Incomplete	The benefits of television to children. (Fragment)
Complete	Television benefits young children in three major ways. (Enumeration of Benefits/Effects)
Question	Why are grades important?
Statement	Grades are important for several major reasons. (Enumeration of Reasons/Causes)
Not Arguable	I want to write about ways to maintain the health.
Arguable	Maintaining good health is crucial. People can maintain their health in many ways. (Process/Enumeration of Suggestions)

5. Topic sentences must not be too specific because very specific statements are factual, not arguable.

⇨ **Example**

Too Specific	Abraham Lincoln was the sixteenth president of the United States.
Effective	Abraham Lincoln's most outstanding quality was his honesty. (Definition)

6. Topic sentences must not be too general because broad statements are difficult to support.

⇨ **Example**

Too General	Overeating is bad.
Effective	Overeating contributes to several health problems. (Enumeration of Effects)

⒟ⒾⓈⒸⓄⓋⒺⓇⓎ
3.2: Evaluating topic sentences

- Evaluate the following topic sentences. Refer to the rules for composing effective topic sentences.
- Identify those that are weak and what is wrong with them.
- Offer a suggestion on how you would correct the problem.
- Rewrite the item to make it more effective.
- If the topic sentence is effective, write "correct" in the space provided.

⇨ **Example**

How to use a library.

This is a fragment. Make it a complete sentence in statement form.

Learning how to use a library is easy if you follow these steps.

1. Learning to surf the net is essential for university students.

....

....

2. Why are Elvis Presley's songs still popular?

....

....

3. I would like to talk about Thomas Jefferson.

....

....

4. Napoleon was an emperor of France.

....

....

ⓄⒾⓈⒸⓄⓋⒺⓇⓎ
3.3: Choosing topic sentences for assignments

- Study the following assignments and the suggested topic sentences that follow.
- Circle the letter of the topic sentence that is appropriate for each assignment.
- Explain your choices.

1. Some students like to study alone, but others enjoy studying groups. Which do you prefer? Discuss two or three advantages of the method you prefer. Include convincing examples, details, and personal experience as support.
   a. There are several advantages and disadvantages of studying alone.
   b. There are two major ways to study.
   c. Studying with others is a good idea for three reasons.

   ....

   ....

2. Living in another country can be exciting. However, sometimes there are customs that might make it hard for visitors to adjust. Describe two or three customs in the U.S. or Canada which might make it difficult for visitors to adjust. Provide convincing examples, details, and personal experience as support.
   a. It is exciting for visitors to live in the U.S. for three reasons.
   b. It is hard for visitors to become accustomed to life in the U.S. because of some strange customs.
   c. The U.S. differs from Malaysia in three major ways.

   ....

   ....

3. Many people value hard work and success. Working hard brings many rewards, such as status, a good income, and a nice home. Despite these benefits from hard work, working too hard can have serious consequences. What are two or three effects of overworking? Provide convincing examples, details and personal experience as support.
   a. People overwork for three major reasons.
   b. Hard work and success are important.
   c. Overworking can cause two major problems.

   ....

   ....

DISCOVERY

3.4: Designing topic sentences for assignments

- Read the following writing assignments.
- In the space provided, write a topic sentence for each one. Follow the rules for writing effective topic sentences.

1. In *Writing Fiction: A Guide to the Narrative Craft,* Janet Burroway wrote, "Remember. Writing is easy. Not writing is hard." Write a short organized response to this quotation by explaining two or three major reasons that writing is hard (or not hard) for you. Use details and examples to support your discussion.

   ....

   ....

2. Kelly Boggs explains the importance of independence in American culture and shows how children are taught to be independent. Choose one trait in your culture and explain why it is important. Also, explain how children are taught to exhibit the trait. Pay close attention to formality, point of view, pronouns, and number agreement.

   ....

   ....

3. Jewells Friend says that people who leave the security of their home cultures to move to another culture to study are heroes. Do you agree or disagree? Discuss three major reasons. Provide examples, details, and personal experience.

   ....

   ....

4. Because the laser is such a powerful device, some people used to fear it. However, recently, scientists have found that the laser has a variety of applications. Discuss four important areas where lasers have been used to the benefit of society. Use specific and convincing examples and details to support your discussion.

   ....

   ....

DISCOVERY

3.5: Writing topic sentences for paragraphs

The following paragraphs are adapted from the article "This Year's Freshmen: A Statistical Profile," from *The Chronicle of Higher Education* (Sec. "Students," 12 January 1996, pp. A34–A35).
- Read each of the following short paragraphs carefully. Read the entire paragraph before deciding on the focus.
- On the lines provided, write a topic sentence that logically introduces each paragraph.
- Follow the rules for effective topic sentences.

1. According to the *Chronicle of Higher Education* (1996), of the American freshmen polled about their activities in 1995, 41% said they had participated in organized demonstrations. Moreover, a mere 22.7% said they had voted in a student election. Only 14.8% had discussed politics, and even fewer, 7.6%, had worked in a political campaign.

   ....

   ....

2. The report shows that 33.9% of the students polled complained of having been bored in class that year. Also, 65% admitted to not having submitted homework assignments on time. A smaller percentage, about one-fourth of the students polled, complained that they had been too overwhelmed to complete their work. Around one-third, or 34%, claimed they had overslept and missed classes or appointments, and 9.7% said they had felt depressed.

....

....

3. First, whereas 83.8% of the freshman women polled had attended a religious service in 1995, 76.9% of the freshman men polled had done so. Also, 87.2% of the freshman women in the survey said they had studied with other students in 1995. However, 81.4% of the freshman men had participated in study groups. More freshman women, 49.6%, had tutored other students than freshman men did, 44.2%. It was also reported that 74.1% of freshman women, as opposed to 65.8% of freshman men, had performed volunteer work. Freshman women, furthermore, were more likely to ask a teacher for advice after class than freshman men were: 21.1% versus 17.7%, respectively. Finally, the *Chronicle* reports that in 1995 more freshman women, 63.3%, had socialized with someone of another racial or ethnic group than freshman men had, 57.9%.

....

....

Journal ENTRY 11

What are college freshmen like in your country?

You have just read some brief descriptions of American freshmen. What are college freshmen like in your country? Discuss their attitude about school, their sociability, their political activism, or another area that interests you. [250-300 words, every other line]

RELEVANT AND CONVINCING SUPPORT

Sources of Support

Having a well-designed topic sentence means nothing if there is weak support. Therefore, you need to collect information for the paper. Where you find support will depend on the purpose and scope of the assignment. One or all of the following sources could be used: personal knowledge and experience, readings in your courses or the library, lecture notes, the Internet, surveys, and interviews.

Regardless of where you find your information, you need to choose support that will be interesting if you want to convince the reader. By brainstorming and listing, you can find direction and sort out the information you have. Do not choose just any example or detail. Pick support that you know the most about and that is the most representative, logical, and convincing. Consider the audience and assignment throughout this process. You do not want to lose the focus of the task.

The subtopics are the main points in the paragraph. Make sure the subtopics you select:
• follow the topic sentence logically.
• are distinctively different (do not overlap).
• belong together (are well matched, at the same level of generality).
• are parallel in form.
• are thought-provoking.
• are logical and appropriate choices that focus on major and representative ideas.

Evaluating Subtopics

The following items contain topic sentences and three subtopics. One of the subtopics in each item is weak. Study the examples and explanations.

1. Technology benefits people's lives in three areas.
   a. Transportation
   b. Industry
   c. The kitchen

Explanation: "Kitchen" is too specific. "The home" would be better.

2. Nonnative students have problems on campus.
   a. Taking notes
   b. Writing compositions
   c. Getting along with roommates

Explanation: The first two subtopics are about academic problems, so the last subtopic does not fit the list because it is about a personal problem. "Participating in class discussions" would be better. The topic sentence would be better stated to include "academic problems."

3. In choosing a school, students should carefully consider the following things.
   a. Caliber of the faculty in their major
   b. Requirements
   c. Work load

Explanation: There is overlap in the last two subtopics since both are related to the work that needs to be done to get a degree. "Cost" may be better for point c.

ⒹⒾⓈⒸⓄⓋⒺⓇⓎ
3.6: **Brainstorming for effective subtopics**

• Complete each of the following unfinished subtopic statements with a logical word or phrase that is parallel to the other items (the same grammatical structure).
• Write a suitable topic sentence on the lines provided.
• Peer-review each topic sentence, using the same guidelines for selecting subtopics in "Sources of Support" on pages 73–74.

⇨ **Example**

I dislike living in big cities because of the air pollution.

I dislike living in big cities because of the crime.

I dislike living in big cities because of the ....*traffic*........ .

Topic Sentences   I dislike living in big cities because of the air pollution, crime, and traffic.

Big cities can be unpleasant places to live for three reasons.

1. I look forward to the future because I plan to.. .
   I look forward to the future because I plan to find a good job.
   I look forward to the future because I plan to get married and raise a family.

   Topic Sentence   ....

   ....

2. A good teacher is well organized.

   A good teacher is ....

   A good teacher is ....

   Topic Sentence   ....

   ....

3. With computers, students can compute complex mathematical problems.

   With computers, students can ....

   With computers, students can ....

   Topic Sentence   ....

   ....

4. In the future, people need to solve the problems caused by pollution.

   In the future, people need to ....

   In the future, people need to ....

   Topic Sentence   ....

   ....

ⒹⒾⓈⒸⓄⓋⒺⓇⓎ

3.7: Solving problems with topic and subtopic sentences

- Bring into class a current draft of a composition you are working on. Discuss the problems you had or are having with your choice of topic and subtopic sentences.
- Explain how you solved them or how you are solving them.
- If necessary, brainstorm in small groups to find more effective subtopics.

Planning Support at All Levels

ANALOGY

Unity is important at every level of generality. The standard expository paragraph is like a pyramid with the topic sentence at the top, or highest level of generality. With each new specific level added for each subtopic, the base of support for the pyramid becomes stronger. Without such support, the pyramid will not stand, and the writer's purpose will not be fulfilled.

Once you have your subtopics, you are ready to develop the next level of generality, the specific support. Remember that you want to dig deeply, so develop support that follows a general-to-specific approach. For every rhetorical pattern, there may be variations in how to structure paragraphs, but effective writers are able to explain and illustrate at various levels. Thus, it is a good idea to keep the following strategy in mind when planning support for an expository paragraph with examples.

THE PYRAMID OF SUPPORT ——————————————————————————

Topic Sentence

↓

Two or More Subtopics

↓

General Explanation of Each Subtopic

↓

General Examples to Illustrate Each Subtopic

↓

Specific Examples, Facts, Details, Statistics, Personal Experiences

↓

Explanation of Specific Examples, Facts, Details, Statistics, Personal Experiences

---

A paragraph is unified if each subtopic is a logical division of the paragraph topic and if the specific support for each subtopic is relevant to that subtopic.

Topic Sentence

This is the topic of the paper. Express it in a statement with the focus you have chosen.

Subtopics

These are the main points, which are more specific than the topic. Plan at least two well-expressed main points.

Explanation of Subtopics

This will include a definition and/or a discussion in general terms of each main point. Plan at least two points of explanation; more is better.

General Examples

These are examples of experiences that people have every day. They may include hypothetical examples (*Let's suppose, Let's say, Imagine that, If*). Plan at least two general examples, but additional examples will provide a more representative range. Include all important details.

Specific Examples

These are specific examples and details of real-life events. This level can include past events and experiences of the writer or other people, case studies, or examples from history (*In my case, Once, The following true story illustrates*). Include all relevant details. Aim for one specific well-developed example or two or more less-developed ones. The examples should contribute to the content and not just repeat the main point word for word.

Explanation of Specific Examples

This explains how an example relates to the main point and why it is relevant. You need to explain the examples to return to the main point. Plan at least two points.

If the discussion stops with the subtopic and a weak explanation, the content is shallow. A discussion which contains all of the above levels, especially specific examples, will be informative. However, you have to keep focused on the assignment or else you may lose control of the content and get off track. Not all the specific ideas underlying a general principle will relate to your topic. This is why you have to be a good critical thinker and be able to select and manage the information. Following are the types of problems you should avoid.

```
┌────────────────────────────────────────────────────────────────────────────┐
│  PROBLEMS WITH PLANNING SUPPORT ─────────────────────────────────────        │
│                                                                              │
│    Type                              Description                             │
│    Uninformative Support            Meaningless, Repetitive Support          │
│    Overlap                          Duplication of Subtopics or Support      │
│    Lack of Unity                    Irrelevant Support                       │
│    Shallow/Sophomoric Thinking      Failure to Develop More Specific Levels  │
└────────────────────────────────────────────────────────────────────────────┘
```

Effective Topic Limitation

One way to avoid such problems is to limit the general topic and dig for support. To do this, write a list that progresses from general to specific. Make sure each new line is related to and more specific than the previous line.

⇨ **Examples**

(General Topic)	TV
(One Aspect of the Topic: Benefits)	Benefits of the TV
(One Benefit)	Entertainment
(One Form of Entertainment)	Entertaining Programs
(Examples of Kinds of Entertaining Programs)	Comedies
(Example of a Comedy)	"Seinfeld"
(Entertaining Aspects of "Seinfeld")	The Humorous Themes in "Seinfeld"

The following example shows a way to limit the same general topic, but with a focus on disadvantages.

TV
Disadvantages of TV
TV Violence
Effects of TV Violence
Effects of TV Violence on Children
How Children Imitate the Violence They See on TV
Violent Games Children Play Because of TV
Cowboys and Indians

Problems with Planning Support

The following examples show what can go wrong if you are not careful limiting the topic. Each example is explained.

Uninformative Topic Limitation

⇨ **Example**

Cigars
Cigar Smokers
Types of Cigar Smokers
Professors Who Smoke Cigarettes

Explanation: Whether or not professors smoke cigarettes is insignificant. However, much more can be said about pregnant women who smoke due to the effects on the fetus. The fact that more and more teenagers are smoking today despite the dangers is also a high-interest topic.

Overlap

⇨ **Example**

TV
Benefits of TV
Get Information
Get Knowledge

Explanation: "Get Knowledge" and "Get Information" overlap; they are very similar. If this happens in a paper, the content will be repetitive.

Lack of Unity

⇨ **Example**

TV
Benefits of TV
Information
News
News Programs
CNN

Explanation: "CNN" is not a news program; it is a news network.

Shallow Thinking

⇨ **Example**

TV
Benefits of TV
Entertainment
Information

Explanation: "Entertainment" and "Information" are equal in value. Each new line should be more specific than the previous one.

ⓓⓘⓢⓒⓞⓥⓔⓡⓨ
3.8: Limiting topics

- Develop seven levels of generalities for each of the following two topics, using the examples on page 77 as a guide.
- Limit your topics by focusing on the advantages (benefits) or disadvantages of each.
- On a separate sheet of paper, peer-review your own work using the questions that follow.

1. Living in Big Cities
2. Having Friends Who Are Native Speakers

peer REVIEW

1. Is there a logical progression from general to specific?
2. Is each new line more specific than (not equal in value to) the previous one?
3. Is there any overlap (unnecessary repetition)?
4. Does each new line relate to the previous ones (unity)?
5. Are the items informative?

ⒹⒾⓈⒸⓄⓋⒺⓇⓎ
3.9: Analyzing and revising for topic limitation

A. Use the same draft you used for Discovery 3.7.
  - This time, analyze it for how well you followed the strategy for topic limitation described on pages 76–79. How specific were you able to get?
  - In small groups, use Peer Review Form 3 from Appendix D to evaluate the drafts.

B. To help you revise your draft(s) and find more examples, do the following:
  - Review the section on planning support at all levels on pages 75–78.
  - Brainstorm for more examples. Limit your subtopics to a level that has three examples.

OUTLINING SKILLS

An outline is a formal organized list of the ideas, explanations, details, examples, and other supporting points in a paper. When organizing a paper, it is easier to write an outline than to write the entire paper. If you have to make changes, do not rewrite every word; simply shift the points in the outline around and cut or add support as needed. It is necessary to learn outlining skills because sometimes a professor will ask to preview an outline before the paper is due and then request the final outline with the paper.

Framing a Paragraph

An outline is a visual representation of the levels of generality. First, the symbols used to signify general ideas are different from those for specific ideas. We will approach outlining by showing how one paragraph is built in layers, beginning with the main points under each topic sentence and adding deeper and deeper support.

Layer One: A, B, C

The main ideas (subtopics) in a paragraph are labeled A, B, C, and so on, and must directly relate to the topic sentence. In the outline model that follows, the subtopics are stated in sentences as models of effective subtopic sentences.

Layer Two: 1, 2, 3

In this level, the supporting points are labeled with Arabic numerals (1, 2, 3, and so on) and the list of supporting points is indented. In this way, the reader can easily identify the supporting points. The rule for unity applies at this level also. Note that in each main division (A, B, C) the supporting points (1 and 2) directly relate to the topic sentence.

Layer Three: a, b, c

This level, consisting of relevant explanations of each subtopic, is labeled with lowercase letters (a, b, c, and so on). This list is also indented. In the following model, the reader can quickly see how the writer plans to discuss each subtopic.

The following is an outline of paragraph 2 from "English Academic Writing: The 'A' Paper."

Model Outline

Topic Sentence: First, the "A" paper has convincing content.

A. To begin with, the content is informative and thought provoking.
  1. The purpose of academic writing
     a. Persuasive approach
     b. Formal tone
     c. Objective thinking

    2. Specific and logical support
      a. Details
      b. Examples
      c. Facts
      d. Statistics
      e. Case studies

    3. Professor's reactions to general support

B. Second, the support is relevant.
    1. Direct relation to the thesis and topic sentences
      a. Writer's topic
      b. Writer's purpose
      c. Writer's method
      d. Writer's opinion

    2. No digression
      a. No "by-the-way" statements
      b. Well-thought-out ideas and supporting points

C. Third, although objective, academic writing can be creative in that the writer is able to demonstrate effective critical-thinking skills.
    1. Depth of thought
      a. Analysis of information
      b. Interpretation of facts
      c. Judgments
      d. Conclusions
      e. Summaries
      f. Defenses

    2. Shallow writing
      a. Weak critical-thinking skills
      b. "Sophomoric" ideas

D. Finally, an "A" paper has a clear purpose, which helps direct the reader, the audience.
    1. Clear objectives

    2. Control of content
      a. Clear ideas
      b. Logical support
      c. Concise discussion

Concluding Remark: Indeed, papers with strong, unified support which demonstrates effective critical-thinking skills are well received by professors.

Rules for Outlining

In addition to the rules for labeling the levels of generality in outlines demonstrated above, there are other guidelines for effective outlining.

Rules for Outlining

   1. **Equivalent Value Rule:** Clearly label the parts of the outline with the appropriate symbols for each level of generality. Remember that the support at the same level of generality should be labeled with the same type of symbol.
   2. **Balanced Support Rule:** Plan at least two subdivisions for each division for balanced, well-developed support.

3. **Parallel in Form Rule**: List the support in parallel form. You can state all the points as sentences or noun phrases. It is a good idea to write out the subtopics as sentences to help with coherence when you write your paper.

4. **Indentation Rule**: Indent for each new level of generality. Levels that are equal in value should have the same indentation.

ⅮⒾⓈⒸⓄⓋⒺⓇⓎ

3.10: **Peer-reviewing model outlines**

• Study the following outlines.
• Imagine the writer is your classmate. Use Peer Review Form 4 from Appendix D to evaluate each outline. Note: Each outline has both strengths and weaknesses, so do not answer yes to all of the questions.

Model Assignment

Much has been said about the role TV plays in people's lives. Some people think TV is a bad influence. Others argue that TV is beneficial to people. What do you think? Discuss the advantages or disadvantages of TV. Provide convincing details, examples, and personal experience.

The Benefits of TV

Outline 1

TV is so related to our daily lives that we cannot even imagine the world without it. TV can give us benefits such as entertainment, information, and education.

A. One major benefit of TV is entertainment.
    1. Joy
        a. Large screen
        b. Stereo sound
    2. Various programs
        a. Movies, sports, comedies, shows, music, soap operas, cartoons
        b. Choosing favorite programs
    3. My favorite programs
        a. Watching TV being my pleasure
        b. Live sports relay

B. Another major benefit of TV is information.
    1. News
        a. Community, country, world
        b. CNN World Today
    2. Living
        a. Weather
        b. Shopping
        c. Utility
        d. Recreation
        e. My weekend plan according to information from TV

C. Finally, TV benefits us because it provides education.
    1. Correspondence class
    2. Adult education
        a. Why TV?
        b. Learning computers

In conclusion, TV is becoming more beneficial in our daily lives when it is used correctly.

Outline 2

TV plays an important role in broadcasting the daily weather information.

A. Importance of weather information
    1. Increased reliability of weather information
       a. improved predictability
    2. Making a daily plan according to the weather
       a. Support of making a decision
       b. Watching the Weather Channel

B. Practical use of the Weather Channel in my life
    1. Some activities depending on the weather
       a. Cleaning and drying clothes
       b. Car wash
       c. Wearing clothes
    2. Memory of a wrong weather report
       a. Rainy picnic

C. Watching warnings on TV about bad weather
    1. Effects of bad weather
       a. Temperature
       b. Wind
       c. Rain
    2. Types of bad weather
       a. Hurricane
       b. Tornado

In conclusion, people benefit from the weather information on TV and make use of it in their daily lives.

CONCLUDING REMARKS

Purpose of Concluding Remarks

The purpose of concluding remarks is to bring the paragraph to a close. The concluding remarks must be unified with the topic sentence and subtopics. Take again the outline on content in academic writing. The topic sentence introduced the topic (content) and limited it to four criteria (convincing ideas, relevant support, effective critical-thinking skills, and strong purpose). The concluding remarks emphasize the need for effective content, which the support has addressed. It also contains a reminder of the benefit of strong content in that professors give such papers high grades because they know the audience will benefit from learning about what effective content is.

Topic Sentence: First, the "A" paper has convincing content.

Concluding Remarks: Indeed, papers with strong, unified support which demonstrates effective critical-thinking skills are well received by professors.

Rules for Composing Concluding Remarks

Complete Conclusions

In complete conclusions, concluding remarks:
- contain a signal (*In conclusion, Indeed, To conclude*).
- recall the limited topic (paraphrase).
- summarize the subtopics (paraphrase if possible).
- contain a final comment (opinion).

Effective Conclusions

In effective conclusions, concluding remarks:
- do not bring up new subtopics.
- follow the paragraph logically.
- recognize all the subtopics

ⓓⓘⓢⓒⓞⓥⓔⓡⓨ
3.11: Composing concluding remarks

Write a short concluding remark for each of the following items.

⇨ Example

> *Topic Sentence:* There are three things that would make me the happiest person in the world.
>
> A. A happy family life
> B. A satisfying career
> C. Inner peace and security
>
> *Concluding Remark:* In conclusion, if I could have a good home life, a challenging job, and inner strength, I would be contented and satisfied with my life.

1. *Topic Sentence:* Living in the dorm benefits nonnative speakers in three ways.

   A. Nonnative speakers can make friends with native speakers.
   B. Nonnative speakers can practice their English.
   C. Nonnative speakers can learn about the customs in the host country.

   Concluding Remark: ....

   ....

   ....

2. *Topic Sentence:* Culture shock has four main stages.

   A. In the first stage, everything in the host culture is exciting and new.
   B. In the second stage, visitors start feeling frustrated due to problems.
   C. After this stage of frustration, visitors start to relax and laugh more.
   D. In the final stage, the visitors start to feel adjusted in the host country.

   Concluding Remark: ....

   ....

   ....

Journal ENTRY 12

Are you in culture shock?

Living in a different country is not easy at times. Some people adjust better/faster than others do. Using the outline in Discovery 3.11, identify which stage of adjustment you are in. Explain two or three reasons that you think you are in that stage. Give personal experience as support. [250-300 words, every other line]

DISCOVERY

3.12: Framing a paragraph outline

- With a partner, compose a complete, formal outline for the following examination question. The topic and subtopic sentences patterns have been supplied for you.
- Plan subtopics and specific support using the layering skills you learned in this chapter.
- Write your own concluding remark.

Examination Question

More and more people are becoming concerned about their physical and mental health these days. In fact, not only do we see an increase in the number of health clubs, we also see a wealth of information published every day on the importance of good health. What are some ways that we can maintain good physical and mental health? Provide examples, details, and your own personal experience or that of someone you know.

Topic Sentence: We can maintain good mental and physical health in three ways.

A. The first way to maintain good mental and physical health is by ....

B. In addition to ...., we can.. .
           (Restate Subtopic A)   (Subtopic B)

C. Perhaps the most crucial way to maintain our physical and mental health is to ....

Concluding Remark: ....

....

....

An effective expository paragraph should have the following elements: topic and subtopic sentences; details, examples, and other relevant support; a concluding remark; effective parallel structure and correct grammar and punctuation; and correct format. If you are attempting to write compositions with more than one paragraph, make sure each body paragraph has the same elements.

Out-of-Class Writing Assignment

- Choose one of the following topics or select a topic from any of the Discovery exercises in this chapter.
- Write a composition [2-3 pages, every other line].

1. Some students like to study alone, but others enjoy studying in groups. Which do you prefer? Discuss two or three advantages of the method you prefer. Include convincing examples, details, and personal experience as support.

2. Living in another country can be exciting. However, sometimes there are customs that might make it hard for visitors to adjust. Describe two or three customs in your country which might make it difficult for visitors from the U.S. or Canada to adjust. Provide convincing examples, details, and personal experience (your own or that of others) as support. Remember to tell the name of your country.

In-Class Writing Assignment

You will be given a time limit in which to write a composition on a topic your instructor will provide [2-3 pages, every other line].

- Plan before you write.
- Allow for time to proofread.
- Use all of the time allowed.

ⒹⒾⓈⒸⓄⓋⒺⓇⓎ
3.13: Peer-reviewing writing assignments

- Use Peer Review Forms 1 and 4 from Appendix D to evaluate one of the writing assignments.
- Study the comments.
- Revise the draft.

SENTENCE TYPES

Sentence variety is valued in academic writing. In other words, you should not depend on one type of sentence, especially the basic patterns. All sentences in English can be classified as simple (basic), compound (fairly basic), complex (advanced), or compound-complex (fairly advanced)

Simple Sentences

All sentences are clauses, and all clauses contain at least one subject and one verb. A sentence which contains at least one subject and one verb is called a simple sentence. This sentence type is basic, so use such sentences minimally in academic writing.

⮞ Examples

He did not study. He did not pass the test. (SV. SV.*)
Steve and his friends are coming to dinner. (SSV.)

*S = subject; V = verb

Compound Sentences

Sentences which contain at least two main clauses joined by a coordinator, a connector, or only a semicolon are called compound sentences. Compound sentences are fairly basic, and it is best to use coordinators sparingly. Instead, use the connectors that have the same meaning or use more complex sentence types.

⮞ Examples

He was tired, so he went to bed. (SV, *so* SV.)
He was tired; as a result, he went to bed. (SV; *as a result*, SV.)
He was stressed out; he could not take the pressure. (SV; SV)

TRANSITIONS I ───

Coordinator	Connectors
for (to indicate meaning)	─────
and	in addition, furthermore, moreover
neither, nor	─────
but	however, on the other hand
either, or	otherwise
yet	nevertheless
so	as a result, therefore, thus

Punctuation of Compound Sentences

To aid readability, use a comma between two sentences that are joined with a coordinator. Avoid frequently beginning a sentence with a coordinator. Also, a comma after a coordinator is not necessary. Such frequent breaks in the flow of thought make sentences choppy.

⇨ **Examples**

Incorrect   Shallow writing is indicative of weak critical-thinking skills. *So* such writing receives low marks.

Correct   Shallow writing is indicative of weak critical-thinking skills, *so* such writing receives low marks.

For sentences joined with a connector, either use a period at the end of the first sentence and capitalize the connector, or use a semicolon at the end of the first sentence and do not capitalize the connector. Either way, use a comma after the connector. Do not replace the period or semicolon with a comma because that would create a run-on sentence.

⇨ **Examples**

Incorrect   Shallow writing is indicative of weak critical-thinking skills, *therefore*, such writing receives low marks.

Correct   Shallow writing is indicative of weak critical-thinking skills. *Therefore*, such writing receives low marks.
Shallow writing is indicative of weak critical-thinking skills; *therefore*, such writing receives low marks.

You can join two closely related sentences together with a semicolon and no connector to make a compound sentence. Do not capitalize the next word, however. Also, do not overuse the semicolon.

⇨ **Example**

We depend a great deal on the people around us; *they* influence us a lot.

ⓓⓘⓢⓒⓞⓥⓔⓡⓨ

3.14: **Using commas and semicolons correctly in compound sentences**

Insert commas (,) and semicolons (;) as needed.

1. Inventions were being patented all the time and great emphasis was placed on the individual to be successful and maybe even famous.

2. English writing is organized at the paragraph level in addition it is organized at the sentence level.

3. Eating salt may not cause high blood pressure in everyone but people who eat low-sodium diets have lower blood pressure on the average.

4. Columbus thought the Native Americans were starving however the Indians were eating better than the Europeans were.

Complex Sentences

Complex sentences are preferred in academic writing. They contain at least one main clause and one dependent (subordinate) clause. Dependent clauses add specific information to main clauses. Whereas main clauses are complete ideas, dependent clauses are incomplete ideas. This means that main clauses can be sentences, but dependent clauses cannot. Therefore, a dependent clause must always be attached to a main clause. Dependent clauses begin with subordinators, which have different meanings.

In the following examples, the dependent clauses are in italics.

➭ Examples

Columbus thought the American Indians were starving *because they did not have meat on their tables.* (SV *because SV.*)

Because he was tired, he went to bed. (*Because SV,* SV.)

I will not take my umbrella *unless it rains.* (SV *unless SV.*)

TRANSITIONS II ————————————————————————————

Coordinator	Connectors	Subordinators
for (to indicate meaning)	———	because since so that
and	in addition furthermore moreover	just as . . . so
neither, nor	———	———
but	however on the other hand nevertheless in contrast	although even though whereas while
either, or	otherwise	———
yet	however on the other hand nevertheless in contrast	although even though
so	as a result therefore thus consequently	———

KINDS OF DEPENDENT CLAUSES

There are three kinds of dependent clauses: adverb, noun, and adjective.

Adverb (modifies verb)

Time	*After you proofread,* hand the paper in.
Cause/Effect	He called home *because he is lonely.*
Conditional	*If you do not stop at this light,* you may get a ticket.
Concession	Sarah failed the test *even though she studied.*
Comparison/ Contrast	*Just as porpoises bear their young live,* so do porpoises. *Whereas Jim is tall,* Tom is short.

Noun (subject or object of verb)

From Information Questions	Where should you put the comma? I do not know *where I should put the comma.*
From *Yes/No* Questions	Does Harry understand? I don't know *whether/if he understands or not.*
From Statements	You are excellent students. We know *that we are excellent students.*

Adjective (modifies noun or pronoun)

Essential (Restrictive)	The person *who just called* is my father.
Nonessential (Nonrestrictive)	My father, *who lives in Oregon,* used to teach composition.

DISCOVERY

3.15: Identifying dependent clauses

- Find and underline the dependent clauses. Identify them as adverb, noun, or adjective clauses.
- If there is more than one dependent clause in a sentence, mark them *(a)*, *(b)*, *(c)*, and so on.

⮞ Example

This stage involves critical thinking <u>because you do not necessarily want to go with the first</u>

(a)

<u>thoughts</u> <u>that cross your mind</u>.

(b)

An adverb clause of cause/effect (a) contains an essential adjective clause (b).

1. "Depth" is the noun for "deep," which is the opposite of "shallow."

2. If a professor comments that a paper is shallow, this means that the writer did not dig deeply into the topic.

3. When professors write textbooks and articles, they seek out their colleagues for feedback in order to revise effectively.

....

4. Although this activity may be hard at first, you will get better at it.

....

5. You may wonder how qualified you are to peer-review.

....

6. Research shows that many people cannot even answer a question on the most basic political issues.

....

Punctuation of Complex Sentences with Adverb Clauses

If a complex sentence begins with an introductory adverb clause, use a comma after the adverb clause. If the adverb clause is at the end of the sentence, do not use a comma.

⮑ Examples

Columbus thought the Native Americans were starving *because they did not have meat on their tables.*

Because the Native Americans did not have meat on their tables, Columbus thought they were starving.

ⒹⒾⓈⒸⓄⓋⒺⓇⓎ
3.16: Using commas and semicolons correctly in complex sentences

- Insert commas (,) and semicolons (;) as needed.
- If a sentence requires no additional punctuation, write "correct" in the space provided.

1. Because shallow writing is indicative of weak critical-thinking skills such writing receives low marks.

....

....

2. You never really know people until you live with them.

....

....

3. The Irish valued their family and their land highly but the Americans valued individualism.

....

....

4. When I looked up at Niagara Falls I could feel the power of the rushing water.

....

....

5. Even though eating salt may not cause high blood pressure in everyone people with low-sodium diets have lower blood pressure on the average.

....

....

6. The Irish had a static economy on the other hand the Americans had a progressive economy.

....

....

Compound-Complex Sentences

Compound-complex sentences are fairly advanced. This type of sentence is a combination of compound and complex patterns. In other words, a complex sentence can be joined to another sentence with a coordinator or conjunction.

⇨ Examples

Because he was sleepy, he put away his homework, and he went to bed.
If it snows too heavily, the streets get slippery, and the buses do not run.

Shallow writing is indicative of weak critical-thinking skills, and such writing, which is often described as "sophomoric," receives low marks.

Main Clauses	Shallow writing is indicative of weak critical-thinking skills. (simple sentence)
	Such writing, which is often described as "sophomoric," receives low marks. (complex sentence)
Dependent Clause	which is often described as sophomoric (nonrestrictive adjective clause)

ⓓⓘⓢⓒⓞⓥⓔⓡⓨ
3.17: Identifying sentence types

In the space provided, identify the sentence types as either simple, compound, complex, or compound-complex.

⇨ Example

Using too many compound-complex sentences may be confusing for the reader.

.................................*simple*.................................

1. This may be because these sentences are long, and using too many long sentences in a paper is not desirable.

....

2. It is hard not to think of self-worth when speaking of self-respect because if people are very disrespectful, they normally do not consider themselves worthy of anything.

....

3. Because some people have gained no self-respect, their "worth" as human beings decreases, and they are promptly labeled as "problems."

    ....

4. The audience is the group of readers whom you are targeting your message to.

    ....

5. TV is so related to our daily lives that we cannot even imagine the world without it.

    ....

6. A paragraph is an organized unit of thought (or group of words) on one topic, and it is the fundamental building block for longer papers.

    ....

RAGMENTS

ANALOGY

A fragment is a piece of something. Imagine a broken window. When a window breaks, it is shattered into several pieces, or fragments, of glass. The window is no longer one unit; in fact, it is no longer a window. Instead, it is a pile of glass. One cannot see clearly through a pile of glass.

In writing, a fragment is an incomplete sentence, which means that it is a piece of an idea, not a whole idea. Just as you cannot see clearly through a shattered window, you cannot understand ideas clearly if they are incomplete. Therefore, the ideas you place between periods must be complete and independent. Phrases and dependent clauses are not strong enough to be used as sentences.

Rules for Correcting Fragments

To correct fragments, do the following:

1. Compose a main clause.

Fragments	If you break a piece of chalk into two pieces. (conditional clause)
	When white sugar is heated. (time clause)
	In addition to listing. (phrase)
Sentences	If you break a piece of chalk into two pieces, the shape and size of the chalk change.
	When white sugar is heated, it changes to caramel.
	In addition to listing, clustering is an effective brainstorming method.

2. Compose a main verb.

Fragments	For example, planning a paper. (phrase)
	A writer who edits and proofreads. (adjective clause modifying "writer")
Sentences	For example, planning a paper can take hours depending on the assignment.
	A writer who edits and proofreads cares about details.

3. Delete the subordinator.

Fragment	Because there is no change in the composition of the chalk. (adverb clause of reason)
Sentence	There is no change in the composition of the chalk. (*because* deleted)

4. Join the fragment to a logical main clause. Use correct punctuation and capitalization.

Fragment   Since there is a lack of interest. There is a great lack of information. (adverb clause separated from main clause)

Sentence   Since there is a lack of interest, there is a great lack of information.

ⓓⓘⓢⓒⓞⓥⓔⓡⓨ
3.18:   Identifying and revising sentence fragments

• If the item is a fragment or contains a fragment, write "frag" on the line.
• Write the sentence correctly.
• If the item is a complete sentence, write "correct."

➪ Example

.........*frag*......... If you cannot answer a question on the TOEFL.

If you cannot answer a question on the TOEFL, try to guess.

1. .... Following an assignment involves understanding its wording and design.

2. .... Because your professors expect good papers.

3. .... For instance, the appearance of the paper when you hand it in.

4. .... An engineer who designs strong bridges.

5. .... The laser is widely used. Since it is so accurate.

6. .... A good solution to problems with grammar.

7. .... To understand the European-American perceptions of the Native Americans and the Africans, it is necessary to look back at the fifteenth century.

8. .... Time expressions, which tell when events occur. They provide transition in papers that are organized in chronological order.

CHAPTER *summary*

- Effective academic writing is convincing because it presents substantial, explicit, and well-organized support.

- Paragraphs have several levels of generality. Make sure the support is unified at each level.

- Topic and subtopic sentences must follow the assignment and be correctly focused.

- The outline is the framework of a paper. It is a crucial step in the planning process. There are specific symbols used to identify the equivalent value in each level (layer) of generality. An outline should be balanced, parallel in form, and logically organized.

- The conclusion should bring the paragraph to an effective close and remain unified with the topic and focus of the paragraph.

- There are four sentence types: simple, compound, complex, and compound-complex. Use a variety of each, but focus on complex sentences. They are preferred in academic writing.

- Write complete sentences. Although fragments are often used in spoken English, they are unacceptable in academic writing.

Chapter 4

Essay Development

CHAPTER TOPICS

- ▶ MANAGING YOUR MATERIAL
- ▶ AN OVERVIEW OF ESSAY DEVELOPMENT
- ▶ THE INTRODUCTION
- ▶ THE BODY
- ▶ THE CONCLUSION
- ▶ REVIEW OF ESSAY DEVELOPMENT
- ▶ PEER REVIEW AND REVISION 2
- ▶ EXEMPLIFICATION
- ▶ TIME SHIFTING

MANAGING YOUR MATERIAL

Journal ENTRY 13

What is national identity?

Is it easy to tell which countries people are from? How do you know people are from the same country? Think of several ways you classify people into cultural groups. Discuss two ways with examples and details. [300-350 words, every other line]

ⓓⓘⓢⓒⓞⓥⓔⓡⓨ

4.1: Dividing an essay into paragraphs

The following essay was written as a take-home exam for a political science course.
- Analyze the following assignment. What is the lead-in? What is the assignment task?
- How would you organize an essay based on this assignment?
- Read the essay answer. With a partner, decide where the paragraphs should begin. Use a paragraph marker (¶) to indicate each indentation.
- Answer the Discussion Questions that follow.

Model Assignment

What is nationalism? Discuss two of the components of national identity and briefly assess the benefits and drawbacks of nationalism as a political force. (Assignment requirements: approximately one typed page, double-spaced, font 12, adequate margins)

Nationalism

1   Nationalism is defined as a nation's shared common thoughts that are stronger than those of other nations. Nationalism can be identified by specific components, such as a common political system, a particular territory, a common enemy, and the same historic background, language, race, original religion, original culture, and economy. One country in which the concept of nationalism is
5   evident is Japan. Japanese nationalism can be identified with two of the components: religion and language. First, Japan's original religion is Shintoism. Shintoism has eighty-eight gods, and the main god is Amaterasu Omikami, God of the Sun. Japan also has religious legends. For example, Japan consists of four islands, and they are children of the gods Izamami and Izanagióa, who are a sister and a brother by blood. Other countries do not have any Japanese gods and religious
10 legends; therefore, we can identify Japanese nationalism by its religion. Another component of Japan's nationalism is language. Japan has its own language, Japanese, and its own written characters, such as Chinese, Katakana, and Hiragana. Japanese characters were based on Chinese at first, but over time the Japanese developed their own original writing system. Now only the Japanese speak and write the Japanese language in this world. Nationalism has benefits and
15 drawbacks. One of the benefits is symbolism because nationalism is an abstraction, but it can be identified with symbols such as national flags and anthems. All states have such symbols, and hanging a national flag and singing a national anthem bring the people of a nation solidarity. In contrast to the benefits, there are drawbacks to nationalism. Violence is a drawback of nationalism as a political force because some citizens express their loyalty to their country with terrorism or wars.
20 In fact, some Japanese soldiers fought with the Japanese government about fifty years ago because they wanted to change the Japanese governmental policy. In most places, people are always fighting because of their nationalism, and it is getting worse. In conclusion, nationalism is very important for a nation; however, it still creates problems, and we do not have any power to solve the problems yet. [351 words]

Ⓠ Discussion Questions

Use what you have learned from the previous essay to answer these questions.

1. Where did you insert the paragraph markers? How did you determine where the paragraphs should begin?
2. Does the essay effectively address the assignment task?
3. With regard to unity, are the supporting points relevant and logically placed?
4. With regard to coherence, does the essay contain clear signals to guide the reader? Also, do the ideas logically follow each other?

As you can see, the more you have to say, the more you have to manage. It was probably easier for you to find the answers to the previous Discussion Questions when the information in the essay was organized and indented to signal new paragraphs.

To convert a paragraph composition into an essay, divide it into several paragraphs and make the topic sentence the thesis statement. The subtopic sentences in your original paragraph will become the essay topic sentences, and the concluding remark will become a full conclusion.

THE TRANSFORMATION FROM A PARAGRAPH TO AN ESSAY ───────

Paragraph		Essay	
Topic Sentence	→	I. Thesis Statement	(Paragraph 1)
A. Subtopic Sentence	→	II. Topic Sentence	(Paragraph 2)
B. Subtopic Sentence	→	III. Topic Sentence	(Paragraph 3)
C. Subtopic Sentence	→	IV. Topic Sentence	(Paragraph 4)
Concluding Remark	→	V. Conclusion	(Paragraph 5)

In this chapter, we will examine the components of longer papers more closely. You will continue to see models that are clearly organized according to the standard classical approach in which a paper has an introduction, a body, and a conclusion. Learning this approach will provide you with a solid foundation in your writing. As you mature as a writer and develop your reading skills in English, you will see ways to vary this classical approach.

AN OVERVIEW OF ESSAY DEVELOPMENT

Essays consist of more than one paragraph and have three major parts: an introduction, a body, and a conclusion. A complete essay contains all of the following elements. (Those elements considered optional have been underlined.)

The introduction contains (usually in this order):
- background information, which attracts or "hooks" the reader.
- a thesis, which limits the topic and states a precise opinion.
- a list of the subtopics, or MAP* points, for the body paragraphs.

The body paragraphs contain:
- topic sentences which follow the MAP points in the thesis.
- transitions introducing each subtopic.
- repetition of the essay topic and precise opinion from the thesis.
- relevant and generous convincing support (unity) and coherence.
- a closing remark (final comment) showing the relevance of the support.

The conclusion contains:
- a paraphrase of the thesis.
- a summary of the main points.
- a closing remark (final comment).

---

* "MAP" is an acronym for *message, audience,* and *purpose.* For more information on MAP points, see page 102 in this chapter.

The following is a model essay from Chapter 1 with the major parts labeled.

Model Essay

Barbara H. Leonhard *(Name)*
ID: 123456 *(ID Number)*
ELSP 003 *(Course)*
C1D1 *(Assignment)*
January 22, 1998 *(Date)*

English Academic Writing: The "A" Paper *(Title)*

1   Academic writing is writing completed in a college or university setting for an academic audience consisting of professors, instructors, teaching assistants, and students. There are several features of English academic writing which make it of value for nonnative speakers to learn. Failure to master the rules for effective academic writing in this culture will affect their success in a course *(Hook)*.

5   Effective English academic writing, particularly the "A" paper, has three characteristics *(Thesis)*. It has convincing content, clear organization, and effective use of the English language *(Map Points)*.

    First *(Transition Signal)*, the "A" paper *(Essay Topic)* has convincing content *(Topic Sentence for Map Point 1)*. To begin with *(Transition Signal)*, the content is informative and thought provoking *(First Subtopic Sentence)*. The purpose of academic writing is to convey knowledge and under-
10 standing of a topic in a persuasive, formal, and objective manner. Such writing is not too general. In order to be convincing, academic writers in Western culture are expected to use specific and logical details, examples, facts, statistics, and case studies to support generalizations. Overly general and illogical content is not well received by professors. Second *(Transition Signal)*, the support is relevant *(Second Subtopic Sentence)*. That is, the support relates directly to the thesis,
15 which clearly presents the writer's topic, purpose, method, and opinion in an essay, and topic sentences, which do the same thing for each developmental paragraph in an essay. Writers are taught not to digress by telling stories or making "by the way" statements, which are out of tone with the assignment despite attempts to be creative and entertaining. All of the sentences contain well-thought-out ideas and relevant supporting points. Third *(Transition Signal)*, although objective,
20 academic writing can be creative in that the writer is able to demonstrate effective critical-thinking skills *(Third Subtopic Sentence)*. The content, that is, has depth of thought. The writer effectively analyzes the information, interprets the facts, makes judgments, draws conclusions, summarizes, and defends opinions. Shallow writing is indicative of weak critical-thinking skills, and such papers, often described as "sophomoric," receive low marks. Finally *(Transition Signal)*, an "A" paper has
25 a clear purpose, which helps direct the reader, the audience *(Last Subtopic Sentence)*. This is because the writer has clear objectives and strong control of the content. The message is clear, logical, and to the point. Indeed, papers with strong, unified support, which demonstrates effective critical-thinking skills, are well received by professors *(Final Comment)*.

    In addition to being convincing *(Transition from Previous Paragraph Topic)*, effective academic
30 writing *(Essay Topic)* in Western culture is well organized according to certain patterns and rules which may vary from culture to culture *(Topic Sentence from Map Point 2)*. The general pattern is described as linear (Robert Kaplan, 1966) *(In-text Documentation)* because of the direct relationship between generalizations and their supporting points *(First Subtopic Sentence)*. Academic papers generally have a deductive approach, in which the generalization is stated first and then supported
35 by specific details, examples, and other kinds of support. Sometimes academic writers use an inductive approach, in which the specific support is given before the generalizations. English academic writing is also *(Transition Signal)* organized on the rhetorical level *(Second Subtopic Sentence)*. There are several classical patterns used: narration, description, definition, process, classification, comparison, cause/effect, and argumentation. The pattern chosen is the method by
40 which the writer will convey the content. This involves learning the organizational cues for the patterns and ways to order the support with these rhetorical devices. The success of a paper depends on how well the writer handles these organizational principles *(Final Comment)*.

    Finally *(Transition Signal)*, good English academic writing *(Essay Topic)* demonstrates sophis-
ticated use of the English language *(Topic Sentence for Map Point 3)*. First *(Transition Signal)*,

45   "A" papers are clearly written at the sentence level *(FIRST SUBTOPIC SENTENCE)*. Not only is organization important at the rhetorical level; it is crucial at the sentence level. Disorganized sentences disrupt the flow of thought in a paper and interfere with the meaning of the passage. Frequent agreement errors, misspellings, incorrect punctuation, and other such problems also demonstrate lack of control of English and distract the reader. Second *(TRANSITION SIGNAL)*, style is important *(SECOND SUBTOPIC*
50   *SENTENCE)*. Effective English academic writing demonstrates control over a variety of sentence types. In Western culture, complex and compound-complex sentences, which contain dependent clauses, are preferred in academic papers. Papers containing too many simple sentences and coordinating conjunctions are considered boring and unimaginative. A wide vocabulary range is another *(TRANSITION SIGNAL)* characteristic of effective academic writing *(THIRD SUBTOPIC SENTENCE)*. Because
55   information is conveyed in content words, weak (basic) vocabulary demonstrates weak thinking. Because effective sentence organization and vocabulary contribute to the content of a paper, writers who have command of the English language are more convincing than writers who cannot articulate complex ideas *(FINAL COMMENT)*.

      In conclusion *(TRANSITION SIGNAL)*, nonnative speakers studying in the U.S. or Canada will
60   benefit from learning what will be expected of them in their academic writing. If the professor's expectations are not met with regard to content, organization, and language, the paper may not be well received *(SUMMARY)*. Mastering the fundamentals of English academic writing will enable nonnative speakers to succeed in their academic studies *(FINAL COMMENT/RESTATEMENT)*. [767 words]

Work Cited *(BIBLIOGRAPHY)*

Kaplan, Robert B, "Cultural Thought Patterns in Intercultural Education." *Language Learning,* 16 (1966), pp.1-20. *(SOURCE INFORMATION)*

THE INTRODUCTION

The main point of a longer paper is found in the introduction, which is the material at the beginning of the paper. The length of the introduction depends on the scope of the topic. If your paper is three pages, the introduction will probably be only one paragraph. If your paper is fifteen pages long, the introduction may be more than one paragraph. (The element considered optional has been underlined.)

The introduction:
- attracts and holds the reader's attention (hooks the reader).
- introduces the general paper topic.
- limits the topic to a manageable focus for the assignment.
- indicates the writer's purpose (to show, to convince, to prove, to entertain, to demonstrate, to inform).
- presents the writer's opinion or attitude about the limited subject in a thesis statement.
- indicates how the topic will be explored (basic enumeration, comparison, contrast, causal analysis, development by example, process, definition, classification).
- provides a MAP (the essay subtopics) for the reader of how the discussion will proceed.

Hooks

Most academic papers begin with a hook, which gets the reader's attention and introduces the topic. Hooks are not required on essay tests; due to the time limit, a strong thesis and MAP are usually all that are needed. There are five kinds of hooks, which can occur alone or in combination: question, quotation, dramatic, funnel, and refutation.

The Question Hook

Asking a question will cause the reader to think about the topic. However, limit your hook to one question. If you ask too many questions, the hook is not effective.

> **Example**

The House of Life

How many decisions do people make in their lives? There could be thousands of decisions in one person's life. However, only a few of them will have a great influence. A metaphor of building a house shows how the five most significant decisions are related to one another and reflect on people's lives. The five most important decisions concern education, career, marriage, residence, and religion. [65 words] (Adapted with permission, Yungjing Hsieh, Taiwanese)

The Quotation Hook

Quoting an expert will give the discussion credibility. Make sure to cite the source accurately.

> **Example**

The Lindisfarne Gospels: A Brief Look at Their History and Decoration

The Lindisfarne Gospels are not only one of the best examples of Northumbrian book illumination, but one of the most well-documented works of art that we have from the late seventh century. Thanks to Aldred's colophon of before 970 AD, we know who wrote the gospels and when and where they were written. The Lindisfarne illuminator combined traditional Hiberno-Saxon motifs with imported elements from the continent, creating a beautiful and sophisticated whole. Hence, the Lindisfarne Gospels are not just important in themselves, but as Janet Backhouse affirms, " . . . (they) thus become a touchstone for the assessment of all other works of art of the period." (2, 66) [108 words] (Adapted with permission, Aimée H. Leonhard, American)

The Dramatic Hook

Describing a scene or telling a story provides a dramatic invitation to the readers.

> **Example**

A Quest for Home

Christmas . . . 1957. Mother, age 30, was pregnant with her fourth child. At 34, she nearly died with her seventh child. Happily married to my father for 33 years, she has committed her life to mothering and all that it entails and also fulfilled duties as a minister's wife. Hers was a private world with public interludes.

Christmas . . . 1981. As a 30-year-old woman, the second oldest of the seven, I have achieved different public goals than my mother could in her day and age. While working toward a Ph.D. in English Linguistics, I busily prepare for 15 hours of teaching a week as a full-time instructor of English as a Second Language. By the time I am 34, I will be well qualified to teach seminars in stylistic analysis and direct an English language program anywhere in the world. Having already given three professional presentations at regional conferences and symposiums, I have found that mine is a public world with private interludes.

The world today is very different for women in the U.S. than it was in the past. Women's priorities have changed dramatically in these three areas: marriage, child-rearing, and education. [197 words]

The Funnel Hook

Stating general points as background for your limited subject presents a "funnel-like" progression from general to specific. Be careful not to start at a level which is too general, however. If you use words from the assignment and follow the assignment task, the level of generality will be acceptable.

☞ **Example**

My Ideal Husband

Love is a wonderful thing with all the happiness, dreams, and future plans that it brings to us. In books, movies, and songs, the most important thing for a happy marriage is great love. However, life is very different from the movies, books, and songs. Even the biggest love in the world is not sufficient for a good marriage. There are a lot of other qualities necessary for a man to be a good husband. Of course, my ideal husband should love me. However, he should also share my ideas, dreams, and future plans, and have a good personality. [99 words] (Adapted with permission, Milena Stanislovova, Bulgarian)

The Refutation Hook

In this kind of hook, summarize an opponent's point of view, or opinion. In the thesis, however, state your point of view. This approach sets up your own argument in a diplomatic way. Use refutation for controversial topics (subjects that create controversy). This is the appropriate type of introduction for an argumentation paper.

☞ **Example**

Forcing Children to Do Things

Forcing children to do things, in general, is good if the child is in danger or too young to make major decisions. Parents may also argue that forcing their child to take up certain hobbies, like the piano, will give the child a well-rounded education and a possible future career in music (*OPPONENT'S VIEW*). However, there are several problems with forcing children to comply: a breakdown in communication between the children and the parents, rebellion, and failure in school (*WRITER'S VIEW*). [77 words]

Thesis Statements

Just as a single paragraph has a topic sentence which introduces the paragraph topic and the writer's opinion and method, so a thesis statement is the most important element of an essay. Thesis statements contain the writer's limited subject, opinion or attitude, and possibly a MAP, which will be discussed in the body of the essay. The MAP is not required, but it is highly recommended because it will enable you to control the topic so that the readers will not get lost.

ANALOGY

Using the analogy from Chapter 3, think of readers as travelers. In your thesis, you are promising to take them on a special trip (topic and opinion). The thesis should tell the readers where they are going (MAP), how they will get there (method), and why they are going on this trip (purpose). The essay should fulfill your promise of a pleasurable, informative, well-directed journey. If the essay lacks unity, that means the trip is disorganized and lacks direction. You have taken the readers to places you never promised to at the beginning of the trip (in your thesis), or you have gone off the road temporarily. Stay on the route and keep your eyes on the road. Not only should all the points and support in the essay be part of the trip plan, it should also be easy for the readers to get to their destination (coherence). All the topic and subtopic sentences should be as clearly stated as road signs. In other words, the topic sentences, subtopic sentences, and any other important organizational cues in the body of the essay are major signs along the way. On a trip, if the road signs are missing, where are the travelers to go? As you can see, the two major rules you learned in

Chapters 2 and 3 still apply to essays: unity and coherence. The only major difference is the length of the trip (the length of the paper).

Thesis statements are expressed in much the same way as the topic sentence patterns were in Chapter 3. Effective and complete thesis statements have the following features. (Those elements considered optional have been underlined.)

Effective thesis statements:

- are complete, grammatical statements (not phrases or questions).
- are not too specific or too general.
- are on one limited subject.
- contain the writer's precise opinion (are not just statements of fact).

Complete thesis statements:

- contain the limited essay topic.
- are arguable (contain a precise opinion about the limited topic).
- show the method of the paper.
- show the audience of the paper.
- show the purpose of the paper.
- <u>contain the MAP points for the paper (body paragraph topics)</u>

Maps (Message, Audience, Purpose)

A MAP* is the list of main points which you will discuss in the body of the essay. Each MAP item, which you choose based on your message, audience, and purpose, will become a paragraph topic. Even if you do not state the MAP in the thesis, you must have a MAP in mind before you write the essay. It is a good idea to state the MAP at the end of the introduction. As you saw from the previous examples of essay introductions, MAPs can be stated as part of the thesis in many ways. Instead of the colon (:), you can say *such as*, and you can also make another sentence with the MAP. Here are variations of the MAPs you saw earlier.

➰ Examples of Thesis Statements with Maps

- However, there are several problems with forcing children to comply. Forcing children to comply can cause a breakdown in communication between the children and the parents, rebellion, and failure in school.
- Women's priorities have changed dramatically in such areas as marriage, child-rearing, and education.
- An "A" paper has three major characteristics: convincing content, clear organization, and effective use of language.

MAP Points

- are relevant.
- are distinctively different (do not overlap).
- belong together (are well-matched, at the same level of generality).
- are parallel.
- are thought-provoking.
- are logical and appropriate choices focusing on major and representative ideas.
- are optional (but highly recommended).

---

*Throughout this textbook, the terms "MAP" and "MAP points" will be used to describe the main points of a composition, essay, or thesis.

D I S C O V E R Y
4.2: Analyzing introductions

- Analyze the following introductions.
- On a separate sheet of paper, list the hook, thesis, purpose, method, and MAP for each.

↪ **Example**

Inventions That Have Revolutionized Our Lives

Compared to 100 years ago, the world of today is becoming so much closer than ever that people can easily attain whatever they want. As Alvin Toffler says in his book, "The Third Wave," modern society is characterized as an information society, in which people's lives are dramatically and unimaginably changed, in fact, to the better. Satellites and computers are good examples of inventions leading to an information society. (Adapted with permission, Jeong-Seog Lee, Korean)

Hook: Quote by an expert

Thesis: Satellites and computers are good examples of inventions leading us to be an information society.

Purpose: To show the reader how satellites and computers are inventions which give us information and, as a result, greatly benefit society

Method: Development by example

MAP: Satellites and computers

1.

The House of Life

How many decisions do people make in their lives? There could be thousands of decisions in one person's life. However, only a few of them will have a great influence. A metaphor of building a house shows how the five most significant decisions are related to one another and reflect on people's lives. The five most important decisions concern education, career, marriage, residence, and religion. (Adapted with permission, Yungjing Hsieh, Taiwanese)

2.

Good Students

University study is challenging. Some students succeed and some do not. What makes some students more successful at academic study than others? It depends a lot on the attitude of the student. Sandy Colhoun, a master's candidate at the University of Missouri School of Journalism, is an example of what professors call a good student. Sandy has a positive attitude about succeeding in an academic setting. He cares about learning, puts in time on his studies, and is interested in the world around him. (Adapted with permission, Vasna Wilson, Thai)

3.

My Ideal Husband

Love is a wonderful thing with all the happiness, dreams, and future plans that it brings to us. In books, movies, and songs, the most important thing for a happy marriage is great love. But life is very different from the movies, books, and songs. Even the biggest love in the world is not sufficient for a good marriage. There are a lot of other qualities necessary for a man to be a good husband. Of course, my ideal husband should love me. However, he should also share my ideas, dreams, and future plans, and have a good personality. (Adapted with permission, Milena Stanislovova, Bulgarian)

4.

Forcing Children to Do Things

Forcing children to do things, in general, is good if the child is in danger or too young to make major decisions. Parents may also argue that forcing their child to take up certain hobbies, like the piano, will give the child a well-rounded education and a possible future career in music. However, there are several problems with forcing children to comply: a breakdown in communication between the children and the parents, rebellion, and failure in school.

Out-of-Class Writing Assignments

The following two Discoveries will get you started on an essay which you will complete in stages in this chapter.

DISCOVERY

4.3:   Composing a thesis statement and MAP

This activity is the first stage of planning for an essay you will complete in this chapter.
• Analyze the following topics. What is the lead-in and assignment design in each?
• Brainstorm on the topics with (a) partner(s).
• Write a thesis statement and a MAP with three MAP points for each topic. Follow the previous rules.

1. Many people agree that a child's educational, emotional, and social development are very important. Children learn a great deal before they are five years old. What are the three most important things (skills, habits, or values) to teach children between the ages of three and four? Provide specific examples, details, and personal experience (your own and/or that of others) as support.

2. Computers have become an important part of everyday life. In many areas, they have become invaluable in doing tasks more efficiently and effectively. In medicine, for instance, they have simplified making diagnoses, cross-checking drug interactions, and maintaining patient information. What advantages have computers brought to academic life? In other words, how has the computer made students' lives easier? Discuss three advantages of computers in academic life. Support the discussion fully with specific examples, details, and personal experience (your own and/or that of others).

DISCOVERY

4.4:   Composing and peer-reviewing an introduction

• Choose one of your thesis statements in Discovery 4.3 and write an introduction for the out-of-class essay.
• Use one of the methods for hooking the audience.
• Use Peer Review Form 5 from Appendix D to evaluate each other's introductions.
• Make the necessary revisions.

THE BODY

Essay Outline Framework

The body comprises the information in the essay. The body will be two or more paragraphs long, depending on the number of MAP points you have. The following sample of an outline framework shows that there is a correlation between the MAP and the topic sentences in the body paragraphs. The body paragraphs are discussed in the order the points are listed in the MAP. Moreover, roman numerals (I, II, III) are used to signify each paragraph in the essay. The rest of the symbols for each paragraph in the body are the same as you learned in Chapter 3. The capital letters A, B, C, and so on show subtopics in each paragraph. Each subtopic should be introduced with clear signals. The numbers 1, 2, 3, and so on indicate more specific support.

I. Introduction
   • Hook
   • Thesis Statement: X, Y, and Z (Map)

II. Topic Sentence 1 (First Map Point, X)
   A. Subtopic Sentence 1
      1. Support
      2. Support
      3. Support
   B. Subtopic Sentence 2
      1. Support
         a. Specific Support
         b. Specific Support
      2. Support

III. Topic Sentence 2 (Second Map Point, Y)
   A. Subtopic Sentence 1
      (Support)
   B. Subtopic Sentence 2
      (Support)

IV. Topic Sentence 3 (Third Map Point, Z)
   A. Subtopic Sentence 1
      (Support)
   B. Subtopic Sentence 2
      (Support)

(Each subtopic sentence should be supported with at least two examples or with one good extended example.)

V. Conclusion
   • Restatement of the Thesis
   • Summary of the Map Points
   • Closing Remarks (Final Comments)

Complete Topic Sentences

An essay outline does not have to contain complete topic sentences for each body paragraph; usually phrases are adequate. However, it will benefit you to write complete topic sentences in the outlines you do for peer review to see if you have control of the assignment task in the essay body. Complete topic sentences include the following elements.

1. A transition signal or phrase is highly recommended. Here are two common enumeration patterns, which are appropriate for an essay following that sample outline framework on the previous page. Use correct mechanics and pay attention to articles.

   ➡ **Example**

Pattern 1	**Pattern 2**
First, _____ .	The first _____ is _____ .
Second, _____ .	Another/The second _____ is _____ .
Finally, _____ .	The other/final _____ is _____ .

   In Pattern 1, do not use *the*. Also, use a comma after the ordinal. Follow the ordinal with a complete sentence. In Pattern 2, however, use *the* with the ordinals and do not use commas. *Another* means "one more in addition"; it can be used for any except the first or last topic sentence. *The other* means "the last one." In other words, there are no others. Follow the ordinal with the subject of the sentence.

2. A restatement of the limited essay topic is also used in a topic sentence. To restate the limited essay topic, use words from the assignment task and paraphrase. That is, use synonyms, different word order, and different word forms.

   ➡ **Example**

   Limited essay topic: Discuss three reasons you chose your major.

   One reason I chose engineering is _____ .
   Another reason for my choice of major is _____ .
   Finally, I decided on engineering because _____ .

3. Each topic sentence should include a MAP point (paragraph topic) from the list in (or near) the thesis. The topics should follow the same order in the body of the essay as they are stated in the MAP list.

   ➡ **Example**

   Thesis: I chose engineering for three major reasons: *personal (family-related) reasons, my strong interest in the field, and the need for engineers in Taiwan.*

      I. First, I chose engineering for *personal (family-related) reasons.*
     II. Another reason for my choice of major is *my strong interest in the field.*
   III. Finally, I decided on engineering because of *the need for engineers in Taiwan.*

4. The topic sentences recall the precise opinion from the thesis. The precise opinion is either implied or directly stated, depending on the nature of the topic.

   ➡ **Example**

   - Culture shock has four main stages: excitement, frustration, humor, and adjustment.
     (The writer enumerates four, not three or five, stages and defines them.)

   - Living in the dorm benefits nonnative speakers in three ways.
     (The writer argues for the benefits, not disadvantages.)

- Life in Taiwan has been greatly influenced by U.S. culture in the foods, the leisure time activities, and the holidays.
  (The writer sees these areas, not others, as the major areas of influence.)

5. The method of development should be clearly stated in the topic sentences. Use terms from the assignment task to state the method.

<u>Method</u>	<u>Terms</u>
Cause	Reason
Classification	Category, kind, type
Compare	Similarity
Effect	Effect, benefit, influence
Difference	Difference
Process	Way, stage, step, phase

6. Unless the essay topic is personal, use content words (not pronouns) in the thesis statement, topic sentences, subtopic sentences, and conclusion.

   ⇨ **Example**

   I. Thesis: Living in the dorm benefits *nonnative speakers* in three ways.

   II. First, by living in the dorm, *nonnative speakers* (not *they*) can make friends with native speakers. (Topic Sentence)

   III. Second, *nonnative speakers* (not *they*) can practice their English in the dorm. (Topic Sentence)
      A. One language skill *nonnative speakers* (not *they*) can practice is reduced speech. (Subtopic Sentence)
      B. *Nonnative speakers* (not *they*) can also learn idioms and slang terms from the *native speakers* (not *they*) in the dorm. (Subtopic Sentence)

   IV. Third, *nonnative speakers* (not *they*) can learn about the customs in the host country if they live in the dorm. (Topic Sentence)

   V. Conclusion: By living in the dorm rather than living alone, *nonnative speakers* (not *they*) can immerse themselves in the host culture. New friendships with native speakers will enable them to develop better English and learn many things about this strange and surprising culture that they may not learn on their own. After all, people never really know others well until they live with them.

Types of Order in Body Paragraphs

In the outlining stage of prewriting, it is a good idea to order the paragraphs logically. There are three basic principles which regulate how to determine the best order: chronology, ranking, and familiarity. As you study these examples, pay attention to the design of each part of the basic outline, especially the wording of the topic sentences.

Chronological Order: Process and Time

The easiest principle is chronological order, which is used for process description (process order) and narration of events (time order).

Process Order

In process order, you must begin with the first step, stage, or phase and end with the last step, stage, or phase. If you try to explain a process with the steps out of order, the reader will get lost, and the results of the process will fail. (You will learn more about process order in Chapter 5.)

⊸ **Example**

    I. Thesis: Adjusting to a new culture is not an easy process at times, but overall it can be a positive experience. Culture shock has four main stages: excitement, frustration, humor, and adjustment.

    II. In the first stage, everything in the host culture is exciting and new. (Topic Sentence)

    III. In the frustration stage, the visitors start having problems. (Topic Sentence)

    IV. After the frustration stage, visitors start to relax and laugh more. (Topic Sentence)

    V. In the adjustment stage, the visitors start to feel at home in the host country. (Topic Sentence)

    VI. In conclusion, getting used to a new and sometimes strange culture can have its low points, but the visitors should feel assured that given time and the development of coping skills, the new way of life may begin to feel as comfortable as the old one.

Time Order

Similarly, with narration of events, begin with the first event and proceed logically in time until you get to the most recent event; this progression is past to present. Although in some cases it might be more effective to start from the most recent event and progress backward, it is usually more logical to describe the past first and then the present rather than to jump around in time. (Narration will be covered in Chapter 5.)

The following outline takes a historical perspective on the European-American perceptions of the Native American and the African. You will read this essay in Chapter 5.

⊸ **Example**

    I. Thesis: To understand the European-American perceptions of the Native Americans and the Africans, it is necessary to look back to the fifteenth century.

    II. In 1492, Columbus sailed across the Atlantic searching for India; instead of India, he discovered the Americas. (Topic Sentence)

    III. The Europeans' views of the Africans were just as prejudiced as their views of the Indians, or Native Americans. Again it is important to go back to the fifteenth century and maybe even further back to understand how the Europeans developed these limited views. (Topic Sentence)

    IV. In Africa (and also in Rome and Greece), there had always been slavery. (Topic Sentence)

    V. With the Renaissance, trade began to flow more freely, and black slaves may have shown up in the marketplace, not en masse, but maybe one or two taken as a curiosity from along the trade routes to India. (Topic Sentence)

    VI. The English had a different view of the Africans than most Europeans on the continent. This view goes back into medieval times and probably even earlier. (Topic Sentence)

    VII. When black slaves were introduced to England, the English were horrified. (Topic Sentence)

    VIII. When the Colonists immigrated to the New World, they carried these ideas with them. (Topic Sentence)

    IX. In conclusion, . . .

Order of Importance: Ranking

The second principle of order involves ranking the MAP points. There are three rankings based on order of importance: equal order, descending order, and ascending order.

Equal Order: No Best

This ranking shows that each MAP point or subtopic is equal in value. Each point carries the same weight in your opinion.

⇨ **Example**

    I. Thesis: Living in the dorm benefits nonnative speakers in three ways.

    II. First, by living in the dorm, nonnative speakers can make friends with native speakers. (Topic Sentence)

    III. Second, nonnative speakers can practice their English in the dorm. (Topic Sentence)

    IV. Third, nonnative speakers can learn about the customs in the host country if they live in the dorm. (Topic Sentence)

    V. Conclusion: By living in the dorm rather than living alone, nonnative speakers can immerse themselves in the host culture. New friendships with native speakers will enable them to progress in their English skills and learn many things about this strange and surprising culture that they may not learn on their own. After all, people never really know others well until they live with them.

Descending Order: Best First

For this order, begin with the most important (largest or strongest) point and end with the least important (smallest or weakest) point. Thus, each point is ranked in descending order.

⇨ **Example**

    I. Thesis: Life in Taiwan has been greatly influenced by U.S. culture in the foods, the leisure time activities, and the holidays.

    II. The first and most important influence the U.S. has had on Taiwan is the food the Taiwanese have adopted from Western culture. (Topic Sentence)

    III. Second, many of the things that people in Taiwan do in their free time have been borrowed from American culture. (Topic Sentence)

    IV. In addition to the foods and the hobbies, American holidays are still another influence on Taiwan. (Topic Sentence)

    V. In conclusion, the daily life in Taiwan reflects American culture a great deal. This Western influence includes the foods, the hobbies, and the holidays people in Taiwan enjoy. Some of the things which were borrowed, such as music and sports, help the Taiwanese to know more about the West. However, some of the new foods, such as hamburgers and potato chips, are not good for their health. Although the Taiwanese may benefit from some Western practices, they should not forget their traditional ways.

Ascending Order: Best Last

For this order, begin with the least important (smallest or weakest) point and end with the most important (largest or strongest) point. Many writers feel ascending order is very effective because the reader is left with the most important point in mind. Note the use of descending order in the following outline on "Kinds of Tornadoes and Their Effects." Because the writer wants the reader to realize how severe and bizarre the effects of tornadoes are, putting the most severe type of tornado last is very dramatic.

⇨ **Example**

    I. Thesis: Tornadoes are classified according to the severity of the tornadic storm as defined on the Fujita Wind-Damage Scale: weak, strong, violent.

    II. The weakest tornadoes, classified as F0 and F1 on the Fujita scale, cause light to moderate damage. (Topic Sentence)

III. Next in rank of severity are F2 and F3 (strong) tornadoes, which cause significant to severe damage. (Topic Sentence)

IV. The most dangerous and frightening tornadoes are the violent F4 and F5 tornadoes, or killer tornadoes, which cause devastating to incredible damage. (Topic Sentence)

V. In conclusion, regardless of strength, all tornadoes can kill, injure, and cause property damage. Such storms are not to be taken lightly. Although fascinating to watch, even the weakest tornado can be an enemy to anything in its path. As one eyewitness said after a tornado hit his Kansas town, "We don't take anything for granted anymore, and we watch the weather like the back of our hand. We watch it day and night." (*Weatherwise*, February/March 1992, p. 29, from Kansas Storms: Destruction, Tragedy, and Recovery, 1991. Diane Silver, editor. Hearth Publishing: Hillsboro, Kansas)

Order of Familiarity

Points can also be ordered according to how well known, familiar, or common they are. It is best to describe familiar ideas before you go to unfamiliar ones. The above outline on tornadoes can be easily adapted to this order.

⇨ Example

I. Thesis: Tornadoes are classified according to the severity of the tornadic storm as defined on the Fujita Wind-Damage Scale: weak, strong, violent.

II. The most common tornadoes are the weak ones, classified as F0 and F1 on the Fujita scale, which cause light to moderate damage. (Topic Sentence)

III. Next in terms of frequency are F2 and F3 (strong) tornadoes, which cause significant to severe damage. (Topic Sentence)

IV. The least common yet most dangerous and frightening tornadoes are the violent F4 and F5 tornadoes, or killer tornadoes, which cause devastating to incredible damage. (Topic Sentence)

V. In conclusion, regardless of strength, all tornadoes can kill, injure, and cause property damage. Such storms are not to be taken lightly. Although fascinating to watch, even the weakest tornado can be an enemy to anything in its path. As one eyewitness said after a tornado hit his Kansas town, "We don't take anything for granted anymore, and we watch the weather like the back of our hand. We watch it day and night." (*Weatherwise*, February/March 1992, p. 29, from Kansas Storms: Destruction, Tragedy, and Recovery, 1991. Diane Silver, editor. Hearth Publishing: Hillsboro, Kansas)

ⒹⒾⓈⒸⓄⓋⒺⓇⓎ
4.5: Composing and ordering topic sentences

- Analyze the following assignment. What is the lead-in? The assignment task?
- Read the introduction and conclusion that follow the assignment.
- On a separate sheet of paper, write three sets of topic sentences. Use equal, descending, and ascending order.

Model Assignment

Most people agree that certain modern inventions, such as the computer, X-ray machine, and laser, have benefited society greatly. However, there are a number of inventions that have hurt society and/or even threaten the existence of life on Earth. Choose three inventions (machines, devices, methods) which are considered dangerous to society and/or the planet Earth. Explain why these things threaten our well-being. Use specific examples, details, and cases (true stories).

I. Introduction

Can people imagine what their lives would be like today without all the inventions and technology of the modern era? Most people emphasize that modern inventions benefit society deeply by making daily life easier. However, only a few people have thought about the negative impact of those inventions. Despite the benefits and all the technological advances that inventions like the automobile, the hand gun, and the television bring to our society, such inventions also cause many problems.

V. Conclusion

In summary, the automobile, the handgun, and the television have damaged our society in a substantive way. Some of the problems that these inventions cause are traffic, pollution, crime, and moral and ethical decline. However, these problems can be avoided or at least diminished provided that people learn to make rational use of such inventions. (Adapted with permission, Licette Galietta, Venezuelan)

ⓓⓘⓢⓒⓞⓥⓔⓡⓨ

4.6: Composing and peer-reviewing an essay outline

- On a separate sheet of paper, complete the following steps.
- Brainstorm on support for the MAP points you listed in Discovery 4.4.
- Use the brainstorming notes to write a formal, complete outline. Refer to the Essay Outline Framework on page 105.
- Use Peer Review Form 6 from Appendix D to evaluate each other's outlines.
- Make the necessary revisions to your outline.

THE CONCLUSION

Conclusions (first addressed in Chapter 3) are longer for essays than they are for single paragraphs. In an essay, you do not need to have a concluding remark in every paragraph since the essay itself has a full conclusion. Following is a review of the rules for effective conclusions. (The element considered optional is underlined.)

Complete conclusions:
- contain a signal (*In conclusion, Indeed, To conclude*).
- recall the limited topic and opinion in the thesis (paraphrase).
- summarize the MAP points (paraphrase if possible) in the same order.
- contain a final comment (opinion).

Effective conclusions:
- follow the essay logically.
- do not bring up new MAP points.
- recognize all MAP points in the summary.

DISCOVERY
4.7: Analyzing essay conclusions

Analyze each of the following conclusions by answering the questions that follow.

⇨ Example

Inventions That Have Revolutionized Our Lives

Introduction

Compared to 100 years ago, the world of today is becoming so much closer than ever that people can easily attain whatever they want. As Alvin Toffler says in his book, "The Third Wave," modern society is characterized as an information society, in which our lives are dramatically and unimaginably changed, in fact, to the better. Satellites and computers are good examples of inventions leading to an information society. [69 words]

Conclusion

In conclusion, material was the sign of power in the past. Today, information is such. Our twentieth-century lives are becoming better and changing dramatically due to inventions such as satellites and computers, opening a road to the information society. Nobody knows what life will be like in the future. [49 words] (Adapted with permission, Jeong-Seog Lee, Korean)

Does the conclusion:

- contain a signal (*In conclusion, Indeed, To conclude*)?   Yes
- recall the limited topic and opinion in the thesis (paraphrase)?   Yes
- summarize the MAP points (paraphrase if possible)?   Yes
- recognize all MAP points in the summary?   Yes
- bring up new MAP points?   No
- contain a final comment (opinion)?   Yes
- follow the essay logically?   Yes

1.

The House of Life

Introduction

How many decisions do people make in their lives? There could be thousands of decisions in one person's life. However, only a few of them will have a great influence. A metaphor of building a house shows how the five most significant decisions are related to one another and reflect on people's lives. The five most important decisions concern education, career, marriage, residence, and religion. [65 words]

Conclusion

The above five reasons—education, career, marriage, residence, and religion—control people's expectations in life. This metaphor illustrates how those five decisions are significant to people's lives. Therefore, people should think patiently and carefully before making important decisions. [38 words] (Adapted with permission, Yungjing Hsieh, Taiwanese)

2.

The Kinds of Tornadoes and Their Effects

Introduction

   Tornadoes are violent twisting wind storms that may accompany thunderstorms. The word "tornado" comes from two Spanish words, *tronada*, meaning "thunderstorm," and *tornar*, meaning "to turn" (Henson, p. 26). More than 1,000 tornadoes strike the U.S. annually, killing or injuring hundreds and causing millions of dollars in property damage. Tornadoes are classified according to the severity of the tornadic storm (or its rank) as defined on the Fujita Wind-Damage Scale: weak, strong, and violent.

Conclusion

   In conclusion, regardless of strength, all tornadoes can kill, injure, and cause property damage. Such storms are not to be taken lightly. Although fascinating to watch, even the weakest tornado can be an enemy to anything in its path. As one eyewitness said after a tornado hit his Kansas town, "We don't take anything for granted anymore, and we watch the weather like the back of our hand. We watch it day and night." (*Weatherwise*, February/March, 1992, p. 29, from <u>Kansas Storms: Destruction, Tragedy, and Recovery</u>, 1991. Diane Silver, 1991) [74 words]

Answer the following questions.

Does the conclusion:

	1	2
• contain a signal (*In conclusion, Indeed, To conclude*)?	....	....
• recall the limited topic and opinion in the thesis (paraphrase)?	....	....
• summarize the MAP points (paraphrase if possible)?	....	....
• recognize all MAP points in the summary?	....	....
• bring up new MAP points?	....	....
• contain a final comment (opinion)?	....	....
• follow the essay logically?	....	....

ⒹⒾⓈⒸⓄⓋⒺⓇⓎ
4.8:   **Composing and peer-reviewing an essay conclusion**

• Write a complete and effective conclusion for the essay you have been working on in this chapter.
• Use Peer Review Form 7 from Appendix D to evaluate each other's conclusions.
• Make the necessary revisions.

REVIEW OF ESSAY DEVELOPMENT

What would you do as a parent to prevent a generation gap?

   Because parents and their children are from different generations, they have different values and perspectives (points of view about life). Such differences can cause conflicts between the two generations. What are some things you would do as a parent to prevent conflicts between yourself and your children? Identify two or three things you could do. Explain them with examples and details. [300-350 words, every other line]

DISCOVERY
4.9: Reviewing essay development

- Use Peer Review Form 8 from Appendix D to analyze and review the following essay.
- Compare your answers in groups.

The Generation Gap
by B. A. Harris

1   When I ask myself what I would do as a parent to prevent a generation gap, I realize that family unity, security for the child, and affectionate love are main factors that will help me to become not a stranger to my children, but a friend.

      In a recent issue of the *Detroit Free Press*, an article on youth hostility asserted that one of the
5   main causes of the generation gap and student revolt is the withdrawal of love by the parents, and that most parents only show an unaffectionate materialistic love by showering their children with unneeded toys, cars, and clothes, or by sending their children to boarding schools for the "best" education, to meet only the "best people." These parents do not realize that what a child considers to be "best" is being home with Mommy and Daddy, enjoying family picnics, and owning a dog named
10   Spot. When a parent is materialistic and withdraws love as a form of punishment, their children grow up to be demanding, spoiled, insecure, hostile, and unable to communicate with their parents.

      The child's ability or inability to communicate is learned through the family, which is the basic social unit. Through it the child is socialized into the pattern of living, and the ideals and morals learned from the family reflect on the child's attitude toward the world. For example, if a child's parents
15   are selfish, unaffectionate, and materialistic, this is the way the child will be also. Furthermore, if a parent is unable to communicate in a proper way with the child, the child in turn will be unable to communicate with the parents.

      Another factor, family unity, strengthens the communication between parents and children. In my home, for example, my family is a working unit: we share, work, sacrifice, and economize together.
20   It is a strong unit strengthened by affectionate love and, thus, emotional security for its members, who depend on one another. The emotional security we feel as a close unit is a gift from my parents—a gift which has weakened any remote chance of there being a generation gap in our home—who have been concerned and eager to know and love their children individually and equally. They have been generous parents not by giving us unnecessary toys, cars, and clothing, but by instilling in us
25   ideals, morals, and emotional security, which cannot be found materialistically.

      Therefore, in my home, we have no generation gap, no hostile youths submitting to radical leaders, no neurotic, spoiled children. I myself can communicate openly and non-aggressively with my parents, who have made themselves my best friends. What is most important, they are there when I need them; I feel secure in knowing they need me, as well, and that they will never send
30   me away unnecessarily.

      Finally, to prevent a generation gap in my home while I am a parent, I will work to make the family a strong and close unit. I will give my children emotional security and not materialistic values. I will be an affectionate mother who will realize that I will need my children as much as they will need me. [524 words] (Adapted with permission, B. A. Harris, American)

DISCOVERY
4.10: Composing and peer-reviewing the first draft of an essay

- Use your revised outlines to write the essay you started in this chapter.
- Use correct essay format.
- Working with a partner or in a small group you have not yet worked with on this topic, use Peer Review Form 8 from Appendix D to evaluate the essay. A new partner will give you a fresh and objective view.
- Make the necessary revisions.

PEER REVIEW AND REVISION 2

Making the Most of the Feedback on Your Writing

As you learned in Chapter 2, the most important part of the writing process is revision, which involves viewing the paper with a critical eye. Your instructor and peer reviewers may make some of the following comments as they analyze and evaluate your paper. It is not easy to hear about the problems in a paper, but your efforts to fix the problems will help you progress with your writing and thus build your confidence.

Off topic   Off focus

Explain   Discuss   Dig deeper

How?   Why?   Who?   When?   Where?

Not Relevant   Not logical   Not convincing

Incoherent   Out of order   Overlapping   Repetitive

What are you trying to express here?

Notice that the comments deal with content and organization, not grammar (agreement, tense, word forms, and so on) or mechanics (punctuation, spelling, and capitalization). Revision involves making major changes, which may require replanning the paper. In other words, you may have to develop stronger support, omit weak support, and reorder your main points. This effort could take a long time, and for a busy student, time is precious. Learning from your instructor's comments and peer reviews will help you to overcome some major problems early on in the writing process so that your time is well spent.

Revision Skills and the Peer Review Process

By now, you have made the connection between the peer review process, your instructor's comments, your revisions, and your grades. Grades are usually based on how well the writer has followed the assignment, the instructor's instructions on how to improve early drafts, and feedback from peer reviews. The peer review forms include questions that are intended to help you to find what is missing or inadequate in your outlines, paragraphs, and essays. As a result, these forms guide you in this critical-thinking process (see Chapter 2, page 32, for a review of critical-thinking skills).

As a result of your instructor's comments and the consistent and constant giving and receiving of feedback in the peer reviews, you should continue to see your (and everyone else's) writing skills improve throughout the semester.

Journal ENTRY 15

In what areas in your writing have you needed to do the most revision so far?

- Review past comments made on your papers by your instructor and on peer review forms by classmates.
- Identify areas where you have had to make the most revisions so far. Do you see any patterns?
- Write a summary of the areas you need to concentrate on the most in the future. [300-350 words, every other line]

ⒹⒾⓈⒸⓄⓋⒺⓇⓎ
4.11: Peer-reviewing a model essay

- Imagine the following essay was written by one of your classmates. Read it carefully.
- Using the skills you have learned so far about writing an essay, use Peer Review Form 8 from Appendix D to evaluate it.
- Compare your answers in groups.

Draft 1

Catch the Three Tigers
by Jung Hee Kang

1   Every year many freshmen start college life with their ambition and challenge. Some students enjoy their school life, but others do not. What are the important qualities to have an enjoyable campus life? How can freshmen adapt to the new environment and be a good student? It is very simple. The three main qualities for this delightful school and being a good student are a positive

5   attitude, obligation of the school's rules, and a clear, firm goal after graduation.

First of all, being a good student requires a positive attitude toward his life. The open-minded and activity provide not only lots of opportunities to make many different types of friends but also various experience to be useful for after the school life. Keeping the challenge is important to the college life.

10   This is a good example to shows how useful having the challenge is. One of my international friends, Mr. Lee, did not speak English very well when he came to the U.S.A. He was also very shy. He was afraid of being spoken by his teacher and classmates. Soon he became to realize that his passive attitude of school and life and his shyness could not be helpful to improve his English. But later on, he changed his attitude. He tried to speak in his classes with his dictionary. He started to

15   say "Hello" to his classmates in order to have some conversation. Also, every time he met the new vocabularies, he asked his American friends to explain the meaning of the words. Now his English has been improved incredibly. Many other international students that he has known envy his excellent English. To have a challenge and positive attitude makes a difference.

Second, obligation of the school's rules is important. Do not miss the classes that you are taking

20   as much as you can. In order to make the classes enjoyable, it is needed to have the good relationship with your teacher and classmates. If you show the effort and passion in the classes, they would not only like you but also respect you. Showing your love and energy to learn something in the classes you will make your school life more productive.

Many freshman students tend to think it is too early to plan their futures after graduation. But I

25   like to stress that it is not early. Right now, I am a second bachelor student. According to my college life in my country, South Korea, it is never early to have an clear, firm goal after graduation. Time never waits for anyone. The sooner you have an organized goal, the better achievement you will have in the future. Believe me. It is based on my previous college life in my country.

These three qualities, positive attitude, obligation of the school's rules and having a clear, firm

30   goal, are essential to have the enjoyable, fruitful college life and being a good student. I am sure these qualities will guarantee you the productive and memorable college life. With three qualities, just go ahead. World will wait you with a big smile. (512 words) (Adapted with permission, Jung Hee Kang, Korean)

⒟ⒾⓈⒸⓄⓋⒺⓇⓎ
4.12: Peer-reviewing for revision

- Now read the student's final draft.
- Note the changes which were made.
- Then complete Peer Review Form 2 from Appendix D.
- Compare your answers in groups.

Final Draft

Catch the Three Tigers
by Jung Hee Kang

1   Every year many freshmen start college life with their rosy dreams and the goals they want to realize in the near future. Some students enjoy their school life, but others do not. What are the important qualities for having an enjoyable campus life? It is very simple. The three main qualities to be a good student are having a positive attitude, observing the school's rules, and making a
5   clear, firm goal for after graduation.

First of all, being good students requires a positive attitude toward life. Open-minded activities provide not only many opportunities to make many different types of friends but also the various experiences are useful for after the school life. This is a good example to show how important it is for students to have a positive attitude in their life. One of my international friends, Mr. Lee, who is
10   studying Chemical Engineering at the University of Missouri, did not speak English very well when he came to the U.S. He was also very shy. He was afraid of being spoken to by his teacher and classmates. Soon he realized that his passive attitude of school and life and his shyness was not helpful for his English. Later on, he changed his attitude. He tried to speak in his classes. He started to say "Hello" to his classmates in order to have some conversation. Also, every time he saw new
15   vocabulary, he asked his American friends to explain the meaning of the words. Now his English has been improved incredibly. Many other international students envy his excellent English. As this example proves, having a positive attitude to school life is imperative, and it can make a difference.

Second, obligation of the school's rules is important. In order to make school life successful, it is necessary for students to attend the classes they are taking as much as they can. Attending
20   classes is mandatory and can help establish a good relationship with the teachers and classmates. If students show their effort and passion in the classes, the teachers and other colleagues respect them. The following example shows how essential it is for students to attend class. When one of my friends, who was born with polio, decided to enter college, her family did not agree with her because all her family members worried that her physical disability would make her frustrated in
25   her campus life. The first main concern that she and her family faced was how she would attend classes regularly because the college that she wanted to go to was located a long distance from her house. Her family was not rich, so they could not afford to buy a car for her. There was no choice but to use public transportation, which took about two hours from her house to the school. However, nobody dissuaded her strong willingness to go to the college. She never missed one class
30   in her college life. She was even on time for a physical education class that was a prerequisite for freshmen. Probably, with her disability, she could have made some excuse for not being in that class, and it probably would have been acceptable to the teacher and other students. But she wanted to observe the school's rules, she said later. Her effort and sincerity toward the classes made a deep impression on her classmates and teachers. As this person's case illustrates, one's
35   devotion to class attendance, despite great odds, can lead to a productive academic life and help one gain the respect of others.

In addition to attending classes, doing the assignments at home is not only one of the most important activities of school life but also basically mandatory for the students. Doing homework and extra study help students to understand lectures which are given in the classes and to make
40   the knowledge theirs. If students do well on assignments and submit papers on time, they will receive good grades. They should try to do each assignment well and to prepare for each class on time. I think that I have learned a great deal of effective information and wide range of knowledge by doing assignments and preparing for each class on time. I have done this since I started to

study at the University of Missouri. As an international student, I think it is too much for me to take four classes, which sometimes deprives me of rest time. Even though I have to spend all day writing, drawing and doing some design work, which does not let me sleep enough, it pays off. I have been praised by the design teacher for doing my design assignments well. Compared to my studying in South Korea, it is hard for me to study in the U.S. As far as I remember, college life in Korea did not require students to put their extra time and energy into studying. In most classes, there were two written tests, which were the midterm and final exam for each semester. I rarely spent all day long to prepare for the tests. I was an easy-going student who did not care about studying. However, now I am facing an entirely different situation in the U.S. I have to go to the library to research the topics given to me in the classes I am taking. Although the assignments give me a lot of stress, I know that doing these assignments and preparing for class on time will be fruitful for me.

Finally, having a clear, firm goal after graduation is vital for good students. Many freshman students tend to think it is too early to plan their futures at the beginning of their college life. However, based on my previous college experience, I like to stress that it is never too early for them to plan their future when they are freshmen. When I started to study at college, I did not have any plan for my future. To tell the truth, I complained about my freshman life because I did not have enough time to hang around with my friends and go to parties. At that time, I thought that I had the luxury of time to get through school. I was just a young girl who had just started campus life. Maybe I was excited about college life and did not try to think about my future. But time passed so fast, and I did not know what to do when graduation came. Many of my friends were the same, but there were a couple of my friends who found the right job because they had spent time learning a foreign language or computer skills. Their early plan paid off for them. On the other hand, I was so regretful of my loose and lazy college life, but it was too late. If I had spent the extra time better by learning computer skills or a foreign language as a freshman the first time, I would have had a different life in Korea, and I would not have come to the U.S. to study for a second B.A. Time never waits for anyone. The sooner you have an organized goal, the better your achievements will be in your future.

These three qualities, having a positive attitude, observing the school's rules and making a clear, firm goal, are essential for students to have an enjoyable, fruitful college life. I am sure these qualities will guarantee a productive and memorable college life. For students with these three qualities, the world will wait with a big smile. [1,254 words] (Adapted with permission, Jung Hee Kang, Korean)

ⒹⒾⓈⒸⓄⓋⒺⓇⓎ
4.13: Peer-reviewing a final draft

You have already peer-reviewed the first draft of the out-of-class essay you started in Discovery 4.3.

- Now with the same people you peer-reviewed with in Discovery 4.10, use Peer Review Form 2 from Appendix D to evaluate the final draft of the essay you have been working on in this chapter. It will also help if you bring the first draft to the peer review session.

EXEMPLIFICATION

Transitions

There are many transitions used in English writing, so it will not be possible to explain all of them in this chapter. Since most of the transitions are rhetorical, indicating the method of development, each chapter dealing with writing patterns will contain the pertinent transitions. In this chapter, we will focus on structures of exemplification.

Structures of Exemplification

There are several structures used to state examples in academic writing. Each structure has rules for word order, sentence organization, and punctuation.

Nouns	Phrases	Connectors	Active Verbs	Passive Verbs
example	such as	for example	include	(be) + characterized as
illustration	such (a[n]/Ø*)	for instance	illustrate	(be) + illustrated by

*"Ø" means no article. *Such* is used with plural and noncountable nouns.

Nouns

Nouns can be subjects or objects, and they can be singular or plural.

example "Pernicious" is *a good example* of a word that is hard to pronounce.
Some good examples of words with silent letters are "doubt" and "psychiatry."

illustration The following true story is *a good illustration*.

Phrase Markers

Phrase markers introduce phrases which contain one or more items, usually a list of nouns. There are four patterns. In each case, the *such as* phrase is placed next to the noun it describes. Pay attention to the use of commas, also.

such as + list

Correct Trees *such as oaks and maples* are deciduous.
(The *such as* phrase modifies an unlimited noun, so commas are not used because the examples are necessary to define the noun.)

Correct Deciduous trees, *such as oaks and maples,* shed their leaves in the fall.
(The *such as* phrase modifies a limited noun, so the commas are used. The examples are not necessary to define the noun.)

Incorrect Trees are deciduous *such as oaks and maples.*

Incorrect Deciduous trees shed their leaves in fall *such as oaks and maples.*
(These sentences are incorrect because the *such as* phrases are misplaced.)

such + noun + *as*

Such trees as oaks and maples are deciduous.
(*Such as* can wrap around the subject of the sentence. Do not use commas. Usually the noun is plural.)

such a(n)/Ø + noun

Some American writers are known for their humor. Mark Twain was *such a writer.*

Some American writers are known for their humor. Mark Twain and James Thurber were *such writers.*
(Use *such a[n]* with a singular noun. Use *such* alone with plural or noncountable nouns. Do not use commas.)

Connectors

Connectors join two sentences (not phrases). If they begin the sentence, use a comma after them. If they follow the subject, use commas on both sides.

for example	Computers are used in many areas. For example, computers are found in banks, hospitals, schools, businesses, and even homes.
for instance	Computers are used in many areas. Computers, for instance, are found in banks, hospitals, schools, businesses, and even homes.
	(Note: A semicolon (;) can be used instead of the period. In that case, do not capitalize the first word in the second sentence.)
	Computers are used in many areas; for example, computers are found in banks, hospitals, schools, businesses, and even homes.

Active Verbs

Different word order is used for these verbs. The verb *illustrate* follows the examples. The verb *include* follows the general idea.

illustrate	Example + *illustrate* + General Idea
	Anger and fear + *illustrate* + negative emotions.
include	General Idea + *include* + Example(s)
	Deciduous trees + *include* + oaks, maples, elms, and sycamores.

Passive Verbs

To form the passive, use a form of the verb *be* + the past participle of the verb. The word order is different for each verb.

(be) characterized as	Examples + *(be) characterized as* +General Idea
	Note: Use *(be) characterized as* to classify or to describe the qualities, traits, or features of something, or to show the distinctive character of something.

Mark Twain *can be characterized as* a humorous writer.

    Example   General Idea

Mark Twain and Woody Allen *can be characterized as* humorous writers.

    Examples   General Idea

(be) illustrated by	General Idea + *(be) illustrated by* +Example
	Many words in English are easy to pronounce. (General Idea)
	This *can be illustrated by* such words as "say," "cat," and "hello."

                                                      (Examples)

ⒹⒾⓈⒸⓄⓋⒺⓇⓎ
4.14: **Analyzing sentences requiring structures of exemplification**

What's missing?
- In the space provided below each sentence, fill in the kind of structure that is missing from the sentence (noun, phrase marker, connector, or verb).
- Then fill in the blank(s) with an appropriate structure of exemplification.

⇨ **Example**

I would like to visit ....*such*........ places ....*as*.......... Scotland and Germany.
......*phrase marker*......

1. Children like to receive various kinds of gifts. ...., they love receiving toys, games, and candy.

   ....

2. Men like to get certain gifts on Father's Day. These gifts .... books and tools.

   ....

3. Nonnative speakers can overcome many problems in this new culture. Some common .... are problems with the food and with the weather.

   ....

4. Some emotions can cause us to feel stressed out. Anger and fear .... these kinds of emotions.

   ....

5. Bright colors, ... red, yellow, and pink, make me happy.

   ....

6. Dark colors, which .... brown and black, are depressing.

   ....

7. Saudi Arabia and Kuwait are .... of countries that are rich in oil.

   ....

8. Red Cross volunteers .... heroes.

   ....

Ⓓ Ⓘ Ⓢ Ⓒ Ⓞ Ⓥ Ⓔ Ⓡ Ⓨ
4.15: Supplying structures of exemplification

- Fill in each blank with a correct structure of exemplification, using the correct form of one of the following phrases.
- Pay attention to the punctuation and grammatical structure of each sentence.
- Spell the structures correctly and use capital letters correctly.
- Use each structure only once.
- The first one is done for you.

examples	for example	~~such as~~	(be) characterized as
such a(n)/Ø	include	such . . . as	(be) illustrated by

1. Negative emotions, ...*such as*........ anger and fear, can cause stress.

2. Good .... of fattening fast foods are french fries, cheeseburgers, and deep-fried fish sandwiches.

3. Dairy products .... milk, eggs, ice cream, yogurt, and cheese.

4. .... words .... "slender," "skinny," and "thin" have similar meanings but different uses.

5. One might catch a cold by touching a person who has a cold. ...., if you kiss someone with a cold, you will probably catch the cold too.

6. Cold germs can live for a long time on contaminated objects. If you touch .... objects, the cold germs will be transferred to your hands.

7. Some expressions in English show how important the sense of sight is. This .... "I see what you mean" and "blind to the truth."

8. Tuxedos and evening gowns .... formal clothes, not informal.

 TIME-SHIFTING

Controlling and Choosing Tenses in Time Clauses

Another skill involved in giving examples is using verb tenses and time clauses, especially when narrating events. Time clauses are dependent clauses which begin with such words and phrases as *when, after, before, until, while, by the time,* and *as soon as.*

General Rules

1. Time clause subordinators can indicate sequential actions (*before, by the time, after, as soon as, until*) or simultaneous actions (*while, as*).

2. If the time clause begins the sentence, use a comma after it, but if the time clause ends the sentence, do not use a comma.

⇨ **Examples**

> John buys popcorn whenever he goes to a movie.
> Whenever John goes to a movie, he buys popcorn.

3. Verb tenses are strictly controlled in complex sentences with time clauses, as the following explanations show.

Choosing Tenses in Complex Sentences with Time Clauses

General Rules

1. If the main clause (independent clause) is in the present or future tense, the time clause (dependent adverb clause of time) is in the present tense. The main clause may contain commands (imperatives) and some simple modals that have present or future meaning.

⇨ **Examples**

> He buys popcorn whenever he goes to a movie.
> After you revise the composition, you need to proofread it.

Please call me when you get home.
Do not hand in the test until you are finished.
We will see our friends when we arrive in New York.
They are going to write the report after they do the experiment.
John will never visit me again as long as he lives.

2. If the main clause is in the past tense, the time clause is in the past tense.

⇨ **Examples**

The jury met for five hours before it reached its verdict.
While the professor was lecturing, the students were taking notes.
As soon as I heard the siren, I pulled over to the side of the road.
I was cleaning the yard when it started to rain.

Perfect Tenses

1. If the main clause is in the present perfect tense, the time clause is in the past tense. The time subordinator is *since* or *ever since*.

⇨ **Examples**

I have lived here since I moved here in 1974.
Ever since/Since he was a child, he has been afraid of snakes.

2. If the main clause is in the past perfect tense, the time clause is past. The time subordinators are *by the time (that)*, *before*, and *when*.

⇨ **Examples**

The bus had already left by the time Jane arrived at the Union.
Joe had already handed in his test when I handed in mine.
My family had already eaten before I got home.

Note: If the time clause begins with *before*, the past perfect tense is not required in the main clause.

My family ate before I *got* home.

3. If the main clause is in the future perfect tense, the time clause is in the present tense. The time subordinators are *by the time (that)*, *before*, and *when*.

⇨ **Examples**

By the time I get home, my family will have already eaten.
The bus will have already left before Jane arrives at the Union.
The other students will have handed in their tests when I hand in mine.

ⓓⓘⓢⓒⓞⓥⓔⓡⓨ
4.16:   Practicing sequence of tenses

A. In the space provided, identify the tenses in the following sentences. Pay attention to the signals in italics.

⇨ **Example**

I *will* never *go* to that restaurant again as long as I *live*.

........future........   simple present

1. When Kathy *lived* at home, she *used to help* her mother a lot.

   ....

2. While people *were watching* the horror movie, somebody *screamed*.

   ....

3. You *have done* several assignments since the semester *began*.

   ....

4. By the time the semester *ends,* you *will have written* many compositions.

   ....

5. Sam *had* just *finished* eating when Mark *called*.

   ....

6. *Do not start* the assignment until you *understand* it.

   ....

B. Fill in the correct tense and form of the verb in parentheses for each time clause. Follow the previous rules for sequence of tenses. Pay attention to the signals in italics.

    ☞ **Example**

        We *were driving* home *when* the accident (occur) ....*occurred*........... .

1. John and Sue *have lived* in Canada *since* they (marry) ....
2. Some students *are going to travel when* the semester (end) ....
3. Joseph *proofread* his composition *before* he (hand) .... it in.
4. *When* you (move) .... here, you probably *felt* excited.
5. *Whenever* my husband and I (go) .... to a ball game, we *sit* as close as we can.
6. Stan *was studying when* I (call) ....

C. Complete the following sentences logically. Follow the rules for sequence of tenses correctly.

    ☞ **Example**

        ....*I worked on my paper*........... until I got tired. Then I went to bed.

1. Whenever you travel, ...
2. By the time Joe got to the theater, ...
3. As soon as the fire broke out in the kitchen, ...
4. I will hand back your compositions when ....
5. Margaret was cleaning while ....
6. I will never shop at that store again as long as ....

Using the Past and Present Tenses in Expository Writing

Earlier you practiced identifying and using tenses by following the rules for using tenses in complex sentences. By now you have done a lot of writing in which there may be a variety of tenses, and knowing when to move from one time frame to another, such as from present to past and back to present, can be challenging. In academic writing, the past and present tense are very common, and if you can learn to use these tenses, you will see immediate improvement in your grammar and content.

The Simple Present Tense

The simple present tense is used to generalize about habits, routines, and customs. Generalizations describe situations that were true in the past, are true now, and will be true in the future. For example, the opening ceremonies for the Olympic Games were the same in the past as they will be in the future. However, the past and future tenses are not used for generalizing about the customs surrounding the Opening Ceremonies at the Olympics; the simple present tense is used for that. We also use the present tense to state facts, such as "There are three kinds of tornadoes" or "Researchers claim they are learning new information about the formation of tornadoes." In expository writing, the present tense is used to explain ideas and give general or hypothetical examples. Such examples explain what usually happens or could happen in certain cases.

Remember that it is a good idea to keep the following strategy in mind when planning an expository essay that uses examples. (For a review of these strategies, see Chapter 3, pages 75–76). Note the tenses to use at each level of generality.

Level of Generality	Tense
Thesis and MAP Points (Subtopics)	present
Topic Sentences	present
Subtopics in Each Body Paragraph	present
Explanation of the Subtopics	present and/or future
General Examples	present and/or future
Specific Examples	past
Explanation of the Specific Examples	past
Return to the Present Time	present and/or future

The Simple Past Tense

Unlike the simple present tense, which is used in general explanations, the simple past tense is used for specific, completed actions in the past. It is the only time you use the past tense. These actions may have happened two minutes ago or twenty years ago. The point is that these specific events are no longer true in the present because they are finished. Such actions can be used as examples to support general points, but they are not used as generalizations.

The following chart shows the simple present and simple past tenses side by side.

THE SIMPLE PRESENT TENSE AND SIMPLE PAST TENSE

Simple Present Tense	Simple Past Tense
Meaning	**Meaning**
General Focus	Specific Focus
True in the past, present, and future	True only in the past
Factual	(Completed past events, actions)
Uses in Academic Writing	**Uses in Academic Writing**
To explain main points	To provide specific examples
To generalize about the subject	(Personal experience, case studies)
To state facts	To narrate historical events
To give hypothetical examples	

↪ **Examples of Transitions/Expressions for the Simple Present and Simple Past Tenses**

Simple Present Tense	Simple Past Tense
Let's say . . .	The following experience illustrates . . .
Let's suppose . . .	In my/my friend's case, . . .
Imagine that . . .	I will never forget the time . . .
Whenever . . . ,/Every time that . . . ,	I still remember when . . .
If . . . , (*present or future conditional*)	Once . . ./One time, . . .
For instance, . . . /For example, . . .	To illustrate,
Adverbs of frequency	(also For example/For instance, . . .)
Modals (*may, might*) and tentative terms	In (*year*), . . .
(*tend to*)	Last year/semester, . . .
In general, . . ./Generally speaking, . . .	A few days/months/years ago, . . .
As a rule, . . .	

Time Shifting in Academic Writing

The previous chart shows a clear difference between the simple present and simple past tenses. You need to learn how to distinguish these tenses in order to time shift from the present (to explain and give general examples) to the past (to illustrate with specific cases).

Notice the writer's use of each level of generality in the following paragraph. The writer uses the present and past tenses appropriately as she moves from one level to another and clearly explains the examples throughout. Use the following labels to identify the time shifts in the example. You will be using these labels again in Discovery 4.17.

LABELS FOR TIME SHIFTS ———————————————————.

(a) Topic Sentence   (d) Transition into Specific Past Example(s)
(b) General Explanation   (e) Explanation of Past Example(s)
(c) General Present Time Example(s)   (f) Return to Present Time/Conclusion

---

[(a) In addition to attending classes, doing the assignments at home is not only one of the most important activities of school life but also basically mandatory for the students.] [(b) Doing homework and extra study *help* students to understand lectures that *are* given in the classes and to make the knowledge theirs. If students *do* well on assignments and *submit* papers on time, they *will receive* good grades. They *should try* to do each assignment well and to prepare for each class on time.] [(c) I *think* that I *have learned* a great deal of effective information and wide range of knowledge by doing assignments and preparing for each class on time. I *have done* this since I *started* to study at the University of Missouri. As an international student, I *think* it *is* too much for me to take four classes, which sometimes *deprives* me of rest time. Even though I *have* to spend all day writing, drawing and doing some design work, which *does not let* me sleep enough, it *pays* off. I *have been praised* by the design teacher for doing my design assignments well. Compared to my studying in South Korea, it *is* hard for me to study in America.] [(d) (As far as I *remember*,) college life in Korea *did not require* students to put their extra time and energy into studying.] [(e) In most classes, there *were* two written tests, which *were* the midterm and final exam for each semester. I rarely *spent* all day long to prepare for the tests. I *was* an easygoing student who *did not care* about studying.] [(f) However, now I *am facing* an entirely different situation here. I *have to go* to the library to research the topics given to me in the classes I *am taking*. Although the assignments *give* me a lot of stress, I *know* that doing these assignments and preparing for class on time *will be* fruitful for me.]

ⓓⓘⓢⓒⓞⓥⓔⓡⓨ
4.17: Analyzing shifts in levels of generality

- Using the previous example as a guide, label the parts of the following paragraph.
- Use some or all of the labels listed above the example. The first one is done for you.

(a)

1   [Finally, having a clear, firm goal after graduation *is* vital for good students.] Many freshman students *tend* to think it *is* too early to plan their futures at the beginning of their college life. However, I *like* to stress that it *is* never too early for students to plan their future when they *are* freshmen, based on my previous college experience in college. When I *started* to study at college,

5   I *did not have* any plan for my future. To tell the truth, I *complained* about my freshman life because I *did not have* enough time to hang around with my friends and go to parties. At that time, I *thought* that I *had* the luxury of time to get through school. I *was* just a young girl who *had* just *started* campus life. Maybe I *was excited* about college life and *did not try* to think about my future, but time *passed* so fast, and I *did not know* what to do when graduation *came*. Many of my friends

10   *were* the same, but there *were* a couple of my friends who *found* the right job because they *had spent* time learning a foreign language or computer skills. Their early plan *paid* off for them. On the other hand, I *was* so regretful of my loose and lazy college life, but it *was* too late. If I *had spent* the extra time better by learning computer skills or a foreign language as a freshman the first time, I *would have had* a different life in Korea, and I *would not have come* to America to study

15   for a second bachelor's degree. Time never *waits* for anyone. The sooner you *have* an organized goal, the better your achievements will be in your future. (Adapted with permission, Jung Hee Kang, Korean)

ⓓⓘⓢⓒⓞⓥⓔⓡⓨ
4.18: Analyzing time shifting

- Read the following passage from an essay based on the outlines you discussed in Chapter 3.
- Then answer the Discussion Questions that follow.

The Benefits of TV

1   TV is so related to daily life that people cannot even imagine the world without it. It can provide benefits such as entertainment, information, and education.
     The first benefit that TV provides is entertainment. It gives people the joy of seeing programs on the large screen and the delight of listening with the stereo sound at home. There are so many

5   programs on TV that people do not hesitate to choose what they want to watch. They can watch

movies, sports, comedies, shows, music, soap operas, cartoons, or whatever their favorites are. When I first came to the U.S. in January this year, I could not find any entertainment. I was told that TV could be amusement. Although sometimes I did not understand exactly what was playing on TV, it did not matter. Colorful images with the loud sound could be enough. Gradually, I grew to
10   enjoy certain programs a lot. Some time ago, I enjoyed the NBA final game, the Chicago Bulls vs. the Seattle Supersonics. I already knew about Jordan, Pippen, and Rodman in the Chicago Bulls, who are popular in my home country. It was a great pleasure that I could watch the live relay of their game on TV.

Discussion Questions

1. Where is the present tense used? Why?
2. Where is the past tense used? Why?
3. How many past examples are there?
4. How are the past examples introduced (transition)?
5. How is the second past example different from the first one?

DISCOVERY

4.19:   Revising problems with time shifting

The present and past tenses are used incorrectly in this adaptation of Jeong-Seog's essay. Find the errors and correct them. There are 14 errors with tense.

1   The second benefit of TV is information. TV broadcasts the news about the community, the

country, and the world. When I was anxious to know what is going on in my homeland, I watch

"CNN World Today." Two months ago, when I turn on the TV for CNN, I am surprised to learn that

North Korea was threatening to come across the DMZ, the Demilitarized Zone. I feel at ease after

5   I hear from a CNN reporter that the invasion does not occur after all. Also, TV was so helpful in

daily life. People could be informed of what the weather will be the next day, where a good place

for shopping was, and what to do when the tap water stops because of the road construction.

When people wanted to go somewhere for recreation, they can also learn where to go and where

to relax. I liked to go on a picnic with my family on the weekends, for instance. When I needed

10   some information for my weekend plans, first I watch TV. If bad weather was in the forecast on the

Weather Channel, I cancel my original plan. Then, I could go shopping or just watch the Disney

Channel at home, which is good for all the members of my family.

ⒹⒾⓈⒸⓄⓋⒺⓇⓎ

4.20:   Using the simple present and simple past tenses

In the following passage from "The Benefits of TV," fill in each blank with either the simple present or simple past tense from of the verb in parentheses. The first one is done for you.

The third reason TV ....benefits....... (benefit) people ....(2)............ (be) that they can

get lessons from TV even if they ....(3).................. (not go) to school. Today everything

..................(4).................. (change) rapidly. What is learned in school can easily become outdated.

Adults eager for more knowledge can use TV. The technology of TV ....(5).............. (make)

it possible for many grown-ups to be re-educated at one time. Compared to the radio, in which

only sound ....(6)......... (be) available, TV ....(7).............. (provide) images, which

.........(8)......... (make) learning more vivid. Today many grown-ups ....(9).............. (have)

difficulty in using computers simply because they ....(10)........... (be) not as sensitive to new

technology as the young ....(11)........... (be). Sometimes they ....(12)........... (feel) out of

date simply because of it. When they ....(13).............. (want) to learn how to use computers,

.........(14)......... (be) it possible with the radio? Once, I ....(15).............. (have) a boss who

.........(16)......... (be) confused about how to use computers. He ....(17)......... (be) too proud

and embarrassed to learn from his staff. He ....(18).............. (tell) me that he ....(19)......... (be)

too old to accept a new thing. However, he ....(20).............. (be) able to find a way to solve his

problem. It ....(21)......... (be) by watching the children's education channel that he can learn how

to use computers.

In conclusion, people ....(22).............. (benefit) from getting entertainment, information, and

education from TV to make use of it in their daily lives. (Adapted with permission, Jeong-Seog Kim,

Korean)

Out-of-Class Writing Assignment

Choose one of your favorite Journal Entries (from this chapter or a previous one) and expand it into a complete 5-paragraph essay with three MAP points. Use all of the skills taught in this chapter.

CHAPTER *summary*

- Complete essays contain an introduction, body, and conclusion.

- The introduction consists of a hook, thesis, and MAP.

- The kinds of hooks include the question, quotation, dramatic, funnel, and refutation hooks.

- The essay outline requires control of each level of generality, which must tie into the thesis, MAP points, and topic and subtopic sentences.

- There are different ways to order the body paragraphs: chronological (process and narration), ranking (equal, ascending, descending), and familiarity.

- The conclusion should be complete and effective. Do not leave the reader expecting more. For a complete conclusion, recall the thesis, restate the MAP, and have a final comment.

- Revision is the most important writing activity. Only through revision can you improve the content, organization, and expression in your papers. Peer review is an important aspect of revision because by getting other readers' reactions, you get positive feedback on your ability to communicate in writing.

- Examples are highly valued in academic writing. There are several transitions used to introduce examples: nouns, phrase markers, connectors, and verbs.

- Controlling tenses in time clauses involves following strict rules. Follow the rules for sequence of tenses. Also, there are specific ways to shift from the present to the past in expository writing. If you can control use of the present and past tenses, you will see progress in your writing.

Chapter 5

Chronological Development (Narration and Process)

CHAPTER TOPICS

► NARRATION

► PROCESS DESCRIPTION

► COHERENCE: OLD IDEA–NEW IDEA

► TIME EXPRESSIONS AND TRANSITIONS

Is there a holiday or celebration in your culture that you wish people in other cultures would adopt?

Cultures share in many ways, such as food, language, and technology. Sometimes cultures actually adopt holidays and celebrations from other countries. Name a holiday or celebration you wish others (such as Americans or Canadians) would adopt from your culture. Describe the holiday or celebration. What happens? Why should people from other cultures adopt it? Be convincing and persuasive. [350-450 words, every other line]

Chronological development, which was introduced in Chapter 4, has two basic forms: narration (time order) and process description (process order).

NARRATION

Narration involves relating events in chronological order from the first event that happened (or happens) to the last event that happened (or happens).

Present narration describes what usually happens during an event that occurs with regularity, like a holiday or a popular ceremony. For such a description, use the simple present tense and adverbs of frequency because you are generalizing. The holiday or ceremony was, is, and always will be celebrated this way.

Past narration describes completed past events, such as historical events, biographies, and past personal experiences (autobiographic material), used to illustrate general ideas. For this focus, use past tenses because the events are complete (or no longer true).

Both present and past narration can be used in assignments to trace the development of something from its origin to the present.

To control a narrative, you need to do the following:

• Understand the time frame you are in and use present and past tense, time expressions, transitions, and time clauses correctly.

• Organize the events in the order they occur(red) from the first event to the last.

Phrases of Time Used in Past Narration

Since narration is used for listing events from past to present, time phrases (references to dates, decades, eras, centuries) are common in narrative writing. Many time phrases include a preposition and a period of time (month, day, year, historic period).

• In 1987, . . .
• Ten years later, . . .
• In the eighteenth century, . . .
• By that time/the end of the year, . . .
• During the war/that period in history/that time, . . .
• Today/In the past, . . .
• On May 1, 1901, . . .
• At the beginning of the century/decade, . . .
• During President Kennedy's term of office, . . .

Have you ever witnessed discrimination against a minority group?

Minority groups include people whose ethnic origin, sexual orientation, religious preferences, or physical or mental health is different from that of the rest of the culture these people are a part of. Have you ever witnessed discrimination against one such group? Give examples of discrimination you have observed against one group and explain two or three reasons that you think people discriminate against this group. Use specific examples and details. [350-450 words, every other line]

ⓓⓘⓢⓒⓞⓥⓔⓡⓨ

5.1: Analyzing a past narrative

The following chronological essay was written in 1980 by an American undergraduate student for an essay test. Note that the writer traces the development of European and American perceptions of Native Americans and Africans from the fifteenth to the nineteenth centuries.

- Read it carefully and circle the time expressions (phrases and clauses).
- Then answer the Discussion Questions that follow.

The European-American Perceptions of the Native Americans and the Africans
by Aimée E. Haynes

1   To understand the European-American perceptions of the Native American Indians and the Africans, it is necessary to look back to the fifteenth century.

In 1492, Christopher Columbus sailed across the Atlantic searching for India, but instead of India, he discovered the Americas. He landed on some islands and called them the West Indies, and it
5   is here where we first get a description of the natives of America. When Columbus returned, he published a description of the Indians and of their immediate neighbors. He said that the natives that he was with were friendly, hospitable, and noble savages. They wore few clothes and were heathens but were peaceful. These Indians, as he called them, told him of another island where the natives were treacherous, cannibalistic, and warlike. From this description that Columbus later published
10   and that traveled through Europe, the Europeans formed the idea that there were two kinds of savages: the noble savage, who was peaceful, and the warlike, cannibalistic, and treacherous savage, who could not be trusted. These views were ingrained in the Europeans, and in the sixteenth and seventeenth centuries, when Europeans, especially the English Colonists, came to North America, they applied these views to all Indians, despite the fact that the Indians differed radically from one
15   another in color, features, speech, and culture.

The Europeans' view of the Africans was just as prejudiced as their view of the Indians, or Native Americans, was. Again it is important to go back to the fifteenth century and maybe even further back to understand how the Europeans developed this limited view.

In Africa, as well as Rome and Greece, there had always been slavery. With the fall of the Roman
20   Empire, black slaves, or North Africans called Moors, were not as much in contact with Europe as they had been previously. Medieval Europe still had slaves, but this was because of religious differences, not because of a difference in skin color. The slaves of medieval Europe were Muslims probably captured in the Crusades. The Europeans felt that these slaves were heathens and therefore could never be free.

25   With the Renaissance, trade began to flow more freely; as a result, a few black slaves were taken to the marketplace as a curiosity from along the trade routes to India. In the sixteenth century, Portugal tried to find a passage to India by sea, sailing around the tip of South Africa. It was the Portuguese who discovered West Africa and brought the first large shipload of black slaves to Europe. Again these slaves were considered a luxury and not used as a labor force.

30   The English had a different view of the Africans than most Europeans on the continent. Based back in medieval times and probably earlier, the English divided good and bad (God and the devil) by the use of two colors, white and black. White to them was the symbol of goodness. Black was everything wicked and evil; in fact, they called the devil the black prince.

When black slaves were introduced to England, the English were horrified. They disliked the
35   Negroes. When the English began to colonize, they saw how useful slaves were, especially for their colonies in Barbados and other islands used for the production of sugar. With the birth of the sugar plantation came the birth of the large-scale slave trade, which was handled primarily by the Dutch and Portuguese. The English had no feeling or care for the Negroes as people. They felt they were simply animals or property that could be owned and worked to death. They did not give the slaves
40   any rights at all.

When the colonists immigrated to the New World, they carried these ideas with them. The South began to obtain slaves because the farmers there grew rice and indigo, and their economy needed the mass workers. Even though England outlawed slavery on the Island of Britain in the eighteenth century, the practice and philosophy of slavery born in England remained in the Americas until the
45   nineteenth century. [668 words] (Adapted with permission, Aimée E. Haynes, American)

Ⓠ Discussion Questions

Answer the following questions about the previous essay.

1. What time expressions did the writer use to trace the development of European attitudes about Native Americans and African Americans?
2. How did the Native American get the name "Indian"?
3. What impression did the Europeans have of the Native Americans after reading Columbus's account?
4. Did the English colonists who came to North America change their view of the Native Americans in any way? Explain.
5. Why did the Europeans have such a limited view of Africans?
6. Who brought the first shipload of black slaves to Europe during the Renaissance? How were black slaves regarded then?
7. How did the English perceive the black slaves? Why? How did their treatment of the blacks change? When?
8. Why did English colonists want black slaves in the New World? Did their treatment of blacks change? When?
9. What are your reactions to this brief history of the European perception of Native Americans and Africans? Has this reading affected your understanding of the historical treatment of African Americans and Native Americans?

Framing Narrative Essays: Time Lines

The most effective way to plan a present or past chronological description is to write a time line. A time line is a list of major, relevant events in chronological order. These events should effectively support a thesis statement.

Study the following time line, which traces the development of one student's interest in philosophy. The student's statement of purpose is in Discovery 5.2.

Model Time Line

Early College Years
- first semester of freshman year—took first class in epistemology
- signed up for another epistemology class and two in phenomenology
- took courses on psychoanalyses

Later College Years
- continued studying psychoanalyses
- studied behaviorism for two years
- studied Jung for one year
- studied Lucan (probably for a year)
- took classes in existential phenomenology (three theory classes and a practicum in psychotherapy)

After Graduation
- worked as a psychotherapist in a university clinic in São Paulo, Brazil
- took courses at the Brazilian Association of Daseinsanalyses

Fall 1997
- moved to Columbia, Missouri
- studied English in the Intensive English Program at the University of Missouri
- attended, as a hearer, the Heidegger Seminar in the University of Missouri Philosophy Department

Winter 1998
- will take courses in the Philosophy Department as a post-bachelor's student

Fall 1998
- hopes to be accepted as a master's student in the University of Missouri Philosophy Department

If your academic goals include applying for a scholarship or getting a graduate degree, for example, you will probably be required to write a statement of purpose. In this statement, you will be expected to trace the development of your interest and experience in your major.

ⒹⒾⓈⒸⓄⓋⒺⓇⓎ
5.2: Analyzing a statement of purpose

- Read the following statement of purpose.
- Then answer the Discussion Questions that follow.

Statement of Purpose for the Philosophy Department
Danielle Pisani Freitas

1   Coming from Brazil with a strong background in existential psychology and a serious interest in studying philosophy, I arrived in Columbia, Missouri, in August 1997 with my husband, who received a Fulbright scholarship for a master's degree in Agricultural Economics at the University of Missouri. Being here in Columbia, Missouri, and looking for an opportunity to continue developing
5   my professional career, I would like to apply to the philosophy department of this university as a candidate for a master's degree.

   My primary reason for seeking a master's degree in philosophy is to complement my career as a psychotherapist. After graduation from college, I worked as a psychotherapist in a university clinic in São Paulo and took courses at the Brazilian Association of Daseinsanalyses. During my
10   academic and professional path, I realized that philosophy could contribute to my development as a psychotherapist.

   Ever since I took my first class in epistemology, during the first year of college, my interest in philosophy has been increasing. I remember, as a freshman, discussing Plato and Aristotle with my friends after class. I really enjoyed those discussions! After that, I decided to take another class in
15   epistemology and two other classes in phenomenology (Husserl). Although I considered those classes very interesting, I had not realized the role that these philosophy courses would later play in my task as a psychologist.

   My first moment of awareness about the importance of studying philosophy happened in my fourth year of college. At that time, I had had four years of psychoanalysis, two years of behaviorism,
20   one year of Jung, and six months of Lucan. In order to decide from which points of view I would interpret my patients' discourse, I asked myself what interested me in each of those theories of personality. From these revealing analyses, I made an important observation. What was important for me as a psychologist studying Freud, Skinner, Jung, and Lucan was my ability not only to understand their theories, but also to grasp the questions that they contemplated as they developed
25   their ideas. In addition, I realized that, as a psychotherapist, I would have to learn how to use my own point of view to comprehend my patients' questions and ideas, rather than simply use the theories of personalities in order to fit my patients into the archetypes I learned. The psychotherapist alone is the main tool used in the analyses sessions. For this reason, it is important for a psychotherapist to

30   develop the ability to understand different ways of thinking and questioning. Because this practice of grasping thoughts and searching for questions also applies to philosophical issues, I realized that studying philosophy would help me as a psychologist. This first insight was the beginning of my genuine interest in studying philosophy.

The utility of philosophical thoughts for psychologists was confirmed for me during my fifth year of college, when I had the opportunity to take classes in the existential phenomenology core. This core
35   was composed of three theoretical classes and a practicum in psychotherapy. In the theoretical classes, I had the chance to read not only Heidegger ("Ser e Tempo"—"Being and Time") but also texts from Binswanger, Merleau-Ponty, and Boss. By reading these texts and applying what I learned to my own practice as a psychotherapist, my interest in philosophy became more serious and meaningful.

40   During the fall of 1997, my first semester here in the U.S., I studied English at the Intensive English Program at this university. I also attended, as a hearer, the Heidegger Seminar in the philosophy department. In the winter of 1998, I will be taking courses in the philosophy department as a post-bachelor's student (PBS). I hope to be accepted into your master's program in the fall of 1998 in order to continue my intellectual and professional development.

45   In conclusion, I want to emphasize my personal interest in studying philosophy and the benefits it can bring to my professional career. Professionally, philosophy will be useful for me not only to help integrate my experience in the Brazilian Association of Daseinsanalyses with the instruction on the philosophical ideas of phenomenology, existentialism, and linguistics, but also to improve my interpreting thoughts and understanding questions, two tasks closely related to those of a
50   psychotherapist.

For these reasons, I hope you will consider my application for graduate studies in the master's program of the University of Missouri Philosophy Department. [726 words] (Adapted with permission, Danielle Pisani Freitas, Brazilian)

Ⓠ Discussion Questions

Answer the following questions about the previous statement of purpose.

1. Where is the writer from?
2. Why is she in Columbia, Missouri?
3. Where does the author state the purpose of the essay?
4. What job did she have after graduation from college?
5. Why is she interested in a master's degree in philosophy?
6. Does the writer address her audience appropriately (tone and point of view)?
7. Do you think she will be accepted into the graduate program? Explain your answer.

Out-Of-Class Writing Assignment: Past Chronology

- Choose one of the following essay assignments and plan the essay by writing a time line.
- Write the essay.
- Use Peer Review Form 9 from Appendix D to evaluate the essay.
- Revise the essay.

Essay Assignments

1. Imagine you are applying for a scholarship (or to graduate school). One of the requirements is to write a statement of purpose in which you trace the development of your interest in your major. Explain to the scholarship committee what past experiences (events and major accomplishments) you have had which contributed to your choice of a major. Use chronological order and a variety of time expressions and coherence devices. (Note: Address your audience in the essay by expressing a strong thesis which states your desire for a scholarship. You want to appeal to the scholarship committee)

2. Develop a complete essay based on Journal Entry 9. Do you know of anyone who overcame a physical or mental disability to accomplish great things? Choose someone you know. Describe the nature of the person's disability and show how the person overcame it.

3. Young people are often influenced by role models, older people who are successful in their careers. Is there anyone who has been a role model for you because of his or her success in a profession? Write an essay in which you trace this person's success. List the relevant events in chronological order. Also, explain how this person's success has influenced you.

PROCESS DESCRIPTION

How can we prevent discrimination?

Identify two or three major things people can do to prevent discrimination. Provide convincing examples and details in your discussion. [350-450 words, every other line]

Process description, the second type of chronological development, is used to instruct the reader on how to do something, how something is done, or how something works. Unlike narration, in which specific past or habitual present events are in focus, the information in a process description is organized in steps or stages with transitions such as:

* *First* or *The first step/stage is . . .*
* *Second, Next, After that,* or *The second step/stage is . . .*
* *Finally, The final step/stage is . . .*

Moreover, in a process description, the present and future tenses (not the past tense) are usually used. Whereas narration describes how something happened in the past (events leading up to a crisis) or what happened/ customarily happens, process describes how something is done. In contrast to narration, which tells a story, process description is usually instructional. The reader is taught how to do something, such as operate a camera, or how something such as a camera functions or works. Descriptions of cycles in nature, such as the life cycle of a plant or animal, are also classified primarily as processes.

Framing Process Descriptions: The Essay Structure

The basic essay structure for process description is not different from what you have learned so far. The content in each part of the essay is specific to the process description itself.

The Introduction

In the introduction, the hook usually contains relevant background information about the process. This may include a definition, especially if the process is technical. For instance, if the topic is "How a Methane Gas Digester Works," the hook should define what this device is. The introduction may also include the purpose of the description and the conditions under which the steps will be completed.

↪ **Example**

> This process is very important/useful/necessary because . . .
> The purpose of this process is to . . .
> This process is completed when . . .

The introduction will also contain a thesis with MAP points. The thesis should contain the essay topic and vocabulary indicating the method of development (process). The MAP will vary depending on whether the process is formal or informal, technical or nontechnical, sequential or nonsequential. In other words, if the process is technical and sequential, the MAP may include steps (chronically ordered action) or stages (a series of related steps).

↪ **Example**

> The life cycle of a tornado consists of four stages: the organization stage, the mature stage, the shrinking stage, and the decaying stage.

However, if the process is nontechnical and nonsequential, the MAP may include a list of ways to do things.

↪ **Example**

> Nonnative speakers can make friends with native speakers on campus in three ways: by joining social clubs, by forming study groups, or by participating in sports.

For more information on the differences between sequential and nonsequential process descriptions, see the section on "Framing the Process Essay: Transitions" on pages 156–158 in this chapter.

Finally, the introduction should make it clear who the audience is. If the purpose of the description is to teach the reader how to perform the process, address the reader as *you*. However, if the reader is simply being informed of the process, do not use *you*. In other words, the process, not the reader, is the focus.
Following are examples of when and when not to address the reader.

↪ **Examples**

How to Do X	(Focus: Instructions directly to the reader)
How X is Done How X Functions (Works)	(Focus: Description of the process itself)

The Body

Body paragraphs are organized according to the type of process description. Follow the MAP points to order the paragraphs. In addition, follow the "Four C's of Process Description" (*clear, complete, convenient, and concise*).

THE FOUR C's OF PROCESS DESCRIPTION

Clear
- The purpose of the process description is clear.
- The process is logically presented.
- The writer describes the necessary conditions, tools and their functions, and requirements.
- The steps and stages are in the correct order.
- The transitions effectively guide the reader.

Complete
- The process includes all the major steps and stages.
- The writer supplies the necessary information on quantities (measurements/amounts), the time it takes for the steps or stages to be completed, and the conditions necessary for the process to occur or be completed.
- The writer warns of any "pitfalls" (possible mistakes) that one may face during the process.
- The writer describes the results of the process.

Convenient
- The process is easy to complete (if it is instructional) or easy to understand (if technical).
- The needs of the audience have been addressed.
- The value of the description is clear.

Concise
- The writer uses the appropriate vocabulary effectively.
- The writer uses grammar effectively, including modals, passive or active voice, simple present or future tense, and time clauses/phrases.

The Conclusion

The conclusion for a process description should restate the thesis, summarize the MAP points, and contain the results of the process. It should also reiterate the importance or benefits of the process.

DISCOVERY

5.3: **Analyzing a technical process description**

- Read the following essay on the life cycle of tornadoes.
- Then answer the Discussion Questions that follow.

The Life Cycle of Tornadoes

1   Tornadoes are violent windstorms in which the air rotates, or twists, causing a funnel-shaped cloud to form from a larger storm cloud. Tornadoes, also called "twisters," are classified on the Fujita Wind-Damage Scale as weak, strong, or violent storms, depending on their wind speeds and the damage they cause. Regardless of the size of a tornado, all tornadoes are formed the

5   same way, but the duration of the tornadic storm will depend on its strength. Understanding how tornadoes are formed and behave is necessary for safety concerns because approximately 1,000 tornadoes occur in the U.S. annually, causing loss of life and millions of dollars in property damage. The life cycle of a tornado consists of four stages: the organization stage, the mature stage, the shrinking stage, and the decaying stage.

10   The first stage is the organization stage. Tornado season begins in the early spring and lasts until fall, but tornadoes can occur at any time if the weather conditions are right. The process is complex and not completely understood. Also, there are several theories, the most familiar of which is the Severe Local Storm Theory.[1] During tornado season, severe thunderstorms, some of which are "parent storms" to tornadoes, occur due to special weather conditions, particularly in Tornado

15   Alley. Tornado Alley is located in the continental plains and Gulf Coast area in the U.S. This area is favorable for thunderstorms to form due to the unstable air masses. Tornadic storms are most likely to occur in the late afternoon and evening because the air is the least stable then.[2] Solar heating is also a factor which contributes to severe storms. As the sun heats the earth, the warm, moist air rises and condenses. During condensation, clouds are formed, and additional heat is released.

20   "If all ingredients are present in the correct proportions, this released heat can lead to . . . severe thunderstorms and tornadoes."[3] When a severe storm develops, the conditions are right for a tornado to form, so the weather service will issue a tornado watch. This means people must pay attention to the weather and listen to weather reports so that they will have enough time to seek shelter if there is a tornado.

25   The massive storms most likely to produce tornadoes are called super cells, which form in unstable areas called squall lines. A squall line is an area of cooler air in front of a cold front moving in from the northwest and heading east. This cold, dry air confronts a warm, moist layer of Gulf air from the southwest. Due to the extreme differences in temperature and pressure, when these

30   fronts collide, the warm air rises quickly, creating an updraft. (A super cell has only one updraft [rising warm air] and one downdraft [falling cool air] contained in the precipitation areas in front of

the updraft, whereas more common storms have several of each. Therefore, a super cell is a more intense storm than the typical thunderstorm.) As the lower layer of warm air rises in the super cell, both layers of air start to rotate (turn or twist) in a counterclockwise motion, creating a mesocyclone (a core of rotation), in which the tornado forms. This intense updraft also causes the formation of
35 hail (ice pellets), which often accompanies tornadoes. Strong updraft and rotation are needed for a tornado to form. Another condition necessary is a rotating wall cloud, which is a dark, low-hanging cloud that starts to form out of the super cell in the southwest edge of the storm. As the winds rotate faster and faster, a funnel-shaped cloud starts to extend downward from the wall cloud. This is the tornado.[2–5] When a tornado is spotted, the weather service issues a tornado warning, which
40 means people must seek shelter immediately due to the dangerous nature of these storms.

The second stage of development is the mature stage, the point at which the tornado reaches its full potential. In this stage, tornadoes differ in size, intensity, and appearance and inflict the most damage. On the average, tornadoes have a short life, which is measured by the length of the path. This is the area where the tornado touches the ground. Not all tornadoes touch down, but the
45 majority do so for a short time. The average life span of a tornado on the ground is less than an hour, and the average path is 2 to 16 miles long and 50 yards wide. Tornadoes travel at 30 miles an hour, on the average, but some have been clocked at 70 miles per hour. People must never try to chase or outrun a tornado because tornadoes may change direction suddenly. Usually tornadoes travel southwest to northwest, but they have been known to skip about erratically.[6]

50 During the mature stage, the tornadoes may change color depending on the amount of moisture in the air, direction of the sunlight, type of debris being sucked up, and location of the storm. Tornadoes occurring in water, called water spouts, are often white. However, tornadoes occurring on land usually turn black as they mature. Often described as "vacuum cleaners," tornadoes pick up everything in their paths—including dirt, trees, semitrailers, livestock, mobile homes, and well-built
55 structures—and toss them around like toys. Because flying debris is the most common cause of tornado deaths, the best thing for people to do is seek shelter away from windows in a basement, storm shelter, or structure enclosed by walls.[6]

It is not always easy to spot a tornado. This is because tornadoes in this stage are sometimes shaped like rain shafts or look like fires. Tornadoes occurring at night are also very hard to spot
60 unless there is a lot of lightning or the tornadoes hit electric lines. The weather conditions and sound of the tornado should leave no doubt as to the nature of the storm, however. The only warning at night may be the distinctive loud roar or squealing sound of the wind, usually preceded by a pelting of large hail and then an eerie silence before the tornado strikes.[3, 6]

The last two stages of a tornado's life are the shrinking stage and the decaying stage. In the
65 shrinking stage, the tornado starts to become smaller or thinner and may appear highly tilted. Sometimes the funnel shape disappears, and a large tornado may "appear to be a large, turbulent cloud near the ground."[6] In the decaying stage, the tornado starts to become disorganized and fragmented. Tornadoes are still dangerous in these stages. The tornado eventually dies as the weather conditions return to normal. That is, the differences in air pressure, temperature, and moisture
70 stabilize, and the tornadic storm ends.[7]

In conclusion, because of the destructive nature of tornadoes, people cannot take them lightly. If people learn to identify the weather conditions that spawn tornadoes, they can take safety measures to protect themselves in the event of a tornado. People need to recognize that each stage of a tornado's life (organization, mature, shrinking, and decaying) is hazardous. Although
75 people cannot prevent tornadoes from occurring, they can heed the warnings and seek shelter long before the silence, the squeal, and the strike. [1,079 words] (Barbara Leonhard, American)

Ⓠ Discussion Questions

Answer the following questions about the previous essay.

1. What is the purpose of the process description? Why is it of value for people to read?
2. What are the four stages in the life cycle of tornadoes? List and briefly define them.
3. What are the three conditions necessary for tornado formation?
4. How long does it take for a tornado to form, live, and die?
5. What warnings does the writer make? Why?
6. What is the difference between a tornado watch and a tornado warning? What do people need to do in each case?
7. Overall, did you find this technical description clear, complete, convenient, and concise? Discuss your answer.

Accuracy in Process Description

The following two statements do not have the same meaning, and only one of them is true.
• If there is a severe storm, a tornado will occur.
• A tornado may occur in a severe storm.

Based on what you just read on the life cycle of tornadoes, you know that the first statement is false. Because the use of *will* shows a definite future result, the writer of the first statement contends that tornadoes definitely occur whenever there is a severe storm. However, not all severe storms produce tornadoes. In other words, there is a possibility that tornadoes will occur during a severe storm. Therefore, a tornado might occur in a severe storm.

Will, may, and *might* are called modal auxiliaries. Auxiliaries are "helping verbs," so they are followed by the base form of the main verb of the clause. To form the negative, place *not* between the modal and the main verb.
• If there is a severe storm, a tornado might occur.
• A severe storm might not produce a tornado.

In a process description (and in other rhetorical methods), accuracy is important. Therefore, it will benefit you to learn the meanings of the most common simple modals.

The chart on the next page lists common simple modals and their meanings with examples. Unless specified otherwise, use present or future tense with these modals.

Notice that some modals, such as *should*, have different meanings.

⇨ Examples

Advisability:	If there is a tornado, you should seek shelter.
	(It is a good idea to seek shelter.)
Expectation:	If you hide in a basement, you should feel safe in a storm.
	(If you hide in a basement, you can expect to feel safe in a storm.)

Also, do not confuse lack of necessity with strong advisability.

⇨ Examples

Lack of Necessity:	You do not have to own a weather radio. (It is not necessary to own one. The consequences are not serious because you can watch TV for weather information.)
Strong Advisability:	You must not try to outrun a tornado.(The consequences can be very serious.)

MEANINGS OF MODALS IN PROCESS DESCRIPTIONS

Meaning	Modal	Example
Ability *(will be able to)*	can	You can follow the development of the storm.
(will not be able to)	cannot/can't	You cannot always spot a tornado at night.
(was/were able to)	could	Before Doppler radar was invented, people could not track tornadic storms accurately.
Possibility *(It is possible that . . .)*	may might can	If you do not seek shelter during a tornado, you might get hurt.
Advisability *(It is a good idea to . . .)*	should ought to had better	You should watch the weather conditions and listen to a weather radio for the latest updates.
(It is not a good idea to . . .)	should not ought not had better not	If there is a tornado, you should not remain outside.
Strong Advisability *(It is strongly advised [not] to . . .)*	must (not)	You must not try to outrun a tornado.
Expectation *(You can expect to . . .)*	should ought to	Once you have found shelter, you ought to be safe from the tornado.
(You can expect not to . . .)	should not	If you follow these instructions carefully, you should not have any problems.
Necessity *(It is necessary to . . .)*	must have to have got to	You must take storm warnings seriously.
Lack of Necessity *(It is not necessary to . . .)*	do not have to	You do not have to own a weather radio to get the latest storm information.
Alternative Solution *(You have choices.)*	can could	To keep posted on the weather, you could watch TV or you could listen to a weather radio.

*Note: *Must* is also used for prohibition, as in *You must not smoke in elevators.*

D I S C O V E R Y

5.4: Paraphrasing statements with modals

The statements in this Discovery exercise are based on the essay "The Life Cycle of Tornadoes."
- Identify each of the following statements as true or false.
- If the statement is false, restate it to make it true.
- Using a modal from the previous chart, indicate the meaning of your restatement.

⮑ Examples

............*False*............ If there is a severe storm, a tornado will occur.

A tornado may occur in a severe storm. (possibility)...

............*True*............ Some tornadoes will not touch down.

1. .... The funnel shape will disappear in the shrinking stage.

....

2. .... Weak tornadoes will not cause death or injury.

....

3. .... Intense updraft will contribute to the formation of hail.

....

4. .... The wind speeds of a violent tornado will be 300 miles an hour.

....

5. .... The duration of a tornadic storm will depend on its strength.

....

6. .... People will always seek shelter if there is a tornado.

....

7. .... People will not chase tornadoes or try to outrun them.

....

8. .... If people seek shelter, they will feel safe.

....

Review of Process Description and Narration

The following chart summarizes the primary differences between the two types of chronological development.

NARRATION VS. PROCESS DESCRIPTION

Narration (Time Order)	Process Description (Process Order)
Tells a story	Instructional
First to last event	First to last stage/step/phase
Examples	Examples
Historical events	How to do X
How X happened	How X functions (works)
Biographies/Autobiographies	How X is done or made
Customary events	
Grammar	Grammar
Past or present tense	Present or future tense

Both methods use:
- Time clauses and participial phrases
- Connectors for chronology
- Active and passive verbs

DISCOVERY

5.5: Identifying narration and process topics

On each line, write N for narration or P for process description according to the type of chronological development the topic requires.

1. .... How Vinegar Is Distilled

2. .... The Development of Greek Temple Architecture

3. .... The Chinese New Year

4. .... The Assassination of John F. Kennedy

5. .... How Plastic is Made

6. .... How to Write a Good Essay

7. .... The Louisiana Purchase

8. .... The Rise and Fall of the Cold War

9. .... An Overview of the Soft Drink Industry

10. .... The Water Cycle

COHERENCE: OLD IDEA–NEW IDEA

What is the most significant change that has taken place in your life since you became a teenager?

Becoming a teenager is a major event in our lives because we are no longer "small children." However, we are not really adults yet. We are still too young to appreciate all of the changes we start to experience. In a way, we are like awkward ducklings turning into swans. What is the most significant change that has taken place in your life since you became a teenager? Describe the change and show its significance. Provide specific examples and details. [400-450 words, every other line]

Using Content Words: Painting a Picture with Words

ANALOGY

One way to use content words effectively in writing is to choose specific (vivid) nouns, adjectives, adverbs, and verbs to inform the reader. A common English saying is, "A picture is worth a thousand words." Think of yourself as an artist. You want to choose your colors carefully to paint a picture that tells the complete story you want to express without wasting canvas.

You do not want the general, ordinary, overused, dull colors. You want to choose specific, fresh, unusual, bright colors which give the details of your story that you are trying to express in your painting. (You will be a more interesting and convincing writer.) The colors you choose and the way you put them together will define your style as an artist because your paintings will not look like everyone else's. (You will have your own writer's voice.)

ⒹⒾⓈⒸⓄⓋⒺⓇⓎ

5.6: Analyzing a description

- Read the following essay in which the writer describes a significant change in her life.
- Circle the descriptive details.
- Then answer the Discussion Questions that follow.

My Benchmark into Womanhood
by Vasna Wilson

1   En route to a Safari in Nairobi, Kenya, I noticed an African woman dressed in a worn-out T-shirt with a red sarong wrapped loosely around her waist. Barefoot, standing in the hot sun, she showed me an African mask, with the intention to make a sale. I looked beyond the mask and
5   noticed a tiny arrow-shaped scar on her face, a tribal mark which symbolizes a transition from girlhood into womanhood. Seeing that mark on her weather-beaten face reminds me today of my own rite of passage into womanhood and why I want to become a photographer.
        During the 1994-95 academic year, I decided to turn my lifelong dream
10   of seeing the world into a reality. With a single backpack, I embarked on my journey to discover the world in a one-year study abroad program, studying

first with Eastern Michigan University on its "European Cultural History Tours" program. The following spring semester, I set sail around the world with "Semester at Sea: A Voyage of Discoveries," offered through the University of Pittsburgh. I visited 65 cities and 35 countries around the globe.

15   My benchmark into womanhood came while I was walking through a poor neighborhood in

Salvador, Brazil. Three women were standing casually in the street, their eyes gazing into emptiness. Each seemed to have something on her mind. They saw me watching them. An unspoken agreement was in the air, and I took a picture, freezing the moment in time. It was then that I realized the power of photography. The click of the button told me that I had left my childhood and the comfort of my mother's home behind to explore the world. Like finding a piece of a missing puzzle, I knew then I had to become a photographer—a storyteller who, with a camera, could use light to bring out the essence of what is in the frame.

As I was documenting my experiences with photography during my trip, I captured every moment before it slipped away. I caught the pink and purple sky as the sun rose over the deep blue Indian Ocean, where one can get lost in the immensity of the earth joining the sky and land, and where dreams become possible. I snapped away one day on a bus packed with people, their belongings, and animals as it meandered to a stop in a small village, where I discovered a street-side entertainer with his cow. I believe it is in the motion of a moment that one can find a passage to connect with other people or places in time, regardless of where they have come from.

Like a caterpillar changing into a butterfly, I came to the University of Missouri–Columbia to study photojournalism in the hope that it will help transform me into a master of my craft. The work I will complete here is the beginning of a new journey, a new exploration of the world and myself, which I hope to show from the eyes of the woman I have become. [504 words] (Vasna Wilson, Thai)

Discussion Questions

Answer the following questions about the previous essay.

1. What kind of hook did the writer use in the introduction: funnel, refutation, or dramatic?

2. Was the hook effective? Why or why not?

3. How does the writer tie the hook into the thesis?

4. What is the purpose of paragraph two? Is it informative? Why?

5. What happened in Salvador, Brazil? Why was this a significant event?

6. Why did the writer feel like a storyteller whenever she took pictures?

7. How has this change in her life affected her career choice?

8. List examples of the writer's use of specific (vivid) language. For instance, instead of writing "I took a trip," the writer used "en route to," "I embarked on a journey," and "I set sail around the world."

Repetition of Content Words: Old Idea–New Idea 1

A good writer demonstrates a wide range of content words (vocabulary) in a paper because these words convey information. The key content words are repeated often to reinforce the topic. They may be repeated in the same form, in another form, or as a synonym or synonymous phrase.

Structures that are often used to restate ideas are *the* + noun (old idea, second-time mention); *such (a, an, X)* + noun (old idea); and *this/that/these/those* + noun (old idea).

DISCOVERY
5.7: Analyzing content words

Analyze the content words in bold in the following paragraph. Identify each as either a) a content word repeated in the same form, b) a different form of a previous content word, or c) a synonym or synonymous phrase. The first five are done for you.

One characteristic that Americans value highly is independence. Throughout history, **Americans** *(a)* (1)

have thought of themselves as pioneers. From settling a new country to opening the frontiers,

that rugged, independent spirit *(c)* (2) has pervaded every aspect of **American** *(b)* (3) life. **Independent** *(a)* (4) people

are admired as being people of strong character. The importance of **independence** *(b/a)* (5) can be clearly

seen in the way **American** (6) children are raised. From the time that **children** (7) are very small, they

are encouraged to **venture out on their own** (8) and try new things. For instance, playing with new

toys is **encouraged** (9) by parents. **Parents** (10) watch proudly as **children** (11) as **young** (12) as two years old

learn how to do things for themselves (13) such as picking out their own clothes and deciding what

they want to eat. As **children** (14) grow older, they are often required to perform household tasks,

like cleaning, to earn their money for things they want. Over time, they are expected to continue

doing things on their own (15), particularly **earning money** (16). Most high school students, for example,

have part-time jobs to **earn money** (17) for things like cars, clothes, and entertainment. **This push** (18)

toward independence continues until the day that children are **encouraged** (19), if not **expected** (20), to

move out **on their own** (21). **American** (22) adults are **expected** (23) to **make their own way in the world with** (24)

little help from others (25). As you can see, **independence** is **a respected trait in American society** (26).

(Kelly Boggs, American)

Time Clauses: Old Idea–New Idea 2

In the previous section, you learned that writers repeat key content words and old ideas to reinforce and develop their topics. Old ideas are often stated in dependent clauses, such as time clauses, rather than in main clauses, where new ideas are introduced. Note the time clauses (represented in italic type) in the following example of a process description.

Distillation: Simple and Fractional

1   The purpose of the following experiments is to practice the purification techniques of simple and fractional distillation. The data will show the boiling point for acetone-water mixture.

        The procedure for simple distillation consists of four steps. First, set up a simple distillation apparatus using a round-bottomed flask. *After you set up the apparatus* (OLD IDEA), add a few boiling chips
5   to a 30-ml 50:50 acetone water mixture. The next step is to collect distillate in a 10-ml graduated cylinder and begin heating the mixture. Next, *while you are heating the mixture* (old idea), record the temperature for every 1 milliliter of distillate. *Once the temperature reaches 100 degrees centigrade* (old idea), discontinue heating the mixture. Finally, plot the various temperatures (*Y*) vs. the number of milliliters collected (*X*) on graph paper. *After you have finished plotting the data* (old idea), connect the
10   points to make a smooth curve. (Kask et al, *Chemistry 133 Laboratory Manual, University of Missouri*, pp. 13-16, William C. Brown Publishers, Dubuque, Iowa, 1995.)

ⓄⒾⓈⒸⓄⓋⒺⓇⓎ

5.8: **Forming time clauses with old ideas**

The following passage is the conclusion of the previous lab report.
• Complete the time clauses with the following old ideas.
• Use each old idea one time. You will use all of the old ideas listed.

        a.   the temperature reaches 100 degrees centigrade
        b.   you have insulated the column
        c.   the mixture is ready
        d.   you have set up the flask on the stand
        e.   the mixture is distilling
        f.   you have added the beads
        g.   the apparatus is assembled

        To perform the experiment for fractional distillation, follow this procedure. First, secure a 100-ml

round-bottomed flask on a ring stand. After ...., place 30 ml of a
                                                                  (1)

fresh 50:50 acetone-water mixture in this flask through a funnel. Make sure the mixture is fresh.

When ...., assemble the fractional distillation apparatus. Once
            (2)

...., loosely pack a minimum amount of glass wool into the bottom
            (3)

of the distillation column to support glass beads. Then add the glass beads. After ....
                                                                                                (4)

...., you may want to wrap the bottom of the boiling flask, the condenser, and the

bottom of the distillation head with aluminum foil to insulate the column. When ....
                                                                                                (5)

............................., distill the mixture slowly. While ...., record the
temperature for every 1 milliliter collected in a 10-ml graduated cylinder. When ....
                                                                                                    (7)
............................., discontinue heating the mixture. Finally, record the data as you did in the simple

distillation experiment. (Kask et al, *Chemistry 133 Laboratory Manual, University of Missouri*, pp. 13-16,

William C. Brown Publishers, Dubuque, Iowa, 1995.)

(6)

Passive Voice

The passive voice is often used in time clauses and phrases with old ideas.

⮌ Examples

As the air temperature falls, rain is precipitated and absorbed by the soil. *After the rain is absorbed* (old idea), the water flows back to the sea, and the process begins again.

When the ingredients start to boil, reduce the heat. *As soon as the heat is reduced* (old idea), cover the pan and simmer the soup for one hour.

Beat the eggs slightly. *Once the eggs are beaten* (old idea), add the flour, milk, and salt.

Formation of the Passive Voice

1. Make sure the verb is transitive (has an object, or receiver). The object receives the action of the verb; the agent performs the action.

⮌ Examples

Transitive Verb	President Carter (agent) vetoed the bill (receiver).
Intransitive Verb	President Kennedy died at a young age. (no receiver).
	(It is not possible to make intransitive verbs passive.)

2. Trade the positions of the agent and the receiver; then add *by* after the receiver.

⮌ Examples

Active Voice:	President Carter (agent) vetoed the bill (receiver).
Passive Voice:	The bill (receiver) was vetoed by President Carter.

Unknown/Unimportant Agent
It is not necessary to include the agent if it is not informative or is not known.

⮌ Examples

The bill was vetoed.
People make all kinds of plastic products these days.
All kinds of plastic products are made these days. (omit *by people*)

DISCOVERY

5.9: Using the passive voice to form old ideas

- Fill in the blank with a time clause that repeats an idea from the sentence above it.
- Use the passive voice.

> **Example**
>
> If a hurricane is approaching, *you should board up your windows.*
>
> ..After the windows are boarded up.., make sure you have enough provisions in the house to help you ride out the storm.

1. First, plan the composition.

   ...., you are ready to write it.

2. Cut the potatoes into long strips.

   ...., deep-fry the strips in hot oil until they are golden brown.

3. Both sides agreed to sign the treaty.

   ...., the war was declared over.

4. See which team can figure out the order first.

   ...., discuss the coherence clues.

5. A scientist proposes a hypothesis.

   ...., the scientist conducts experiments to test the hypothesis.

6. First, wash the car thoroughly and rinse it.

   ...., you are ready to wax it.

TIME EXPRESSIONS AND TRANSITIONS

Time Expressions

Time expressions, which tell when events or steps occur(red), provide transition in papers organized in chronological (time and process) order. Time relationships can be expressed in prepositional phrases, time clauses and phrases, connectors, and verbs.

You have already practiced with time clauses (formation and use of old ideas), active and passive verbs, and prepositional phrases of time (time lines). This section will address time phrases, connectors and verbs of chronology, and transitions in process description. Learning how to form and manipulate time expressions will help you improve your sentence organization and fluency.

Participial Phrases of Time with Active Verbs

Time clauses can also be reduced to participial phrases if the subjects in the main clause and time clause are the same. Given that the subjects are the same, you can form the participial phrase by deleting the subject in the time clause and then changing the verb in the time clause to the *-ing* form. (If a pronoun is used in the main clause in place of the proper noun, it might be necessary to replace it with the proper noun.) This process is easy to do if the verb is in the continuous tense because all you have to do is delete the subject and *be* from the time clause.

Forming Participial Phrases of Time with Active Verbs

1. Make sure the main clause and the time clause refer to the same subject.

➫ **Examples**

> While *Lewis* was exploring the Maria's River, *he* had a fight with the Blackfeet Indians.
> (*Lewis* and *he* refer to the same subject.)

> After *Monroe* arrived in Paris, *he* signed a treaty with Napoleon.
> (*Monroe* and *he* refer to the same subject.)

2. If the verb in the time clause is in the continuous tense (*be* + *-ing* form of the verb), just delete the subject and *be*. Then proceed to Step 4.

➫ **Example**

> While ~~Lewis was~~ exploring the Maria's River, he had a fight with the Blackfeet Indians.
> While exploring the Maria's River, he had a fight with the Blackfeet Indians.

3. If the verb in the time clause is not in the continuous tense, delete the subject and change the verb to the *-ing* form.

➫ **Example**

> After ~~Monroe~~ arriv~~ed~~ ^(ing) in Paris, he signed a treaty with Napoleon.
> After arriving in Paris, he signed a treaty with Napoleon.

4. Replace the pronoun in the main clause with the proper noun (if necessary).

➫ **Examples**

> While exploring the Maria's River, ~~he~~ ^(Lewis) had a fight with the Blackfeet Indians.
> While exploring the Maria's River, Lewis had a fight with the Blackfeet Indians.
> After arriving in Paris, ~~he~~ ^(Monroe) signed a treaty with Napoleon.
> After arriving in Paris, Monroe signed a treaty with Napoleon.

When deleting the subject from the time clause, be careful to avoid the misplaced modifier—an adjective that modifies a word or phrase other than the one it is intended to modify.

➫ **Example**

Original	After Monroe arrived in Paris, Napoleon decided he had no need for Louisiana.
Incorrect	After arriving in Paris, Napoleon decided he had no need for Louisiana. (Napoleon did not arrive in Paris; Monroe did.)

The Use of the Present Perfect in Process Description

Often in process description, the present perfect tense is used in time clauses.

⤳ Examples

After you *have mixed* the dry ingredients, add a cup of milk.
When you *have added* the milk, mix the batter.

The participial phrases are formed this way.

After having mixed the dry ingredients, add a cup of milk.
Having mixed the dry ingredients, add a cup of milk.
After mixing the dry ingredients, add a cup of milk.

Note: Although *After having mixed* is grammatically correct, it sounds more awkward than *Having mixed* or *After mixing.*

⤳ Example

Study the participial phrases in this version of the paragraph you read earlier.

Distillation: Simple and Fractional

1   The purpose of the following experiments is to practice the purification techniques of simple and fractional distillation. The data will show the boiling point for acetone-water mixture.
    The procedure for simple distillation consists of four steps. First, set up a simple distillation apparatus using a round-bottomed flask. *After setting up the apparatus,* add a few boiling chips
5   to a 30-ml 50:50 acetone water mixture. The next step is to collect distillate in a 10-ml graduated cylinder and begin heating the mixture. Next, *while heating the mixture,* record the temperature for every 1 milliliter of distillate. *Once the temperature reaches 100 degrees centigrade* (no change, different subject), discontinue heating the mixture. Finally, plot the various temperatures *(Y)* versus the number of milliliters collected *(X)* on graph paper. *Having finished plotting the data,* connect the
10   points to make a smooth curve. (Kask et al, *Chemistry 133 Laboratory Manual, University of Missouri*, pp. 13–16, William C. Brown Publishers, Dubuque, Iowa, 1995.)

Note that the time clause in the following sentence was not changed to a participial phrase because the subjects are not the same.

Once the temperature reaches 100 degrees centigrade (no change, different subject), discontinue heating the mixture.

The time clause in *After you have finished plotting the data* was changed to the present perfect tense (*Having finished plotting the data*) because the subject of both the time clause and the main clause is *you.*

Participial Phrases of Time with Passive Verbs

For passive verbs, which contain the past participle, simply omit the subject and be. Retain the past participle. Never change a passive verb to an active verb in this process. You must make all the other necessary changes, however.

Forming Participial Phrases of Time with Passive Verbs

1. Make sure the main clause and the time clause refer to the same subject.

⤳ Examples

When Lewis was asked to head an exploratory expedition west to the Pacific, he refused at first.

After Lewis was asked to head an exploratory expedition west to the Pacific, he refused at first.

(In both sentences, *Lewis* and *he* refer to the same subject.)

2. Delete the subject. For time clauses that begin with *when* or *until*, delete *be;* for time clauses that do not begin with *when* or *until*, change the simple form of *be* to the *-ing* form.

↪ **Examples**

> When asked to head an exploratory expedition west to the Pacific, he refused at first.
> After being asked to head an exploratory expedition west to the Pacific, he refused at first.

3. Replace the pronoun in the main clause with the proper noun (if necessary).

↪ **Examples**

> When asked to head an exploratory expedition west to the Pacific, Lewis refused at first.
> After being asked to head an exploratory expedition west to the Pacific, Lewis refused at first.

Do not make participial phrases with time clauses that begin with time subordinators containing *as* (*as, just as,* and *as soon as*).

Active Voice:
Correct Sentence	As soon as I finished eating, I started studying.
Incorrect Phrase	As soon as finishing eating, I started studying.

Passive Voice:
Correct Sentence:	As soon as Lewis was asked to head an exploratory expedition west to the Pacific, he refused.
Incorrect Phrase:	As soon as asked to head an exploratory expedition west to the Pacific, he refused.

⒟⒤⒮⒞⒪⒱⒠⒭⒴
5.10: Reducing time clauses to participial phrases

- Study each of the time clauses in the following paragraph.
- If it is possible to change the time clause to a participial phrase, rewrite it in the space provided.
- If it is not possible to change the time clause, write "not possible."
- The first and last ones are done for you.

The Water Cycle

(1) The water cycle is a natural process in which water changes form and moves from place to place on the earth. (2) All of the earth's water comes from the sea. (3) The process begins when the sun radiates heat. (4) When this happens, sea water evaporates, making water vapor. (5) After the water vapor forms, it begins to rise. (6) While it rises, it cools. (7) When the water vapor cools, it condenses. (8) As the vapor condenses, clouds form and move toward high land. (9) When the clouds reach high land, the air temperature falls. (10) As the air temperature falls, rain is precipitated and absorbed by the soil. (11) After the rain water is absorbed, it flows back to the sea, and the process begins again.

1. *not possible* ....

2. ....

3. ....

4. ....

5. ....

6. ....

7. ....

8. ....

9. ....

10. ....

11. After being absorbed, the rain water flows back to the sea, and the process begins again.

Connectors Used for Chronological Description

Connectors join two sentences. There are two kinds of chronological connectors: sequential and simultaneous. If the two sentences indicate sequential actions, the first action is stated first. The connectors used in this case are *afterward*, *after that*, *then*, and *next*. Do not use a comma after *then*; use a comma after other connectors.

Action 1.	**Connector(,)**	**action 2.**
(Sentence)	(Sequential)	(Sentence)

⇨ Example

Lewis and Clark crossed the Rockies. After that, they separated and explored different rivers.

Mix the dry ingredients. Afterward, add the milk.

If the two sentences indicate simultaneous actions, begin with the longest action or the action which started first. Connectors that indicate simultaneous actions include *meanwhile*, *at the same time*, and *in the meantime*.

Longer, earlier action.	**Connector,**	**shorter action.**
(Sentence)	(Simultaneous)	(Sentence)

⇨ Example

The water vapor condenses. In the meantime, clouds are formed.

Heat the milk. Meanwhile, beat the eggs.

Verbs for Chronological Order

Verbs give information about stages in both narration and process.

Stage	Verb
Early Stage	begin, start
Middle Stage	continue, proceed
Final Stage	finish, end

Study the use of connectors, verbs, phrases, and clauses of time in the following lab report.

Distillation: Simple and Fractional

1   The purpose of the following experiments is to practice the purification techniques of simple and fractional distillation. The data will show the boiling point for acetone-water mixture.
     The procedure for simple distillation consists of four steps. Begin *(VERB)* by setting up a simple distillation apparatus using a round-bottomed flask. After setting up the apparatus, add a few boiling 5   chips to a 30-ml 50:50 acetone water mixture. The next step is to collect distillate in a 10-ml graduated cylinder and begin heating the mixture. Meanwhile *(SIMULTANEOUS CONNECTOR)*, record the

temperature for every 1 milliliter of distillate. Once the temperature reaches 100 degrees centigrade, discontinue heating the mixture. At this point *(SEQUENTIAL CONNECTOR)*, plot the various temperatures *(Y)* versus the number of milliliters collected *(X)* on graph paper. After plotting the data, connect the
10   points to make a smooth curve. (Kask et al, *Chemistry 133 Laboratory Manual, University of Missouri*, pp. 13–16, William C. Brown Publishers, Dubuque, Iowa, 1995.)

Framing the Process Essay: Transitions

There are two kinds of process description: sequential (chronological stages, phases, and steps) and non-sequential (a list of suggestions).

Sequential Process

To indicate chronological order in a sequential process, use transitions such as time clauses and phrases, connectors, and verbs for chronological order. Also, use the following enumeration signals to list the steps or stages.

Enumeration Signals to State the Main Stages, Steps, and Phases

The first step (stage or phase) is _____ .   First, _____ .

The second step (stage or phase) is _____ .   Second, _____ .

The final step (stage or phase) is _____ .   Finally, _____ .
                                       (Infinitive or Gerund Phrase)   (Main Clause)

Caution: Do not overuse ordinals.

Study the use of structures for sequential process in the following lab report.

Simple Distillation

1   The procedure for simple distillation consists of four steps. First *(ENUMERATION SIGNAL)*, set up a simple distillation apparatus using a round-bottomed flask. After setting up the apparatus *(TIME PHRASE)*, add a few boiling chips to a 30-ml 50:50 acetone water mixture. The next step is *(ENUMERATION SIGNAL)* to collect distillate in a 10-ml graduated cylinder and begin heating the mixture.
5   Meanwhile *(CONNECTOR)*, record the temperature for every 1 milliliter of distillate. Once the temperature reaches 100 degrees centigrade (time clause), discontinue heating the mixture. At this point *(CONNECTOR)*, plot the various temperatures *(Y)* versus the number of milliliters collected *(X)* on graph paper. After plotting the data *(TIME PHRASE)*, connect the points to make a smooth curve. (Kask et al, *Chemistry 133 Laboratory Manual, University of Missouri*, pp. 13–16, William C. Brown Publishers,
10   Dubuque, Iowa, 1995.)

ⒹⒾⓈⒸⓄⓋⒺⓇⓎ
5.11:   **Brainstorming on a sequential process**

• Choose one of the following simple sequential processes to describe to a partner.
• Use a variety of sequential transitions.
• Place old ideas before new ideas.

Topics
How to Operate a Camera (or another common device)
How to Make Rice (or another simple dish)
How to _____ (Choose a sequential process in your major.)

Begin the process description with a thesis statement.

➯ **Examples**

Informal _____ is not difficult if you follow this procedure.
(Gerund Phrase)

Formal The procedure for _____ involves/consists of the following steps.

Nonsequential Process

For a nonsequential process, use transitions for additional ideas.

Enumeration Signals

The first/second/final way _____ is _____ .
(Infinitive Phrase) (Infinitive Phrase)

The most important measure to take is _____ .
(Infinitive or Gerund Phrase)

To begin with/First/Second/Finally, _____ .
(Main Clause)

Connectors (for additional suggestions)

Moreover/In addition/Furthermore/Also, _____ .
(Main Clause)

Phrase Markers (old idea–new idea)

In addition to/Besides _____ , _____ .
(Old Idea, Noun Phrase) (New Idea, Main Clause)

Phrases for alternatives

One way/Another way/Still another way _____ is _____ .
(Infinitive Phrase) (Infinitive Phrase)

Study the use of structures for nonsequential process in the following essay.

Tornado Safety

1   Tornadoes, which are severe rotating windstorms, cannot be prevented. Ways to predict these storms, however, are improving due to Doppler radar, which tracks the development of storms and indicates areas where wind rotation is occurring. If the weather conditions are right for a tornado, a tornado watch is issued. If a tornado is actually spotted, a tornado warning is issued. People

5 should take the following precautions in the event of a tornado in order to remain safe.
    The measures people take initially will depend on whether there is a tornado watch or a tornado warning. First (*ENUMERATION SIGNAL*), if there is a tornado watch, people should stay informed by listening to the radio or watching TV for the latest weather information. In addition (*CONNECTOR*), they could purchase a radio with a weather band, which continually broadcasts the current weather

10 conditions. If a tornado is actually spotted, on the other hand, a tornado warning is issued and, depending on the location of the tornado, a siren is sounded. The most important safety measure (*ENUMERATION SIGNAL*) in this case is to seek shelter right away in a house or other well-built structure and stay away from windows. More people die in tornadic storms because they are hit by flying debris in the strong winds, so people should get as many walls between them and the tornado as

15 possible. They could hide in a closet or, best yet, the basement. Another good place is (*FORM OF*

Other) an underground storm shelter.

In addition to (*Phrase Marker*) taking the above precautions, there are several things people should not do. One mistake would be (*Phrase for Alternative*) to stay in a mobile home. Mobile homes are easily destroyed in tornadic storms. Moreover (*Connector*), people should not try to outrun or even
20   chase tornadoes. As fascinating as tornadoes are, even the weakest tornadoes can kill. Therefore, people should get out of their cars and lie down in a low area, such as a ditch. They could also (*Connector*) seek shelter under a highway overpass. Another (*Phrase for Alternative*) fatal mistake would be to try to videotape the tornado. People could get killed by flying debris if they stay outside or next to windows just to capture the tornado on film. Finally (*Connector*), people should not leave
25   their shelter until the sirens are turned off or until the weather reports indicate that the tornado has dissipated. Only when the conditions are safe should people venture outside to survey the damage.

In conclusion, although tornadoes cannot be prevented, people can protect themselves if they pay attention to the weather conditions and listen for watches and warnings. People should also (*Connector*) educate themselves on the appropriate actions to take and avoid making fatal mistakes
30   in judgment when a tornado is spotted. [468 words] (Barbara Leonhard, American)

ⒹⒾⓈⒸⓄⓋⒺⓡⓎ
5.12:   Brainstorming on a nonsequential process

- Choose one of the following nonsequential processes to describe to a partner.
- Use a variety of nonsequential transitions.
- Place old ideas before new ideas.
- Use third-person plural to sound objective.

Topics
How Nonnative Speakers Can Improve Their English
How to Quit Smoking (or any other bad habit)

Begin the description with a thesis statement.

⤳ Example

> Smokers can ultimately quit smoking if they follow these guidelines from the Department of Health, Education and Welfare (HEW).

Out-of-Class Writing Assignment: Process Development

- Choose a topic and write a process order essay.
- Use the appropriate transitions for sequential or nonsequential process description.
- Use Peer Review Form 9 from Appendix D to evaluate your essay.
- Revise the essay.

Essay Assignments

1. Write an essay about how you triumphed over a difficult situation. Describe the problem you (or someone else) had. Then explain the steps you took to solve it. How did you feel before and after you solved this challenging problem? Provide specific and relevant details.

2. Write an essay about how to solve a major problem in your country. Describe the problem. Then be complete and informative as you describe each step (or measure) people in your country could follow to solve this problem.

CHAPTER *summary*

- There are two forms of chronological order: narration (time order) and process description (process order).

- Narration involves relating events from the first to last event. Examples of narration are historical events and biographies/autobiographies, which are related in the past tense; and customary events, such as holidays, which are related in the present tense. To plan a narrative paper, write a time line on which you list major events from past to present.

- Process description involves explaining how to do something, how something functions, or how something is done in steps and stages, which may or may not be sequential. Process description requires the present and future tenses. A process description should be clear, complete, convenient, and concise (the four C's of process description). In a sequential process description, discuss the stages, phases, or steps with transitions for chronological order. In a nonsequential process description, discuss the ways, measures to take, or things to do using transitions for additional ideas.

- Instead of depending too much on the modal *will*, which states a definite future event, use other simple modals (such as those for ability, possibility, advisability, expectation, necessity, lack of necessity, prohibition, and alternative solution) to convey other meanings. Not all future events can be accurately predicted, so using the other simple modals will enable you to be more accurate.

- Effective vocabulary can make or break a paper. Part of planning a paper is finding the right words and increasing your vocabulary range. Choose words which convey your message vividly and concisely. Also, use appropriate repetition (old idea–new idea). Instead of using the same words over and over, find synonymous phrases or clauses, and change the word forms. Use pronouns correctly if you do not need to repeat a key word.

- Both process and narration require effective use of time clues: time clauses and phrases, time connectors, and active and passive verbs. For effective coherence with these structures, use old ideas (in dependent clauses and phrases) before new ideas (in main clauses).

References for "The Life Cycle of Tornadoes" and "Tornado Safety"

1. "Climate and Weather: The Local Severe Storms Theory," *Encyclopedia Britannica*, 1997 ed., [http://www.eb.com:180/], May 1997.
2. Davis, Gode, "Tornado," *Popular Science*, October, 1988: 65-69, 108.
3. Doswell, Charles, A. and Ostby, Frederick P., *A Kansas City Area Guide to Severe Thunderstorms and Tornadoes*, Kansas City, Missouri: National Severe Storms Forecast Center, August 1982.
4. Darkow, Grant L., "Questions and Answers About Tornadoes," handout, Atmospheric Science Department, University of Missouri–Columbia, revised May 1985.
5. "Tornadoes," *Encyclopedia Britannica*, 1997 ed., [http://www.eb.com:180/], May 1997.
6. "Tornado Safety: Surviving Nature's Most Violent Storms," U.S. Department of Commerce, U.S. Printing Office, 1982.
7. "Tornadoes!" [http:www.txdirect.net/%7Emsattler/tornado.htm], May 1997.
8. U.S. Federal Emergency Management Agency Fact Sheet, "At Home Tornado Preparation and Safety Tips," [http://www.fema.gov/fema/tornado/html.]
9. _____, "Backgrounder: Tornadoes," [http://www.fema.gov/fema/tornado/html.], May 1997.
10. _____, "Tornado Safety Tips Brochure," [http://www.fema.gov/fema/tornado/html.], May 1997.

Chapter 6

Comparison/Contrast Analysis

CHAPTER TOPICS

▶ STRIKING COMPARISONS/CONTRASTS

▶ METHODS OF COMPARISON/CONTRAST

▶ ANALOGIES

▶ TIME ORDER

▶ STRUCTURES OF COMPARISON

▶ STRUCTURES OF CONTRAST

▶ USE OF OLD IDEAS IN BLOCK FORM

Are people basically the same?

Make a chart of basic similarities and/or differences between people from two different cultures. Decide if you agree or disagree with the above question. Bring the chart to class.

ⒹⒾⓈⒸⓄⓋⒺⓇⓎ
6.1: Discussing cultural differences

Discuss the following questions in groups.
- In what major ways (areas) do cultures differ? List the major ways and provide examples.
- What problems can these differences between cultures cause? List the major problems and give examples.
- Report your findings to the class.

In this chapter, you will learn how to analyze, organize, and state similarities and differences. Comparison/Contrast studies are common not only in many academic fields but also in daily life. The most common reason for comparison/contrast analysis is to show superiority. For example, people may need to compare/contrast merchandise in a store before deciding which product to buy. Likewise, students usually compare/contrast colleges and universities in order to determine which one to attend.

Another purpose for comparison/contrast analysis, especially in academic writing, is to draw analogies, or to compare the abstract and the concrete. For instance, you learned earlier in this book that the process of writing (abstract) is similar to planning a trip (concrete). In addition, comparison/contrast analysis might focus on either similarities or differences to explain a problem or refute a stereotype. A writer could also argue that two topics that appear very different are also similar in many ways.

Finally, comparison/contrast analysis is used to show changes over time (chronological). A paper examining traditional vs. modern ways of life, for example, would be organized chronologically. The following chart summarizes the five major reasons for comparison/contrast analysis.

REASONS FOR COMPARISON/CONTRAST ANALYSIS ——————————

<u>Purpose</u>	<u>Thesis (example)</u>
To show superiority (*contrast*)	Topic X is better than Topic Y.
To make an analogy between an abstract and a concrete thing (*compare*)	Topic X is (like) Topic Y.
To show that X and Y are more similar than different (*compare*)	Topics X and Y have striking similarities.
To show that X and Y are more different than similar (*contrast*)	Topics X and Y are different in many ways.
To show changes over time: past vs. present (*contrast*)	Topic X has changed greatly in the last _____ years.

In this chapter, you will also learn how to organize comparison/contrast essays. There are two methods: alternating form and block form. In alternating form, the topics are examined point by point. In block form, they are discussed separately. The following chart illustrates the differences between the two methods.

METHODS OF COMPARISON/CONTRAST ANALYSIS ——————————

<u>Alternating</u>	<u>Block</u>
Topics X and Y are discussed point by point.	Topics X and Y are discussed separately.

II. Point of Comparison/Contrast 1
    A. Topic X
    B. Topic Y
	II. All about Topic X
	    A. Point of Comparison/Contrast 1
	    B. Point of Comparison/Contrast 2

III. Point of Comparison/Contrast 2
    A. Topic X
    B. Topic Y
	III. All about Topic Y
	    A. Point of Comparison/Contrast 1
	    B. Point of Comparison/Contrast 2

STRIKING COMPARISONS/CONTRASTS

As you have just learned, comparison/contrast analysis has a specific purpose. It is very unlikely that a professor will ask you to only state similarities or differences; the professor will expect you to use the comparison/contrast method to prove a point. A typical academic assignment might require that you disprove a stereotype or explain the causes of a problem. To do so, you might need to demonstrate that there are striking similarities or differences between the topics. For example, the model essay in Discovery 6.2 shows that the striking differences between the Irish and the American cultures caused misunderstandings between the two groups when the Irish immigrated to the United States.

DISCOVERY
6.2: Analyzing a contrast essay

- Read the following essay carefully.
- Then answer the Discussion Questions that follow.

The Differences Between Irish Peasant Society and American Society
by Aimée E. Haynes

1   The Irish peasant society was very different from the American society to which the Irish immigrated. The two main, or root, differences between the Irish and the Americans were their different economic situations and almost opposite philosophies. All other differences—such as class systems and economy, technology, language, views of the individual and the family, and

5   religion—seemed to stem from these two.
    The Irish economy was very static; it did not and could not go anywhere. The people lived from year to year on a subsistence level. There were no industries or any type of constructions of that sort. They had to get their livelihood directly from the soil. The Protestant landlords owned all of or most of the land and rented it out to tenants. They in turn rented out portions of land to poorer

10   peasants called cottiers. In Ireland, it was very important, almost essential, to have land. If one did not have land, he was nobody. People in Ireland needed land so that they could plant potatoes for food so that they could live. The Irish subsisted almost entirely on potatoes.
    The Irish class system was integrated with and as static as its economy. The people were born into their classes and could rarely escape from them. If one were born to a family without land,

15   for instance, it was probable that as long as he stayed in Ireland, he would become nothing but a landless laborer, who could not move up the economic or class ladder. The landless laborers, in fact, were thought to be the lowest class and despised by those that had land. The only exceptions to this rule were the priests. Priests were considered very holy and were revered regardless of whether or not they or their fathers owned land. One example of how much reverence the Irish

20   felt for their priests is seen in the book <u>Wildgoose Lodge and Other Short Stories</u>, by William Carelton. The story is "The Lough Derg Pilgrm."

        "When we got into Pedigo, we found the lodging-houses considerably crowded. I contrived, however, to establish myself as well as another, and in consequence of my black dress, and the garrulous industry of my companion, who stuck close to me all

25   along, was treated with more than common respect." (1, p. 97).

    Basically no one in Ireland wanted to be without land, yet at the beginning of the nineteenth century, there were too many people for the land to support them all. It was virtually impossible for all the people to continue to rely on the land for their food and livelihood, and yet in Ireland there were no big cities with industries for people to work in. Consequently, many Irish immigrated to

30   America, but a great many died as well.

America, on the other hand, had a very progressive economy as well as an extremely fluid class system. The people in America believed in progress and had many cities with industry as well as a great deal of rural countryside. One Irish immigrant said,

35
"... this country ... is an agricultural and a manufacturing country which produces immense employment both of the labors of the field and of the mechanical arts." (2, sec. 4).

With these greater opportunities for employment and money, there was also the promise of even greater social status. Again, as with Ireland, the classes and the economy were joined. In America, the most unskilled base job went to a man that was considered low in the social scale, but if that
40 man did well and rose to a better job (something that was impossible in Ireland), he also rose in social status. The Irish came to America extremely unskilled from the American point of view. Because of lack of skills, the Irish had to enter life in America at the bottom of the social ladder. The only people below the Irish were the black slaves.

The Irish and Americans differed regarding technology. The Irish had very little if any at all. They
45 farmed the same way that their fathers and their fathers before them had. Hence, their farming methods were rather primitive in that they used only plows and oxen rather than advanced farming equipment. Because of this, if the Irish had enough money to buy land for a farm, they simply were not skilled enough on the whole to make a living from farming in America, compared to Americans. In contrast, although the Americans were less rural minded, they were so progressive that their
50 rural lifestyles were permeated with technology. With their tractors, they were able to maintain very large farms as opposed to the small-acre plots of the Irish.

Another great difference between the Irish and the Americans was their differences in philosophy toward life as shown in their language. The Irish were really very passive toward their world. They believed that they had no control over it, but they took it in stride. They did not try to change the
55 world that they lived in; at the most they left it and immigrated someplace else. Their language reflects this passivity for their environment. According to Dr. Kerby Miller in Emigrants and Exiles: Ireland and the Irish Exodus to North America, the Irish would say, "The road twisted me upon you," while the English equivalent would be, "I met you on the road."[2] This example shows that English is far more aggressive than the Gaelic or Irish language. Whereas the Irish also tended to look
60 inward and not deal with the world, the Americans were very outgoing and embraced the world.

Due to differences in philosophy, these two cultures differed with regard to individualism and family. The two most important things to the Irish were their families and their land. In Ireland, the family unit was more important than the individual. Because of the harsh environment in Ireland, the Irish could not survive alone. The people were poor and needed to depend upon their family,
65 friends, and neighbors for help in time of need. This need to rely upon their fellow man was even considered when people were deciding who they should marry, as related by Tomas O'Crohan.

"She made it plain to the old couple what a responsibility anyone was taking on himself if he didn't marry near home, but made an alliance with a family that lived a long way off and wouldn't be in a position to lend a hand on a rainy day." (3, pp. 144-5).

70 The Irish emphasized the clan and thought of themselves as a large family willing to help their brother in time of need. A functioning unit made up of many parts, they always thought about their actions in terms of how they would affect the family rather than how it would benefit the individual.

Whereas the Irish were dependent on others, the Americans put great emphasis on being aggressive and individualistic. The family, or clan, was not as important to Americans as was self-
75 reliance and individual success. They loved change, moreover, and believed in a rosy future as well as progress. They wanted and believed that they could make their world better and better. Inventions were being patented all the time, and great emphasis was placed on the individual to be successful and maybe even famous. People looked up to men who were individuals who had had it rough yet made it; they were successful. The American Dream was to go from nothing and
80 by sheer will power and personality become somebody great and respected.

Another difference stemming from differences in philosophy was religion. The Americans were, on the whole, Protestant, while the majority of the Irish peasants that immigrated to America were Catholic. Not only were the Irish Catholic, but they were not purely Catholic; their philosophies were

85 a combination of paganism and Catholicism. The Americans, however, thought of themselves as a very civilized, sophisticated, and cultured society. There was little or no room for superstition. Their religion reflected their belief in reality, facts, and science, progress and technology.

The Irish Catholics, on the other hand, were very superstitious. Some good examples of this superstition and fear of the unknown can be seen in some of the short stories in <u>Wildgoose Lodge and Other Stories</u>. One example is from a story called "The Lianhan Shee."

90
> "In the meantime, Mrs. Sullivan had uncorked her bottle of holy water, and plentifully bedewed herself with it, as a preservative against this mysteriouse woman and her dreadful secret." (1, p.54).

Not only were the Irish very superstitious, but they also practiced pagan rites. They visited holy places that really had nothing to do with Christianity but were a carry-over from pagan practices.
95 An example of one of the pilgrimages is in the short story "The Doughberg Pilgrim" by William Carelton in his book <u>Wildgoose Lodge and Other Stories</u>.

These pagan practices were not quite as obvious to the Americans as the Irish wake was. It is thought that it was the Irish wake that distressed the Americans the most. The Irish wake was described in detail by Tomas O'Crohan in <u>The Islandman</u>.[3] Basically a wake was like a party. There
100 were a lot of games, food, and drink. In the past, at wakes, the Irish had mock marriages and even a great deal of sex, or "fertility" rites. The Irish must have felt that if they showed as much life as possible to death, death would not spread to any more of them.

The games, drinking, and merrymaking all took place in front of the house of the deceased. Now if this practice by the Irish were not bad enough to Americans, there was also keening. In the past,
105 keening had been done by a group of professional keeners, who were paid to keen. The keening was a high-pitched lyrical song that sang the praises of the deceased. The more the keeners were paid, the more lavish were the praises. As time went on, the art of keening was forgotten. In the early nineteenth century, it degenerated into a high-pitched howl that the whole group of party makers joined into. When the Irish tried to continue these ancient customs, wakes and keening, in
110 America, it quite upset their American neighbors.

In contrast, the American society was not only Protestant but based on the philosophies of the New England Puritans. Funerals at this time, therefore, were somber affairs with much weeping, intense grief, and silence. The people wore black to the funerals, and if the person who died was a close relative, or a husband or a wife, the bereaved were expected to wear black and mourn
115 their loss for a year. Thus, for Americans at this time, the keening, games, and merrymaking were sacrilegious and intolerable. They looked upon the Irish as barbarous animals, and many of these stern Americans were so concerned with the morality they were taught that they were incapable of accepting the Irish and their customs.

In conclusion, the Irish encountered many problems when they immigrated to the United States.
120 Many were very poor and arrived in the states penniless. Many immigrants spoke Gaelic predominantly, and those that could speak English usually were not proficient at it. Their religion was different from that of Americans. The Irish were Catholic, while the Americans were Protestant. Their philosophies toward the individual differed as did their philosophies on life in general. The Irish passively accepted life, whereas the Americans aggressively embraced it and tried to mold it. The Irish peasants were predominately rural and somewhat primitively so; however, the Americans were
125 industrial and progress-oriented. The Irish were poor and lived on a subsistence level, never looking ahead, just living a day-to-day existence, but the Americans had enough to eat and money in the bank. Americans could look forward to a future, while the Irish could not even conceive of one. All of these differences and others made it very difficult not only for the Irish who immigrated to America but for the Americans who let them into their country, as well. [2,010 words] (Adapted with
130 permission, Aimée E. Haynes, American)

Bibliography

1. Carelton, William. <u>Wildgoose Lodge and Other Stories</u>. Cork and Dublin: The Mercier Press, 1973.
2. Miller, Kerby A. <u>Emigrants and Exiles: Ireland and the Irish Exodus to North America</u>. New York: Oxford University Press, 1985.
3. O'Crohan, Tomas. <u>The Islandman</u>. New York: Oxford University Press, 1979.

Discussion Questions

- Answer the following questions about the previous essay.
- Then, on a separate piece of paper, complete the study chart that follows. The chart has been started for you.

1. In what five ways did the Irish immigrants who came to America in the nineteenth century differ from the Americans? Where did these differences stem from?
2. Where are these differences stated?
3. What is the writer's purpose for the contrast analysis of the Irish and the Americans?
4. Are the differences explained fully and clearly?
5. What cultural conflicts occurred due to these differences?
6. Is the conclusion effective?
7. Imagine you are going to be tested on the contents of the previous essay. Make a study chart on the next page. List the five major points of contrast between the Irish and Americans on the left. In columns on the right, list major terms, examples, and/or details. The first point of contrast is done for you. Note: You will need these notes for an assignment in Chapter 8.

Study Chart

Major Differences Between Irish Immigrants and Americans

Points of Contrast	The Irish	The Americans
1. Class Systems and Economy	static class system/ economy	progressive, fluid class system/economy
	upward mobility not possible	upward mobility possible
	rural; farms	urban; industry
	subsistence tied to land ownership or labor on the farms	skilled labor
2. Technology		

METHODS OF COMPARISON/CONTRAST

As the chart on page 162 shows, there are two ways to organize a comparison/contrast essay: alternating and block form. This section will illustrate each method.

Developing a comparison/contrast essay begins with brainstorming. When analyzing the similarities and/or differences between two people, places, or things (let's say Topic X and Topic Y), you first need to look for points upon which to base the comparison/contrast. These points are called points of comparison or contrast. You discovered in the previous essay, for instance, that the Irish and the Americans could be contrasted based on the following points:

- Class systems and economy
- Technology
- Language
- Views of the individual and the family
- Religion

ⓓⓘⓢⓒⓞⓥⓔⓡⓨ
6.3: Finding points of contrast

What points of contrast would you use for the following general topic?
- Brainstorm with partners. On a separate sheet of paper, list as many points of contrast as you can.
- Then choose the three strongest points. Be careful not to overlap the points.

> Topic: You have to choose a good university to attend. You have narrowed your choices down to School X and School Y. What are the things you need to consider in making your final decision?

After finding convincing points of contrast, you can organize them in one of two ways for a contrast essay: alternating form (point by point) or block form (discussing one and then the other).

Alternating Form

In the alternating method, the essay is organized point by point. The points of contrast are used as the topics for the paragraphs, and the two things being contrasted (such as the two schools) are the subtopics in the paragraphs. A complete, formal outline for alternating form usually follows this pattern.

<u>A Contrast of X and Y</u>

  I. Introduction (Include the hook and thesis with a MAP listing the points of contrast: 1, 2, and 3.)

 II. Topic Sentence: Point of Contrast 1
   A. Topic X
       1. Support
       2. Support
   B. Topic Y
       1. Support
       2. Support

III. Topic Sentence: Point of Contrast 2
   A. Topic X
       1. Support
       2. Support
   B. Topic Y
       (develop support as shown previously)

IV. Topic Sentence: Point of Contrast 3
   A. Topic X
   B. Topic Y

  V. Concluding Paragraph (with a summary of the MAP points of the paragraphs in the body, a restatement of the thesis, and a final comment)

Discovery 6.4 shows a model outline that uses alternating form to contrast two schools (School X and School Y). Let's say you found three good points of contrast for Schools X and Y: cost, quality of teaching, and study facilities. Because the purpose of contrasting two schools is to show superiority, the thesis should state your opinion about which school is better for you. To avoid unnecessary repetition and make your point emphatically, it would be better to discuss School X first in each paragraph if your choice is School Y.* Also, you need to discuss the same points for each school. You cannot, for instance, discuss tuition and dorm expenses for School X vs. cost of textbooks and lab fees for School Y; these points cannot be contrasted.

---

*This is the recommended order for superiority and does not necessarily apply to the other purposes for comparison/contrast studies.

ⓓⓘⓢⓒⓞⓥⓔⓡⓨ
6.4: Analyzing a model outline in alternating form

- Study the following outline.
- Then answer the Discussion Questions that follow.

A Contrast of School X and School Y

I. It is not easy to find a good school. I have considered many schools, but School X and School Y seem to be the best choices. These schools differ in many ways. School Y is a better school for me than School X with regard to cost, quality of teaching, and study facilities.

II. First, School Y is more affordable than School X.
   A. School X
      1. Tuition and fees
      2. Dorm
   B. School Y
      1. Tuition and fees
      2. Dorm

III. In addition to its affordability, School Y's faculty is superior to School X's.
   A. School X
      1. Professors' reputations
      2. Teaching methods
   B. School Y
      1. Professors' reputations
      2. Teaching methods

IV. Finally, School Y provides much better study facilities than School X does.
   A. School X
      1. Library
      2. Computer labs
   B. School Y
      1. Library
      2. Computer labs

V. After analyzing the differences in cost, the quality of teaching, and the study facilities in Schools X and Y, I have decided to attend School Y. It stands out as the better choice because it is more affordable, the faculty is superior, and there are excellent study facilities.

🄠 Discussion Questions

Use the previous outline to answer the following questions.

1. What is the hook?
2. What is the thesis? The writer's purpose?
3. What kinds of information are contained in each topic sentence?
4. In each paragraph, what is always Point A? Point B? How are they ordered?
5. Are the subpoints (1, 2, . . .) the same in all the paragraphs? Why or why not?
6. Is the conclusion complete and logical? Why or why not?

Block Form

In the block method, the topics being compared/contrasted are discussed in separate paragraphs. One paragraph is about Topic X, and the other is about Topic Y. The same points of comparison/contrast are the subtopics in the paragraphs. A complete, formal outline for a contrast analysis in block form usually looks like this.

A Contrast of X and Y

I. Introduction (Include the hook and thesis with a MAP listing the points of contrast: 1, 2, and 3.)

II. Topic Sentence: All about Topic X
    A. The First Main Point: Point of Contrast 1
        1. Support
        2. Support
    B. The Second Main Point: Point of Contrast 2
        1. Support
        2. Support
    C. The Third Main Point: Point of Contrast 3
        (etc.)

III. Topic Sentence: All about Topic Y (Use paragraph-to-paragraph transition.)
    A. The First Main Point: Point of Contrast 1
        1. Support
        2. Support
    B. The Second Main Point: Point of Contrast 2
        1. Support
        2. Support
    C. The Third Main Point: Point of Contrast 3
        (etc.)

IV. Concluding Paragraph (with a summary of the MAP points of the paragraphs in the body, a restatement of the thesis, and a final comment)

Discovery 6.5 shows a model outline that contains the same information as the model outline in Discovery 6.4, only in block form. Again, note that the better choice is discussed last, and the same points are contrasted in each part.

ⒹⒾⓈⒸⓄⓋⒺⓇⓎ

6.5: Analyzing a model outline in block form

- Study the following outline.
- Then answer the Discussion Questions that follow.

A Contrast of School X and School Y

I. It is not easy to find a good school. I have considered many schools, but School X and School Y seem to be the best choices. These schools differ in many ways. School Y is a better school for me than School X with regard to cost, the quality of teaching, and study facilities.

II. School X is an average school.
    A. Cost
        1. Tuition and fees
        2. Dorm
    B. Quality of teaching
        1. Professors' reputations
        2. Computer labs

      C. Study Facilities
        1. Library
        2. Computer labs

III. In contrast to School X, School Y fits my needs better.
    A. Cost
       1. Tuition and fees
       2. Dorm
    B. Quality of teaching
       1. Professors' reputations
       2. Teaching methods
    C. Study Facilities
       1. Library
       2. Computer labs

IV. After analyzing the differences in cost, the quality of teaching, and the study facilities in Schools X and Y, I have decided to attend School Y. It stands out as the better choice because it is more affordable, the faculty is superior, and there are excellent study facilities.

Discussion Questions

Use the previous outline to answer the following questions.

1. How is the block form outline similar to the alternating one?
2. What kinds of information are contained in each topic sentence?
3. In each paragraph, what is always Point A? Point B? Point C? How are they ordered?
4. Are the subpoints (1, 2, . . .) the same in each paragraph? Why or why not?

DISCOVERY

6.6: Reviewing alternating and block form outlines

- Use all of the following information to organize a contrast of the two topics provided.
- Find the three points of contrast and order the information logically.
- Write two complete, formal outlines, one block form and one alternating.
- Include the introduction, body (including topic sentences), and conclusion. The outlines will contain the level of subpoints 1, 2, 3. Use only the information given. Do not add information.

Topics

- Life in the Dorm with a Roommate
- Life in Your Own Apartment

Information

- Have control of noise levels
- Cost
- Do not pay utility bills
- Have interactions with roommate and neighbors
- Social diversions
- Study environment
- May have conflicts with roommate's study routine
- Do own shopping and cooking
- May get noisy
- Pay utilities and rent
- Do not have to compromise with your study routine
- Do not need to buy furniture
- Have more opportunities to speak English
- Have more privacy
- Includes room and meals
- Do not need a study hall or lounge
- May need to buy furniture
- Have a study hall and lounge
- Have fewer interactions with neighbors
- Can join clubs
- Have fewer opportunities to speak English

ANALOGIES

Writers also find similarities between unlikely partners to create analogies, or metaphors. An analogy is a comparison of an unfamiliar, usually abstract idea and a familiar, usually concrete thing. For example, Robert Burns, a famous Scottish poet, defined love by comparing it to a red rose in his poem, "A Red Red Rose." He wrote, "My love is like a red red rose that sweetly blooms in Spring." Readers may not understand the notion of love until they examine the characteristics of a rose. A rose is beautiful; likewise, love is beautiful. A rose is red (the color of passion), and love is passionate. A rose smells sweet; similarly, love is tender and pleasing. Just as a rose has thorns, which sting those who come too close or are careless with it, so love hurts those who mishandle it. Thus, although love and a rose at first appear incomparable, upon analysis, the similarities enabled Burns to reveal a universal truth about love.

ANALYSIS OF BURNS'S ANALOGY

Thesis: My love is like a red red rose that sweetly blooms in Spring.

Concrete (Specific, Tangible)	Abstract (General, Intangible)
A rose is beautiful.	Love is beautiful.
A rose is red.	Love is passionate.
A rose smells sweet.	Love is sweet and pleasing.
A rose has thorns which sting.	Love hurts.

Textbooks frequently contain analogies. The following is an analogy that was used to explain "depth of thought" in Chapter 3.

⮕ Example

Depth of Thought

1   "Depth" is the noun for "deep," which is the opposite of "shallow." If a professor comments that a paper is shallow, this means the writer did not dig deeply into the topic. The ideas are very general, and the support is lacking. In effect, it is a boring paper with weak critical thinking. The following analogy may present a more vivid definition of "depth of thought."

5   A good writer is like a scuba diver. Let's say you are in the Florida Keys on spring break doing some scuba diving, and you want to see the coral reefs. What can you see of the coral reefs from the beach? Sometimes they are visible from the surface, but they are not as vivid and clear from here. *As a writer, you would be too distant from the topic at this point.* You need to get closer. If you want to see the coral reefs more closely, you need to get in the water and start wading. Deeper and deeper you go, and the water is up to your knees, your waist, and your neck. Although you are closer to your goal, either the water is too shallow or you are too far away from the reef. *As a writer, you cannot discuss your topic in detail yet because the ideas are too shallow; although you can see some details, you are still too far away, too general.* Finally, you plunge into the water, and deeper and deeper you swim until you are next to the coral reefs. *As a writer, it is at this point you are able to become specific and vivid. You can paint this picture with words for the reader.* It is here the colors, shapes, and size of the reef are revealed. You can see all the plants and animals living on and around the reef. You can feel the water around you; it is cool and clear. Fish swim past you and possibly nibble on you. You are awed and possibly transformed by this miracle of nature before you. *As a writer, you have to invest yourself in the writing and reveal part of yourself in your opinions, reactions, personal experiences, and understanding of the world. If you love your topic, your reader will too.*

This analogy illustrates that every detail is informative; the more details, the more informative and descriptive the writing is because it shows "depth of thought." Perhaps the reader of a vivid description of the coral reefs will want to see the reefs too. The fewer the details, however, the less persuasive the writing is because it is "shallow." The writer did not dive in close enough to the reefs, and such distance from the heart of the topic is not inspiring.

When explaining analogies, you can use alternating or block form. Analogies focus primarily on similarities; you do not need to acknowledge the differences between the topics.

ⒹⒾⓈⒸⓄⓋⒺⓇⓎ
6.7:   **Analyzing an analogy**

The following essay compares an abstract idea to a concrete one.
• Read the essay.
• Then answer the Discussion Questions that follow.

The House of Life
by Yungjing Hsieh

1   How many decisions do people make in their lives? There could be thousands of decisions in one person's life. However, only a few of them will have a great influence. A metaphor of building a house shows how the five most significant decisions are related to one another and reflect on people's lives. The five most important decisions concern education, career, marriage, residence, and religion.

5   First of all, education can be one of the earliest decisions that people make. Like building a house, they have to draw an outline first. By the time I was sixteen years old, for example, I had chosen a senior high school in order to prepare to go to the university. In addition, I decided to study science and major in nutrition or dietetics. Similarly, the blueprint also decides where the house is located, what the size is, and what it looks like.

10   Second, just as people's choice of career is influenced by their education and by some characteristics of the jobs they want, so the process of building a house is determined by the blueprint and by the available materials. To illustrate, I will see if the company I am interested in has insurance for its employees, a good retirement plan, an attractive salary, chances for advancement, and other benefits. The same is true with constructing a house. The foundation of the house should be stable
15   enough for the house to stand for a long time.

After settling down with a good job, it is time to consider another big decision—getting married. Marriage is the bridge from single life to family life. After building the foundation of a house, people begin to buy furniture and fill the empty house with many things that complement it. These choices are similar to the ones people make when they decide whom to marry, what their family plans are,
20   and how to raise their children.

At that point, people will need to make another essential choice—residence. This decision is settled not only for themselves but also for their children and possibly their children's children. The people building the house may look for good surroundings, including a quiet environment, convenient transportation, and a nice neighborhood. Similar to choosing a residence, how the yard is landscaped
25   may influence others' first impressions of the house.

Unlike the previous four decisions, religion concerns a person's spiritual life. Decorations in a house and religion are similar in that both involve independent and mental decisions. Moreover, both play important roles in one's inner life and the atmosphere of a house.

The above five decisions—education, career, marriage, residence, and religion—control people's
30   expectations in life. This metaphor illustrates how significant those five decisions are. Therefore, people should be patient and think carefully while they are building their lives. [466 words] (Adapted with permission, Yungjing Hsieh, Taiwanese)

ⓠ Discussion Questions

- Answer the following questions about the previous essay.
- Complete the analysis on a separate sheet of paper.

1. What is the writer's analogy? How does the writer develop it? Complete the following chart to help you analyze the analogy. Write the concrete (specific, tangible) ideas on the right and the abstract (general, intangible) ideas on the right.

Analysis of Analogy

Thesis: Life is like a house.

Concrete	Abstract
People are going to make a home for themselves. (Topic)	*People are going to make major decisions in life. (Topic)*

2. Is the analogy clear and complete? That is, are there enough details to show the similarities? Can you think of other supporting points that could be added?

In-Class Writing Assignment

- With a partner, develop an analogy, choosing one of the following thesis statements or one of your own.
- To plan the analogy, make an organized chart listing both the concrete and abstract features (as you did in Discovery 6.7).
- Use the vocabulary provided and a variety of structures of comparison.
- Read your analogy to the class.
- Then use Peer Review Form 10 from Appendix D to evaluate your analogy.

1. Thesis Statement: Life (or Love) is like a game.

   - rules to follow
   - turn-taking
   - foul play
   - good sportsmanship
   - fair play
   - chance, lucky moves
   - strategies
   - the consequences of cheating
   - scorekeeping
   - fun
   - stress
   - team player
   - coaches and referees

2. Thesis Statement: Life (or Love) is like a roller coaster.

   - slow start
   - very fast
   - thrilling
   - scary
   - dangerous
   - full of surprises
   - ups and downs
   - sudden dips
   - unexpected turns
   - cannot jump off
   - a screeching halt (stops very suddenly)
   - want to get on again

Are you a driver or a passenger in life?

Life is like a long journey in a car. On this journey, some people like to be the drivers, and some people like to be the passengers. What kind of person are you? Do you like to do the driving or do you like to ride along? Discuss two or three reasons for your choice with examples. [300 words, every other line]

TIME ORDER

The Past vs. the Present

Chronological order is sometimes used in comparison/contrast analysis. In a history class, you may be asked to compare or contrast the past and the present. Let's say you are asked to contrast your country now with your country 30 to 50 years ago. If you were to use your notes to write an outline, you would find points of contrast and organize them.

Block form may be the better method for time-order comparison/contrast because it is easier to control verb tenses and time expressions, and the changes over time are more distinctive. Alternating form is possible, however, if the chronological structures are used effectively. No matter which form you use, always discuss the past first.

Block Form

I. Introduction

II. My country 30 to 50 years ago
   A. Point of Contrast 1
   B. Point of Contrast 2
   C. Point of Contrast 3

III. My country today
   A. Point of Contrast 1
   B. Point of Contrast 2
   C. Point of Contrast 3

IV. Conclusion

Alternating Form

I. Introduction

II. Point of Contrast 1
   A. My country 30 to 50 years ago
   B. My country now

III. Point of Contrast 2
   A. My country 30 to 50 years ago
   B. My country now

IV. Point of Contrast 3
   A. My country 30 to 50 years ago
   B. My country now

V. Conclusion

6.8: **Brainstorming on time-order contrast analysis**

In groups, discuss the following questions, taking notes on a separate sheet of paper.
Note: You may need to refer to these notes later on in this chapter.

1. In what areas has your country changed in the past 30 to 50 years? List the specific changes. These are the points of contrast.
2. How has your country changed in each of the areas you listed? List support for each point of contrast.
3. Why has your country changed in these areas? List the reasons.
4. Are the changes for the better? Explain your answers.
5. Write an appropriate thesis statement that you could use for an essay about your own country based on the above analysis. Include a MAP and a precise opinion about the changes.

Journal ENTRY 22

Is your country changing for the better or for the worse?

The more developed countries get, the faster they change. Think of ways that your country has changed in the last 30 to 50 years. Are these changes for the better? Discuss two or three major changes. Provide convincing examples and details. [500-550 words, every other line]

Tracing Events: Developments from Past to Present

Another assignment you may have is to trace the development of (or changes in) something. This means to begin in the past and proceed to the present in chronological order. Always begin in the past; it is confusing to trace the development of something backwards. Also, do not jump around from past to present and back to past. Moreover, the assignment might call for comparisons or contrasts to be made as each new stage in the development is compared or contrasted with the previous ones.

6.9: **Analyzing a model essay tracing events**

The following essay test answer was written by an American undergraduate student. She ranks the kinds of Greek temple architecture in chronological terms beginning with ancient times and ending with the present time.
• Identify the time-order transitions and contrasts.
• Then, on a separate sheet of paper, complete the study guide that follows.

A Brief History of Greek Temple Architecture
by Aimée E. Haynes

1   The Greeks were a "natural" people. Their deities were very human in their actions but represented all the things of nature that surrounded the early Greeks. In the Archaic Period, the first temples built to these nature deities were built of wood. Perhaps the columns were originally tree trunks, carved and eventually fluted. It is unknown exactly what these first temples were like as none remain today.

5   The first type of temples that are still present today are the marble temples of the early Doric order. The Doric order in the beginning was stiff, heavy, and impressive, not unlike the early Greek Kouros, a type of stone sculpture of the Archaic Period. This type of monument depicts a youthful athlete with a rigid, geometric posture. As the ancient Greeks advanced, learning proportion in both sculpture and architecture, they became more realistic and more true to what the human figure looked like and what the true temple should look like.

10   The Parthenon is the climax to the perfection both of architecture in the Doric order and in the sculpture of the human body. The Parthenon's shafts are no longer squat and heavy-looking. The capitals, once very large and massive, are much smaller and more modest in the Parthenon. This slimming of the shafts and the reduction of the heavy capital give the Parthenon an airy, other-world quality that the early Doric temples did not have. The sculpture that is on the Parthenon (done by Phidias or his undersculptures) is also airy, more godlike, and more flexible; all the sculptures are beautiful and perfect. The sculptures of men are almost godlike with perfect bodies and tranquil faces.

The next phase of Greek architecture is the classical Ionic order. The Ionic order is much more decorative and even more fluid than the Parthenon and the Doric orders. A perfect example of a totally Ionic temple is also found in the Acropolis in Athens: it is the temple of Athena Nike. Its columns are longer and thinner than its neighbor on the Acropolis, the Parthenon. The triglyphs and metopes give way to one continuous frieze. The capitals are no longer just square-shaped stones or blocks of marble but are decorative and look like shells or jelly rolls. The classical Ionic order was decorative, but it too was simple.

25   The last phase of Greek architecture was the Corinthian style. It was not much used and was overly ornate. It perhaps also reflects the Hellenistic Period. Whereas the sculptures during the Classical, Doric, and Ionic orders were serene and godlike, the statues of the Hellenistic Period are emotional and active. They reflect incredible agony and extreme happiness, passion, pain, and joy. Corinthian architecture is extremely ornate. Its capitals are made up of large palmettes that can be viewed from all sides, unlike the Ionic "sea shell" capital.

The Corinthian order was not used much by the Greeks because at about the time it developed, the Peloponnesian War broke out. Athens eventually fell. Athens was bankrupt near the end of the fourth century due to the excessive building on the Acropolis. The Greeks were weakened from lack of money and soon lost power during the Peloponnesian War. Because of their financial deficiencies and because of the wars, there was very little large-scale building anywhere in Greece. The Acropolis was the last architectural feat of the Hellenes.

The Greeks, as I said before, used wood in the beginning to build their temples. The wood was then replaced by marble and stone. All of the Acropolis is in marble. This marble had a soft white look that was painted in places to give it added beauty and freshness. Marble was also used for the friezes and sculptures on the temples, and later, as seen in the Erechtheum (Ionic order) on the Acropolis, bronze grills were used to replace walls or close in openings between columns. Bronze was used for sculpture all through the Greek Archaic, Classical, and Hellenistic Periods.

Greek architecture is still in use today. When architecture reaches such a state of perfection as the Parthenon did, it is always awe inspiring. [684 words] (Aimée E. Haynes, American)

Ⓠ **Discussion Questions**

Use the above essay to answer the following questions.

1. Which words and phrases indicate time order?
2. Which words and phrases indicate contrast?
3. On a separate sheet of paper, complete the following study guide by making a chart in which you list the characteristics of each type of temple. (The chart has been started for you.) Finish the characteristics of the temples of the later Doric order. Then continue the study guide. Include all the temple types.

Study Guide for History of Greek Architecture

Type of Temple	Characteristics		Examples
1. Archaic	materials:	wood	
	columns:	carved, fluted tree trunks	
	statues:	stone; rigid, geometric posture	Kouros
	sculpture:	bronze	
2. Early Doric order	materials:	marble	X
	style:	stiff, heavy, oppressive	
	shafts:	squat, heavy-looking	
	capitals:	large, massive	
	sculpture:	bronze	
3. Later Doric order			Parthenon

Journal ENTRY 23

How has traditional house design in your culture changed in the last 30 to 50 years?

As times change, so do patterns of living. People change their ways to follow trends. What was fashionable years ago may not be fashionable now. This is true for clothing and cars. Why not houses? How has traditional house design in your culture changed in the last 30 to 50 years? Why? Describe the changes in house design and explain why there were changes. [500-550 words, every other line]

ⒹⒾⓈⒸⓄⓋⒺⓇⓎ
6.10: Brainstorming on comparison/contrast topics

- On a separate sheet of paper, complete the following brainstorming activity by yourself.
- In groups, compare the charts. To do this, each person should speak about his or her chart.
- Make revisions to your chart and hand it in as your assignment.

Brainstorming Activity

1. Are there mainly similarities or differences between the lifestyle in the U.S. or Canada and in your country? List at least three major areas. Choose areas that reflect each culture's values. For instance, do not just list food preferences. Explain why a certain diet or custom related to that diet is important.

2. On a separate sheet of paper, make a chart like you did in Discovery 6.2, showing the similarities or differences between the lifestyles in your country and the U.S. or Canada.

3. Write an appropriate thesis statement with a MAP.

Out-Of-Class Writing Assignment

- Develop an arguable point (thesis) for a contrast essay on one of the following topics. Your MAP should have three main points of contrast (differences).
- Write a complete, formal outline. Use either alternating or block form.
- Use Peer Review Form 11 from Appendix D to evaluate your outlines in groups.
- Revise your outline and write the first draft of the essay.
- Use Peer Review Form 12 from Appendix D to evaluate the essay.

Topics

1. In Discovery 6.8 and Journal Entries 22 and 23, you discussed changes that have taken place in your country in the last 30 to 50 years. One change you may or may not have thought of is in the way in which females are raised and treated in your society. Contrast the way females in your culture were raised and treated in the past with the way they are raised and treated today. Discuss each point of contrast, using specific examples and details which contrast the traditional vs. contemporary values in your culture. Illustrate with specific cases of people you know, such as your mother or grandmother(s).

2. Based on your brainstorming notes in Discovery 6.10, write a contrast essay of lifestyles in the U.S. or Canada and your country. Explain why these differences are significant. If you have primarily found similarities, write a comparison essay.

In the following sections, you will practice structures of comparison (similarity) and structures of contrast (difference), as well as coherence techniques used in comparison essays. The comparative structures include thesis statement patterns, topic sentence patterns, and internal transitions (connectors, phrase markers, and clause markers). This section will also include information that compares dolphins and porpoises, which you will need to complete Discovery 6.11.

STRUCTURES OF COMPARISON

The following chart will be used in the examples and exercises that follow.

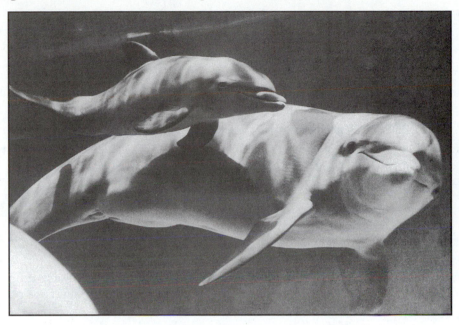

Dolphins and Porpoises: Similarities

1.	*Biological classification:*	Mammals (warm blooded; nurse their young for a year or more); Members of toothed-whale (*Odontoceti*) suborder of *Cetacea* (possess teeth)
2.	*Dietary habits:*	Eat marine fish and larger vertebrates
3.	*Skull shape:*	Telescoped
4.	*Skin:*	Smooth with rubber-like texture; a layer of rubber underneath the skin (insulation)
5.	*Tail:*	Propelled by a horizontal tail; the same graceful up-and-down tail movement
6.	*Fins:*	Two fins (forelimbs); a high triangular-shaped dorsal fin (like that of a shark) on the back
7.	*Speed:*	Can travel at speeds of 25 mph or faster
8.	*Respiratory system:*	Have lungs; breathe through a single nare (blowhole) at the top of the head
9.	*Communication:*	Make sounds for navigation, communication, and location of prey
10.	*Sociability:*	Travel in herds; strong sense of community (stay with the same herd for life)

Thesis Statements

The thesis statement contains the two topics being compared, a main verb, and a term for similarity. A MAP listing the similarities might follow the thesis statement. Note that the topics (X and Y) precede the verb.

⇨ **Examples**

Dolphins and porpoises have several major *similarities*: physical features, sociability, and
  (X)   *(Y)*   *(NOUN)*   *(MAP)*
communication.

Dolphins and porpoises have several *characteristics in common*: physical features, sociability,
  (X)   *(Y)*   *(NOUN PHRASE)*   *(MAP)*
and communication.

Dolphins and porpoises *are similar* in several major ways: physical features, sociability, and
  (X)   *(Y)*   *(be + ADJECTIVE)*   *(MAP)*
communication.

Topic Sentences

Each topic sentence that examines similarities contains both topics of comparison, a verb, a term for similarity, and a phrase (or clause) listing the point of similarity. Each topic sentence should also contain a transition. Note that the topics (X and Y) have various positions in the topic sentence patterns.

⇨ **Examples**

Dolphins and porpoises *are similar regarding* the way they swim.
  (X)   *(Y)*   *(be + ADJECTIVE)(PHRASE*   *(POINT OF SIMILARITY)*
                                         MARKER)

Dolphins *are similar* to porpoises *with regard to* the way they swim.
  (X)   *(be + ADJECTIVE)*   *(Y)*   *(PHRASE MARKER)*   *POINT OF SIMILARITY)*

Dolphins and porpoises *are similar* in that they swim the same way.
  (X)   *(Y)*   *(be + ADJECTIVE)*   *(POINT OF SIMILARITY)*

Another *similarity* between dolphins and porpoises is the way that they swim.
    (NOUN)   *(X)*   *(Y)*   *(POINT OF SIMILARITY)*

Internal Transitions

The internal transitions include connectors, phrase markers, and clause markers. These structures provide coherence between the sentences in each paragraph.

Connectors

The connectors for similarity, *similarly* and *likewise,* are used between two complete sentences. The first sentence is a statement about one of the topics of comparison, and the second sentence is about the second topic. The second sentence paraphrases the information in the first sentence. A semicolon can be used instead of a period, but do not capitalize the next word.

⇨ **Example**

The dolphin breathes through a blowhole on top of its head. *Similarly/Likewise,* the porpoise
          (SENTENCE ABOUT X)   *(PARAPHRASE ABOUT X)*
has a nare through which it breathes.

The dolphin breathes through a blowhole on top of its head; *similarly/likewise,* the porpoise
          (SENTENCE ABOUT X)   *(PARAPHRASE ABOUT X)*
has a nare through which it breathes.

Phrase Markers

The phrase markers for similarity, *like* and *similar to,* are used with nouns. Usually a phrase of similarity begins the sentence and is set off by a comma.

⇨ Example

Like/Similar to the dolphin, the porpoise breathes through a nare, or a blowhole, on the top
(PHRASE MARKER)   (NOUN: X)   (NOUN: Y)   (MAIN CLAUSE)
of its head.

Clause Markers

The only clause marker for similarity is *just as,* which precedes a dependent clause about one of the topics of comparison. The main clause follows *so*. The main clause can be reduced to an auxiliary followed by the second topic of comparison.

⇨ Examples

Just as the dolphin breathes through a nare on the top of its head, *so* the porpoise has a
(DEPENDENT CLAUSE ABOUT X)   (MAIN CLAUSE ABOUT Y)
blowhole for breathing.

Just as the dolphin breathes through a nare on the top of its head, *so* does the porpoise.
(DEPENDENT CLAUSE ABOUT X)   (AUXILIARY + Y)

ⒹⒾⓈⒸⓄⓋⒺⓇⓎ

6.11: Using structures of comparison (similarity)

* Using the following structures of comparison, write complete sentences on the similarities between dolphins and porpoises.
* Use each structure only once.
* Pay attention to capitalization while planning the sentences.

1. similar to	5. likewise
2. like	6. similarly
3. one similarity	7. just as . . . so
4. are similar to	8. are similar with regard to

1. ....

....

2. ....

....

3. ....

....

4. ....

....

5. ....

....

6. ....
....

7. ....
....

8. ....
....

STRUCTURES OF CONTRAST

The following chart will be used in the examples and exercises that follow.

A porpoise   A dolphin

Differences Between Dolphins and Porpoises[1, 2, 3]

Feature	Dolphins	Porpoises
Number of species	40	5 or 6
Habitat	primarily U.S. waters	worldwide, but rarely south of North Carolina
Length	average: 2.1 to 3.0 meters long (can reach up to 4.6 meters)	smaller than dolphins
Dorsal Fin	prominent, broad-based, crescent shaped, and pointed at the tip	small, rectangular, blunt-tipped
Head	large, rounded	smaller, rounded
Snout	long, sharp, beak-shaped, flat	very short, indistinct
Teeth	round, cone-shaped	flat, triangular
Sociability	playful, outgoing, friendly to people	serious, wary of people

Thesis Statements

Thesis statements for contrast essays include both topics of contrast and terms for contrast analysis, such as *different* and *differences*. The thesis might also contain a MAP listing the points of contrast.

⤸ **Examples**

> Dolphins and porpoises have two major *differences:* physical features and sociability.
> *(X)*　　　*(Y)*　　　　　　　*(Noun)*　　　　　　　*(Map)*

> Dolphins and porpoises *are different* in two ways: physical features and sociability.
> *(X)*　　　*(Y)*　*(be + Adjective)*　　　　　　*(Map)*

Topic Sentences

Each topic sentence in an alternating contrast analysis contains both topics of contrast, a verb, a term for contrast, and a point of contrast (difference). Each topic sentence should also contain a transition. Note the word order in each pattern.

⤸ **Examples**

> Dolphins and porpoises *are different regarding* their size.
> *(X)*　　　　　*(Y)*　*(be + Adjective) (Phrase　(Point of*
> 　　　　　　　　　　　　　　　*Marker)　Contrast)*

> Dolphins *are different* from porpoises *with regard to* their size.
> *(X)*　*(be + Adjective)*　　*(Y)*　*(Phrase Marker) (Point of*
> 　　　　　　　　　　　　　　　　　　　*Contrast)*

> Dolphins and porpoises *differ* in that they are not the same size.
> *(X)*　　　　　*(Y)*　*(verb)*　　*(Point of Contrast)*

> The second/Another *difference* between dolphins and porpoises is size.
> *(Transition)*　　　*(Noun)*　　　　　*(X)*　　　*(Y)*　*(Point of*
> 　　　　　　　　　　　　　　　　　　　　　　*Contrast)*

Internal Transitions

Connectors

The major connector for contrast essays is *in contrast*. Place this connector between statements about each of the topics of contrast. A semicolon can be used instead of a period, but do not capitalize the next word.

⤸ **Examples**

> Dolphins can grow up to 4.6 meters in some species. *In contrast*, porpoises are generally
> 　　　　*(Sentence About X)*　　　　　　　*(Connector)*　　*(Sentence About Y)*
> smaller than dolphins.

> Dolphins can grow up to 4.6 meters in some species; *in contrast*, porpoises are generally
> 　　　　*(Sentence About X)*　　　　　　　*(Connector)*　　*(Sentence About Y)*
> smaller than dolphins.

Phrase Markers

The phrase markers for contrast essays are *unlike, in contrast to,* and *different from*. These structures are followed by nouns. A phrase of contrast usually begins the sentence. Put old ideas in phrases.

⤸ **Example**

> *Unlike/In contrast to/Different from* dolphins, porpoises are small.
> 　　*(Phrase Marker)*　　　　　*(Noun: X)*　　*(Main Clause About Y)*

Clause Markers

The clause markers for contrast statements are *whereas* and *while*. These structures are followed by subjects and verbs. The dependent clause can precede or follow the main clause. Note that a comma is used in each position. Put old ideas in dependent clauses.

⇨ **Examples**

Whereas/While dolphins are large, porpoises are small.
(CLAUSE MARKER)   (DEPENDENT CLAUSE   (MAIN CLAUSE
                          ABOUT X)   ABOUT Y)

Porpoises are small, *whereas/while* dolphins are large.
(MAIN CLAUSE ABOUT Y)   (CLAUSE MARKER)   (DEPENDENT CLAUSE
                                                  ABOUT Y)

ⓓⓘⓢⓒⓞⓥⓔⓡⓨ
6.12:   Using structures of contrast

- Using the following structures of contrast, write complete sentences on the differences between dolphins and porpoises.
- Use each structure only once.
- Pay attention to capitalization while planning the sentences.

1. are different regarding	5. in contrast to
2. are different from	6. in contrast
3. differ in that	7. whereas
4. different from	8. while

1. ....
   ....

2. ....
   ....

3. ....
   ....

4. ....
   ....

5. ....
   ....

6. ....
   ....

7. ....
   ....

8. ....
   ....

USE OF OLD IDEAS IN BLOCK FORM

There are two major ways to achieve coherence in comparison/contrast essays. One way is to use what you just learned: structures of comparison and contrast. Another way is to repeat old ideas. Earlier in this textbook, you practiced this coherence technique with enumeration devices. The necessary repetition of old ideas is just as important when stating similarities and differences, especially in block form essays.

Some people think block form is easier to use than alternating because all you have to do is state the characteristics of Topic X and then state the characteristics of Topic Y. However, you need to tie the two parts of the essay together effectively, especially in longer essays. To do this, it is necessary to remind the reader briefly of the information about Topic X while you are discussing the characteristics of Topic Y. The comparison/contrast structures are used for the recall of old ideas.

DISCOVERY

6.13:   **Analyzing the use of old ideas in a block form essay**

- Study the following two versions of a short essay on the differences between dolphins and porpoises.
- Then answer the Discussion Questions that follow.

Version 1

1   Dolphins and porpoises share several characteristics, which often causes people to be confused or misled to believe these sea mammals are one and the same. However, dolphins and porpoises are different in many ways.

   People may be more familiar with dolphins since they are sociable and friendly to humans. In fact,
5   due to their playful and outgoing nature, dolphins not only perform in amusement parks but also are used to provide therapy for troubled children. Moreover, dolphins comprise 40 species primarily found in U.S. waters. Most species of dolphins are 2.1 to 3 meters long, but some can reach 4.6 meters. The dolphin has a large, rounded head and a long, sharp snout that is flat and beak-shaped. Its teeth are round and cone-shaped. Its prominent dorsal fin, which is located on its back, is broad-based,
10   crescent-shaped, and pointed at the tip.

   Porpoises are serious and wary. Since they avoid people, they are not usually in the public eye. There are 5 or 6 species of porpoise found worldwide, and rarely south of North Carolina. Its body and head are small, and its snout is very short and indistinct. Its teeth are flat and triangular. Its dorsal fin, located on its back, is small, triangular, and blunt-tipped.

15   Once people learn the distinguishing features of dolphins and porpoises, they will no longer confuse them as members of the same species. [229 words]

Version 2

1   Dolphins and porpoises share several characteristics, which often causes people to be confused or misled to believe these sea mammals are one and the same. However, dolphins and porpoises are different in many ways.

   People may be more familiar with dolphins since they are sociable and friendly to humans. In fact,
5   due to their playful and outgoing nature, dolphins not only perform in amusement parks but also are used to provide therapy for troubled children. Moreover, dolphins comprise 40 species primarily found in U.S. waters. Most species of dolphins are 2.1 to 3 meters long, but some can reach 4.6 meters. The dolphin has a large, rounded head and a long, sharp snout that is flat and beak-shaped. Its teeth are round and cone-shaped. Its prominent dorsal fin, which is located on its back, is broad-based,
10   crescent-shaped, and pointed at the tip.

   Unlike dolphins, porpoises are serious and wary. Since they avoid people, they are not usually in the public eye as much as dolphins are. There are fewer species of porpoises than there are of dolphins, around 5 or 6 as opposed to 40. Whereas dolphins live close to the U.S., porpoises are

15 found worldwide, and rarely south of North Carolina. The body and head of the porpoise are smaller than those of the dolphin. Also, in contrast to the dolphin, which has a long, distinctive snout, the porpoise has a short, indistinct snout. The teeth of the porpoise are very different from those of the dolphin because they are flat and triangular, not round and cone-shaped. Dolphins and porpoises also have distinctively different dorsal fins as well. In contrast to the dolphin's fin, which is large, rounded, and pointed at the tip, the dorsal fin on a porpoise is small, triangular,
20 and blunt-tipped.

In conclusion, once people learn the distinguishing features of dolphins and porpoises, they will no longer confuse them as members of the same species. [319 words]

 Discussion Questions

Based on Version 1 and Version 2, answer the following questions.

1. Which version sounds better? Why?
2. In Version 2, what is the topic of paragraph two? Does the writer ever refer to porpoises? Why not?
3. In Version 2, what is the topic of paragraph three? Does the writer refer to dolphins? Why?
4. In Version 2, how is the paragraph on porpoises tied to the one on dolphins?
5. In Version 2, in the paragraph on porpoises, what kind of information is in the main clauses? Which information is in the dependent clauses and phrases of contrast? Why?
6. In Version 2, paragraph three, does the writer repeat the old information word for word or is the old information paraphrased?
7. Where are old ideas placed most of the time in Version 2, before or after new ideas?
8. Which paragraph in Version 2 is the most different from that in Version 1?

Journal ENTRY 24

Have your views of the world changed since you were a child?

Your current views of the world might be very different from your views of the world when you were a child. Choose two or three major differences and discuss them in block form. Provide convincing examples and details. [500-550 words, every other line]

DISCOVERY

6.14: Reviewing structures of comparison and contrast

- Read the following essay.
- Then fill in each blank with a structure of comparison or contrast.
- Pay close attention to number agreement and mechanics.

Cultural Differences Between the U.S. and Venezuela
by Licett Galietta

Before visiting the United States for the first time, I was a little scared because I knew I would find here people with values and customs different from mine. After a few days of living in the U.S. and sharing with American people, I was surprised and delighted with the many points in common between American culture and Venezuelan culture. Despite the ...., (1) however, I could not avoid feeling shocked over the noticeable .... (2) between both cultures regarding family, friendship, and rules of politeness.

.... First, the definition (3) of "family" differs. When talking about their family, Americans generally think of their immediate family, which is the parents and their children. That is the impression I have gotten from the American people I have met since I came to the United States. ...., (4) when Venezuelans talk about their family, they generally think about a more extended idea of family. When I think of my family, for example, I think of not only my parents, brothers, and sister, but also my grandparents, aunts, uncles, and cousins. Second, these cultures have different ideas about distance between family members. In America, when the children grow up, they frequently leave their parents' home and go to live in another city. For this reason, American families do not get together with much frequency. .... Americans, the members of (5) Venezuelan families tend to live close to one another, most likely in the same city. This fact allows them to have a closer relationship due to sharing more moments together and helping one another. For example, ... American families meet only on special dates or (6) occasions like Christmas, Thanksgiving, weddings, and funerals, Venezuelan families also meet on Sundays to have lunch and socialize together, or they take vacations together during holidays and on days off. Indeed, unlike American families, Venezuelan families have closer relationships among the members.

.... To begin with, social (7) distance has different rules in each culture. In America, the people are so concerned about respecting other people's privacy that friends always keep some distance from each other. That is, they usually maintain physical distance between each other. Also, Americans usually avoid asking for help from their friends unless it is absolutely necessary. Unlike Americans, Venezuelans consider a friend almost like a relative. It is perfectly normal to come physically close to a friend, give him or her a hug or a kiss, or shake his or her hand. Because Venezuelans believe that a friend is a person one can rely on if there is problem, they would not hesitate in asking a friend for help. Another .... between both cultures is the relationship between neighbors. While (8) the relationship between neighbors in America is usually limited to just greetings, in Venezuela, neighbors generally become friends. For example, in the place I live, the neighbors may drop over for coffee in the afternoon and socialize with us. They would also offer their help if we need it. For example, they look after our home when we are traveling on vacations. In these respects, the American concept of friendship is different from the Venezuelan one.

.... First, these cultures (9) differ with regard to directness. For example, Americans tend to be very direct. They get to the point with no preamble. Sometimes, this direct way of saying things may be considered rude by people from other cultures. It is not that Americans are impolite. On the contrary, they are very polite because they always say thank you and please, and they try to moderate their statements by using tactful expressions. However, in Venezuelan culture, people tend to make a few statements suggesting the point before getting to it, so the person is somehow prepared to hear what is going to be said. Another difference between both cultures .... rules of (10) politeness involves some questions or topics that people are not supposed to ask or talk about. In American culture, it is considered impolite to ask another person about his or her age, especially if she is a woman. Also, people should avoid talking about certain topics like religion, salary, or weight. In contrast, asking about age or talking about religion, salary, or weight in Venezuelan culture is not a transgression. Consequently, it is acceptable for a friend to ask another friend how much she or he weighs or what her or his salary is. It is important for Americans and Venezuelans to be aware of these differences in politeness in order to avoid misunderstandings.

In summary, although American and Venezuelan culture have some similarities, they are different in several ways. The American concepts of family, friendship, and politeness are different from the Venezuelan ones. For this reason, when I came to America, I had to adapt myself to this new culture. (Adapted with permission, Licett Galietta, Venezuelan)

CHAPTER *summary*

- Comparison is the analysis of similarities; contrast is the analysis of differences.

- There are five main purposes of comparison/contrast analysis: to show superiority of one topic over another, to draw analogies that help explain abstract ideas, to show changes over time (the past vs. the present) or to trace events, to reveal surprising similarities (to possibly refute a stereotype), or to reveal surprising differences (to possibly refute a stereotype).

- Two methods are used to organize comparison/contrast essays. One is the alternating method, in which the two topics are examined side by side around the points of comparison or contrast (body paragraph topics). Alternating form is easier for the reader to follow than block form because the topics are presented side by side, and it is easier for the reader to remember the information. The other is the block method, in which the two topics are examined separately and the points of comparison or contrast are the paragraph subtopics. This method is especially useful with past vs. present contrast analysis. It may be easier to control the tenses if you discuss the past in one part of the essay and the present in the other part. Also, use block form if you have incomplete information.

- Special structures are used in comparison/contrast essays. First, the thesis statement and topic sentence patterns require both topics being compared or contrasted, special terms for comparison or contrast, and points of comparison or contrast. Also, the internal transitions for both comparison and contrast are classified as connectors, phrase markers, and clause markers. Although the word order and punctuation for these structures of similarity and difference are the same, the vocabulary is different. Use a variety of these structures in your comparison/contrast essays.

- The cohesion device old idea–new idea (which was covered in previous chapters) is also used in comparison/contrast essays, especially in block form. In the second part of the discussion in a block form essay (Topic Y), the reader may need to be reminded of old information (Topic X). Recall old information in dependent phrases and clauses, and put old information before new.

References
1. "Dolphin," Compton's New Media, Inc., 1993, [http://www.ucsc.edu/mb/creatures/dolphin-1.html], April, 1996.
2. "Dolphins and Porpoises," Compton's Learning Company, 1990-1992, [http://www.well.com/user/bridge/dolphins and porpoises_147.html].

Chapter 7

Cause/Effect Analysis

CHAPTER TOPICS

- ▶ ANALYSIS OF CAUSE
- ▶ IDENTIFYING LOGICAL CAUSES: CRITICAL THINKING
- ▶ ANALYSIS OF EFFECT
- ▶ STRUCTURES OF CAUSE
- ▶ STRUCTURES OF EFFECT

ANALYSIS OF CAUSE

Cause/Effect analysis is a fundamental pattern implemented across all disciplines of academic writing. An analysis of causes involves a search for reasons or factors contributing to a situation. For example, in a sociology class, you might examine the causes of a social problem, such as crime or drug abuse. For an assignment in a psychology class, you might be asked to research the factors contributing to depression.

An analysis of effect involves investigating the result or consequences of a situation. In a geology class you might be asked to examine the effects of a natural disaster, such as a typhoon, earthquake, or volcanic eruption. In a health science class, you might have to write about the symptoms of an illness, such as acquired immune deficiency syndrome (AIDS).

In this chapter, you will learn how to determine logical causes and effects, order them appropriately, and frame essays of cause and effect. You will also learn how to organize sentences using cause/effect structures. The discoveries and journal entries in this chapter will help you learn how to gather information for some of the out-of-class writing assignments.

Journal
ENTRY 25

Are you under stress because of your workload in school?

It is late in the semester, and your schoolwork is probably piling up. Are you feeling stressed because of the workload in your classes? Why or why not? Discuss two or three reasons with specific examples and details. [approximately 700 words, every other line]

ⓓ ⓘ ⓢ ⓒ ⓞ ⓥ ⓔ ⓡ ⓨ
7.1: Discussing stress and burnout

Discuss the following questions with partners. Take notes on a separate sheet of paper; you will be using them later in this chapter.

1. Do you ever feel stressed? How do you know when you are under stress? How do you feel or act?
2. What causes you to feel stressed? List as many reasons as possible.
3. Is stress ever a good thing? Why or why not?

ⓓ ⓘ ⓢ ⓒ ⓞ ⓥ ⓔ ⓡ ⓨ
7.2: Discussing a model analysis of cause

- Read the following passage from a paper written for a course on human resources management.
- Then answer the Discussion Questions that follow.

Burnout in the Healthcare Sector
by Pattie Malone

1   Introduction
      Stress is a part of everyday life and, to a certain degree, is healthy for an individual. Chronic stress, however, is not healthy for an individual, and chronic stress results in burnout. Burnout is defined in lay terms as physical or emotional exhaustion, especially as a result of long-term stress.
5   Researchers have commonly found that individuals in the human services professions, such as health care, are more susceptible to burnout than individuals in other professions (Maslach, 1982; Pines and Aronson, 1988; Patrick, 1984; Weber, 1991). Today, the economic, political, and regulatory pressures in the healthcare industry have made an already stressful environment even more so (Dubnicki, 1991). The purpose of this study is to determine what burnout is, why it is so prevalent
10   in the healthcare sector, and what human resources management can do to prevent burnout.

      Burnout Defined
      Pines and Aronson (1988) define burnout as a state of physical, emotional, and mental exhaustion caused by long-term involvement in emotionally demanding situations. Physical exhaustion comes in the form of low energy, chronic fatigue, and weakness. Emotional exhaustion is characterized by
15   the development of negative attitudes toward oneself, work, and life itself.
      Maslach (1982) defines burnout as a syndrome of emotional exhaustion, depersonalization, and reduced personal accomplishment that can occur among individuals who work with people. Emotional exhaustion is characterized by lack of energy. This kind of emotional state is also referred to as "compassion fatigue." Depersonalization is the development of detached, callous, or even
20   dehumanized response signals. It is the treatment of people as objects rather than as humans. Reduced personal accomplishment is the experience of a decline in a feeling of competence. It is a loss of self-esteem. Though there is some discrepancy as to the components of burnout, both researchers agree that burnout is not an isolated phenomenon. The researchers also agree that burnout frequently occurs in a wide variety of people, especially those working in human services
25   and at all levels of management. Another point of agreement is that there are internal and external factors that contribute to burnout.

      Internal Factors That Lead to Burnout
      There are several internal factors that lead to burnout. Burnout tends to occur in educated individuals. It occurs more frequently in individuals with 2 to 4 years of college education than in
30   individuals who have gone on to postgraduate studies. Younger individuals in new careers are also more prone to suffer from burnout. In addition, single people are more susceptible than married individuals. This is due to the lack of support that younger, single individuals experience (Maslach, 1982).
      There are certain personality traits that make one more susceptible to burnout. A person who
35   is weak and nonassertive when dealing with people is more prone to burnout. A person who is

impatient and intolerant is also more susceptible. A person who lacks self-confidence, has low ambition, and is reserved and conventional is also prone to burnout (Maslach, 1982).

External Factors Particular to Health Care That Lead to Burnout

Burnout is especially problematic in the healthcare sector for a multitude of reasons (Weber,
40   1991). First, healthcare professionals are constantly exposed to emotionally demanding situations (Pines and Aronson, 1988). It is stressful to consistently be the one to help others. Nurses are particularly prone to burnout because of the constant care they must provide to their patients.

Second, the rate of change in the healthcare sector places all healthcare workers in a constant state of flux. Change is stressful, and change is what has characterized the healthcare field in the
45   last decade (Kaye, 1989). Change has occurred in a variety of ways. The payment mechanism has shifted from retrospective to prospective. Medical technology results in a change in the provision of care. Mergers, downsizing, and re-engineering are organizational changes that impact individuals.

A third reason that burnout occurs in healthcare professionals and administrators is that many healthcare institutions are being financially squeezed. The financial distress of the organization
50   becomes emotional distress for the individual. The stress of "doing more with less" can only be borne for so long (Weber, 1991).

Another reason burnout is a frequent occurrence in health care is that the public has begun to question the efficiency and competency of healthcare professionals. Society has decided that health care costs too much. Health care was 12.2% of the gross national product of the United
55   States in 1990 (Sonnefeld et al, 1991). A study has shown that, when compared to health care in other major industrialized countries, health care in the United States costs more per person and per service, is less accessible to many of its citizens, is provided at a more intensive level, and offers comparatively poor gross outcomes (Schieber et al, 1991). Facts like these are frequently cited as proof that the entire healthcare system needs revamping.

60   The president of the United States and members of Congress have been debating for healthcare reform, but they cannot agree on the type. Meanwhile, employers and individuals are demanding better healthcare services in terms of quality and efficiency. Healthcare professionals feel they have little control over what is happening to them and to their future, and it is this lack of control that causes burnout (Weber, 1991).

65   Many individuals entered the healthcare field when it was not perceived as an industry. Those individuals chose that field so that they could provide humanitarian care to the ill. Today, these healthcare professionals resent and resist its transformation to a business environment (Kaye, 1989). Providing health care may have once been a humanitarian mission, but it is certainly a business today. Healthcare professionals are now having to deal not only with the stress in the provision of
70   health care, but also with the stress of the business operations associated with this provision of health care.

Other External Factors That Lead to Burnout

There are other external factors that cause burnout. These factors, while not specific to the healthcare field, are added stress factors. They include poor organization and management, poor
75   interpersonal communication, and an absence of positive feedback (Pines and Aronson, 1988). Healthcare providers, once glorified as being mavericks, must now be a part of healthcare teams. In order to best serve the patient, these teams must communicate effectively with each other; however, little has been formally done to help the providers become adept in doing so.

The last three external factors to be addressed that cause burnout are work overload, bureaucracy,
80   and institutional rules and regulations. A workaholic mentality is what characterizes many individuals in the healthcare sector. One consultant on strategic planning for hospitals commented that being stressed out was a status symbol (Weber, 1991). Bureaucratic red tape is another external factor that causes burnout. The amount of paperwork involved in receiving reimbursement from Medicare, Medicaid, and third-party payers is but one example of the bureaucratic labyrinth that one must deal
85   with in health care. Institutional rules and regulations are also a cause of burnout. For the healthcare provider, the quality assurance programs of prospective, concurrent, and retrospective review assuredly adds to the stress of providing care.

There are general external factors that add stress to the workplace. There are also external factors particular to health care that compound the stress level. It is the combination of these external

90   factors that makes burnout so prevalent in the healthcare sector. [1,204 words] (Adapted with permission, Pattie Malone, American)

Bibliography (Sample Entries)

American Heritage Dictionary; second college edition. (1985). Boston, MA: Houghton Mifflin.

Dubnicki, D. (1991) Keeping the flame alive. Seven steps to remedy burnout. Health Care Forum Journal. 34 (6), 24-5.

Foulkes, F.K., and Livernash, E.R. (1989). Human resources management: cases and texts. Englewood Cliffs, NJ: Prentice-Hall.

Hall, D.T. and Williams, R. (1971) Organizations and individual response to external stress. Administrative Science Quarterly. 16, 533-547.

Kaye, G.H. (1989). Multis, mergers, acquisitions and the health care provider. Nursing Management. 20 (4), 54-62.

Discussion Questions

Use the previous paper to answer the following questions.

1. When is stress a problem in daily life?
2. What is chronic stress?
3. Which professionals seem most affected by burnout?
4. What are the major causes of burnout, according to the introduction?
5. What is burnout, according to Pines and Aronson?
6. On a separate sheet of paper, make a study chart of the internal and external factors that lead to burnout. Organize it logically and include important details.

IDENTIFYING LOGICAL CAUSES: CRITICAL THINKING

In the previous paper, the writer went into great detail about the causes of burnout. She did not limit the discussion to only one or two obvious causes, such as overwork or lack of appreciation. Instead, she gathered information from a number of sources and organized the causes into logical categories. Likewise, if you were writing a paper for a health science class on the causes of cancer, you would need to make a complete list of all the factors contributing to the incidence of cancer. When identifying the causes of a situation, it is important to give comprehensive coverage in the analysis, be logical, and find appropriate sources.

Giving Comprehensive Coverage to the Causal Analysis

When analyzing the causes of a situation, realize that there may be more than one cause. Consider all the possibilities and do not oversimplify. For instance, if your assignment is to write a paper on the causes of heart disease, do not focus on only one cause, such as smoking. There are other causes of heart disease, such as heredity, lack of exercise, a high-fat diet, and stress. Likewise, in a paper on the causes of cancer, you would not want to argue that cancer is caused primarily by pollution. Studies show that in addition to the environment, there are other factors that can contribute to the development of cancer, such as heredity, smoking, a lowered immune system, and stress.

Simplistic Thinking   Stress causes cancer.
Accurate Thinking   Cancer is caused by a number of factors: heredity, environment, smoking, and lowered immunities, to name a few.

Imagine that you have to write a paper on the causes of stress in your life. You have already discussed this topic in Discovery 7.1. Take the following stress test to measure your level of stress more accurately.

ⒹⒾⓈⒸⓄⓋⒺⓇⓎ
7.3: Identifying causes

Measure your current level of stress by completing the following checklist.
• Place a ✓ next to each event that you have experienced in the past year.
• Count the total number of checkmarks.
• Determine your stress level using the scale for the levels of stress that follows.
Note: You will need the information from your test later on in this chapter.

1. Making a major move ....
2. Family vacation ....
3. New baby ....
4. Getting married ....
5. Financial problems ....
6. Time management problems ....
7. Inheriting or winning money ....
8. Physical illness ....
9. Physical injury ....
10. Hospitalization ....
11. Death of someone close ....
12. New job ....
13. Victim of a crime ....
14. Conflict(s) at school ....
15. Conflict(s) at work ....
16. Separation from loved ones ....
17. Change in time spent with friends ....
18. New boy/girlfriend ....
19. Reduction in leisure activities ....
20. Starting a diet ....
21. Stopping smoking or drinking ....
22. Legal problems ....
23. Car accident ....
24. Other _____ ....
25. Other _____ ....

SCALE TO MEASURE STRESS LEVEL ──────────

Number of checkmarks	Stress Level
0-3	Mild
4-6	Moderate
7 or more	High

Adapted with permission from Mueser, Kim T. and Susan Gingerich. <u>Coping with Schizophrenia:
A Guide for Families</u>. Oakland, California: New Harbinger Publications, 1994, p. 157.

Ⓠ Discussion Questions

Use the above test to answer the following questions.

1. Did you include any other causes of stress in Journal Entry 25 and Discovery 7.1 that are not listed here?
2. Do you feel this test is an accurate way to measure stress? Why or why not?

Being Logical: Avoiding the Post-Hoc Fallacy

1   When you search for causes of a situation, be careful with how you interpret chronological events. Sometimes two events related chronologically are causally related. The water cycle is a good example. When the sun heats the earth (action 1), water evaporates (action 2). When water evaporates (action 3), clouds are formed (action 4). Such chronological events are causally related 5   because heat is needed for evaporation. Also, if water does not evaporate, clouds do not form.

However, not all chronological sequences involve cause and effect. Just because two events occur sequentially does not mean that the first event causes the second one. Let's say you have an important job interview. You would like to wear your blue suit, which is your favorite, but it is at the dry cleaner's. So now you have to select another suit. As it turned out, you did not get the job 10   that you interviewed for. Why not? There may be some very logical reasons, such as insufficient experience or not meeting all of the job requirements. It would be illogical, however, to reason that you did not get the job because you did not wear your favorite suit.

This type of faulty reasoning is called the post-hoc fallacy. In Latin, the expression for this fallacy is *post hoc, ergo propter hoc*, which means "after this, therefore, because of this." However, an 15   action that immediately follows another one is not necessarily the result of the first action. To avoid post-hoc thinking, carefully consider whether the chronological events are actually related causally.

ⒹⒾⓈⒸⓄⓋⒺⓇⓎ
7.4: Identifying post-hoc reasoning

Write P if the events in each sentence are an example of post-hoc thinking or C if the events are causally related.

1. .... When George was a child, he never brushed his teeth. He has several cavities.

2. .... Last night, Sally went to bed with wet hair. This morning, she woke up with a cold.

3. .... When I blew out the candles on my birthday cake, I wished for a new car. The next day, I won a new car.

4. .... The arteries leading to Joe's heart clogged. Joe had a heart attack.

5. .... I was thinking about my sister all day yesterday. She called me last night.

6. .... It rained hard for two weeks. The river overflowed.

7. .... The Smiths watched game shows every day since they got married. They divorced last month.

8. .... We ate chicken that was tainted with salmonella. We contracted food poisoning.

Finding Appropriate Sources

As with any assignment, causal analysis should be credible and accurate and should reflect current research. Quite often people hold mistaken beliefs about the cause of a situation. They may not realize that current scientific research has identified specific causes and ruled out others. For example, when information about the AIDS virus first surfaced in 1983, people knew so little about it that they began to speculate about its causes. At first, people believed that the virus was airborne or that it could be transmitted by simply touching the infected person. They also believed that one could catch AIDS in a swimming pool. Current scientific research has since debunked (refuted) those beliefs by proving that AIDS can be transmitted only through direct contact with blood or bodily fluids. Now that many of these myths have been disproved, AIDS patients are receiving more effective medical treatment and scientists have been able to make major advances in finding a cure.

This example illustrates that beliefs of the past might not hold true today. In order to identify logical causes and avoid post-hoc thinking (e.g., "If someone who has AIDS touches my hand, I will get AIDS."), it is important to consult a number of sources. The following activity demonstrates the value of using current research to identify logical causes.

🄳🄸🅂🄲🄾🅅🄴🅁🅈
7.5: Discovering causes

Complete Parts A, B, and C in order. Do not skip or read ahead.

A. The following questions test your knowledge of the causes of mental illness. Under Column X, circle T if the statement is true or F if the statement is false.

	X		Y	
1. Mentally ill people are possessed by demons.	T	F	T	F
2. Mental illness is caused by poor parenting.	T	F	T	F
3. Mental illness is the result of weakness of character.	T	F	T	F
4. Chemical imbalances in the brain cause mental illness.	T	F	T	F
5. Drug abuse causes mental illness.	T	F	T	F
6. A lack of education contributes to mental illness.	T	F	T	F
7. Strokes result in mental illness.	T	F	T	F
8. Mental illness can be inherited.	T	F	T	F
9. Mental retardation (slow mental development) is related to mental illness.	T	F	T	F
10. Structural and brain abnormalities can lead to mental illness.	T	F	T	F

B. Now read the following paper on the causes of mental illness.

The Facts About Mental Illness

1   The process of scientific discovery is very important in people's lives. Often what people think is true may be based not on the facts, but rather on superstition, fear, and speculation. Valid scientific research refutes commonly held myths and, thus, improves the quality of people's lives. This has been the case with theories on the causes of mental illness and treatment of the mentally ill.

5   According to the National Alliance for the Mentally Ill (NAMI), a support and advocacy organization "dedicated to improving the lives of people with severe mental illnesses" (NAMI Advocate 2), people used to believe that mental illnesses were caused by demonic possession, poor parenting, weak character, strokes, drug abuse, or a lack of education. Also, mental illness was confused with mental retardation. Because of this ignorance, no one knew how to treat the mentally ill. For example, it
10   was believed that drilling a hole in the head of a mentally ill person would release the demons. However, NAMI claims that such theories and practices only served to stigmatize, blame, and punish the mentally ill, not cure them.

Unfortunately, the misguided thinking of the past lingers today. The mentally ill are misjudged and discriminated against in many areas, such as health care and housing. Although these people are disabled by their disease, they cannot get adequate insurance to treat their illness. Due to their
15   illness, they cannot work. Thus, they often cannot get adequate housing. In fact, NAMI reports that one-third of the homeless are mentally ill.

Current research shows that many mental illnesses are the result of chemical imbalances in the brain, genetics, and structural and brain abnormalities, or are viral in nature. Such mental illnesses
20   have now been classified in the mental health field as "no-fault" brain disorders because they are no fault of the patient. In fact, it has been established that the severe mental illnesses are treatable, organic disorders, like heart disease or diabetes. These discoveries have lead to the appropriate treatment for and care of people who have the major mental illnesses, such as schizophrenia, manic depression, obsessive/compulsive disorder, and major depression, all of which "can profoundly
25   disrupt a person's ability to think, feel, and relate to others" (NAMI Advocate 2).

NAMI maintains that people should no longer stigmatize the mentally ill. It reports that given the proper medication, at least 80% of those with major mental illnesses can now lead productive lives. Therefore, the mentally ill deserve equal opportunities for adequate insurance coverage, health care, and housing.

30   Indeed, due to scientific inquiry, people should no longer attribute the causes of mental illness to coincidences and superstitions (folk beliefs). Rather than blaming, fearing, or persecuting the mentally ill, people should be helping them get the appropriate treatment to stabilize the illness and to lead productive lives.

[Source: NAMI Advocate (Sept./Oct. 1997), p. 2 and other materials from the National Alliance
35   for the Mentally Ill, 200 N. Glebe Rd., Suite 1015, Arlington, Virginia, 22203-3754. NAMI is described as a grassroots, family, and consumer-support and advocacy organization dedicated to improving the lives of people with severe mental illnesses. NAMI web-site: http://www.nami.org]

C. Now turn to page 159 and take the test again. Circle the answers in Column Y. Have your answers changed? Why?

....

....

....

....

....

Journal ENTRY 26

Do you know of any myths or theories which have been disproved by modern science?

You have just seen examples of theories that have been disproved by contemporary research. Do you know of any other myths or theories that are no longer considered true because scientific discoveries have since disproved them? Describe how science has disproved these theories. [600 words, every other line]

Ordering Causes

Once you determined the causes of a situation, you need to order them logically. Each major cause is a MAP point.

Order of Importance

One way to order the causes is to consider their relevance (or importance). As you learned in Chapter 4 (Essay Development), you can rank MAP points using equal, ascending, or descending order. The following examples show ascending order (least to most relevant or important).

   I. Thesis: A number of factors contribute to heart disease.
  II. One cause of heart disease is lack of exercise.
 III. The second major cause is a high-fat diet.
 IV. The most significant cause is smoking.

↪ Examples

Weak Thinking	People who watch too much TV will divorce.
Clear Thinking	People with serious problems communicating might divorce.

You also need to consider whether the causes combine to contribute to a situation or whether one cause logically precedes another, like in a chain reaction. Keep in mind that the causes that contribute to a situation might not be causally related to one another. In the following example, the causes (lack of exercise, a high-fat diet, and smoking) do not share a cause/effect relationship with one another. However, all three factors can lead to heart disease.

More Than One Cause

Cause ⇒
Cause ⇒ ⇒ ⇒ Effect
Cause ⇒

↪ Example

Lack of exercise ⇒
High-fat diet ⇒ ⇒ ⇒ Heart disease
Smoking ⇒

Chain Reaction

In a chain reaction, one event happens, which causes another event. The second event in turn causes a third event. The chain of events continues until the cycle stops. For more information on chain reactions, see page 215 in this chapter.

Cause ⇒ Effect ⇒ Cause ⇒ Effect ⇒ Cause ⇒ Effect
   (X happens, which leads to Y, which causes Z)

↪ Example

   ⇒ Smoke enters the bloodstream.

    ⇒ Smoke burns holes in the arteries.

     ⇒ The holes fill up with fat.

      ⇒ The arteries eventually get clogged (completely fill up with fat).

       ⇒ Due to this, the blood cannot get to the heart.

        ⇒ A heart attack occurs.

Familiarity

Another way to order causes is to rank them by level of familiarity. The most familiar (common or dominant) cause is usually listed first. The least known cause is listed last.

↪ Example

    I. Thesis: Some students cheat for several reasons.
   II. The most obvious reason is to get good grades.
 III. Another common cause of cheating is laziness.
 IV. Finally, students cheat because they think no one will care if they do.

Classification/Categorization

Finally, you can classify the causes by category. Classification is a common method of organization in academic writing. In this method, the writer sorts through information and organizes it into categories (groups) according to the characteristics the different types (or kinds) of information have in common. To complete this process logically, the writer needs to name the categories by identifying the principle that defines the relationships between the pieces of information. In other words, the writer needs a "principle of classification."

For example, in the paper "Burnout in the Healthcare Sector," the writer organized the causes of burnout according to the relationship of each factor to the healthcare workers (principle of classification). Some information seemed to relate to the personal lives of the healthcare workers, while other information did not. The writer discovered that the information could be classified into two categories: internal (personal) and external (work-related).

The writer also set up two clearly distinctive categories; there was no overlap (factors that existed in both categories). There would be overlap, for example, if the writer used the following three categories: personal causes, work-related causes, and job-related causes. The second and third categories would more than likely have had the same causes. Similarly, the writer sorted the information logically into each category. That is, all the personal factors were separate from the work-related categories. An example of illogical classification would be if the writer listed personality and level of education as work-related causes, or changes in the system and financial problems at the company with personal causes.

ⒹⒾⓈⒸⓄⓋⒺⓇⓎ
7.6: Ordering causes

Imagine you are going to write a paper about the causes of stress in general. How would you organize and order the causes of stress?
- Using the stress test from Discovery 7.3, brainstorm in small groups on ways to order the causes of stress.
- Use one of the following possible approaches or one of your own.
- Report to the class.

    <u>Possible Approaches</u>
    Classification of causes (types, kinds, factors)
    Ranking of importance (least to most stressful)
    Familiarity (most common to nonnative speakers)
    Chain reaction (one thing leads to another; a cycle)

Framing the Essay of Cause

Once you have your MAP points, you need to design the thesis statement and write the topic sentences. Follow the rules you learned in Chapter 4, except use terms for causal analysis to indicate the method of development. These terms include *cause, reason,* and *factor.* There may also be a verb of cause, such as *contribute to, lead to,* or *result in.* The following patterns can be used for thesis statements, MAPS, and topic sentences in a causal essay.

Thesis Statement Patterns

In the thesis, enumerate (list) the causes in the order that you have determined to be the best for your purpose.

There are several causes of (reasons for) _____, including X, Y, and Z.
(EFFECT)   *(MAP POINTS)*

A number of factors contribute to _____, including X, Y and Z.
(EFFECT)   *(MAP POINTS)*

Note in the following examples that the terms for causal analysis are the subjects of the statements and that the effects are stated as objects. The actual causes are given in the MAP

➩ Examples

There are several causes of heart disease, including lack of exercise, a high-fat diet, and smoking.
(EFFECT)   *(MAP POINTS)*

A number of factors cause heart disease, including lack of exercise, a high-fat diet, and smoking.
(EFFECT)   *(MAP POINTS)*

Topic Sentence Patterns

In each topic sentence, use a transition, a term for causal analysis, and the appropriate MAP point.

One cause of _____ is _____ .
(EFFECT)   *(CAUSE)*

Another/The second/third/final reason/cause/factor is _____ .
(CAUSE)

In addition to _____, _____ can cause mental illness.
(OLD CAUSE)   *(NEW CAUSE)*   *(EFFECT)*

Note the word order and placement of the effects in the following examples. Also, notice that you can repeat old paragraph topics as transitions to a new topic.

➩ Examples

One cause of mental illness is genetics.
(EFFECT)   *(CAUSE)*

Another cause is chemical imbalances in the brain.
(CAUSE)

In addition to genetics, chemical imbalances in the brain play a role in the development of
(OLD CAUSE)   *(NEW CAUSE)*

mental illness.
(EFFECT)

🅓🅘🅢🅒🅞🅥🅔🅡🅨

7.7: Identifying and ordering causes

• On a separate sheet of paper, brainstorm on the following topics. Determine relevant causes.
• Order the causes logically.
• Write thesis statements, MAPS, and topic sentences to show your order.

Topics
Causes of Student Failure
Reasons for Urbanization
Causes of a Social Problem in Your Country

⤳ Examples

> I. Thesis: A number of factors contribute to heart disease.
> II. One cause of heart disease is lack of exercise.
> III. The second major cause is a high-fat diet.
> IV. The most significant cause is smoking.

Out-Of-Class Writing Assignment

- Choose one of the following topics for an essay of cause.
- Write an outline and first draft.
- Then use Peer Review Form 13 from Appendix D to evaluate the first draft.

Topics

1. Use your notes from Journal Entry 25 and Discoveries 7.1 and 7.3 to write about the common causes of stress among nonnative speakers. Focus on three major causes. Provide convincing examples, details, and personal experience (your own or that of others).
2. Do you know anyone who has dropped out of school? One study reported that 40% of freshmen drop out of (leave) college. Discuss three major reasons that you think so many students drop out during their first year of college. Provide convincing examples, details, and personal experience. Use your notes from Discovery 7.7.
3. Choose another topic from Discovery 7.7. Focus on three major causes. Provide convincing examples and details.

Analysis of effect

How can students prevent stress and burnout?

You have explored the causes of stress and burnout in school. How can students prevent getting stressed out (or burned out)? Discuss two or three things students can do to relax. Provide specific examples and details, including personal experience (your own or that of others). [600-700 words, every other line]

In the first part of this chapter, you learned how to determine and order logical causes and how to frame essays of cause. You also learned the importance of thinking logically and giving comprehensive coverage to the causal analysis. The same critical-thinking skills apply to the analysis of effects.

Determining Effects

An analysis of effects involves determining the results (or consequences) of an event or situation. These consequences must logically follow the event or situation in order for the relationship to be considered causal. Therefore, it is important to avoid post-host thinking when searching for effects. For example, advertisers use post-hoc thinking to sell products by appealing to your emotions instead of your common sense. They want to convince you to believe that if you buy their product, such as a new motorcycle, you are going to be a "cool" person or have a more exciting life. However, the logical result is that you have a new means of transportation.

➡ **Examples**

Post-hoc thinking:	If you buy this motorcycle, you will be "cool" and have a more exciting life.
Logical thinking:	If you buy this motorcycle, you will have a new means of transportation.

To avoid faulty thinking, consider that there may be more than one effect; do not oversimplify by stating only the most obvious effects. Consult a number of sources on the topic in order to become more informed on the range of effects.

➡ **Examples**

Simplification of effects:	As a result of smoking, people get cancer.
A range of effects:	According to the Academy of Family Physicians, smoking can lead to cancer, heart disease, strokes, emphysema, ulcers, gum disease, high blood pressure, smoker's cough, sore throat, and decreased athletic ability.

Ordering Effects

The rules for ordering effects are the same as those for causes; the only difference is that the focus is on effects. First, effects can be ordered by importance, as the following example of descending order illustrates.

➡ **Example**

    I. Thesis: Violent tornadoes cause devastating to incredible damage.
    II. The worst effect of violent tornadic storms is loss of life.
    III. Second, violent tornadoes cause extensive property damage.
    IV. Finally, violent tornadoes can also impact the economy of the areas they strike.

You can also order effects in a chain reaction, but make sure to supply all the steps in the chain of events in order to present a logical analysis. Third, effects can also be ordered according to familiarity. Begin with the most familiar effect.

➡ **Example**

    I. Thesis: People with the flu sometimes experience complications.
    II. The most common complication is a bacterial infection.
    III. Problems can occur with inflamed sinuses, bronchi (the two main branches that lead to the lungs), muscles, or ears.
    IV. Finally, nonbacterial diseases, which are less common but still very serious, can also occur.

Finally, the same rules you learned for classifying causes apply to classifying effects. One way to classify effects is to organize the effects into logical categories, such as internal and external. Another way is to determine when the effects occur. Thus, the principle of classification is chronological order. In other words, do the effects occur right away (immediate effects) or do they occur later (remote effects)? In order to be accurate and logical, it is important to consider whether the effects are immediate or remote. To practice these two classification methods, complete the following Discovery exercises.

ⒹⒾⓈⒸⓄⓋⒺⓇⓎ
7.8: Ordering effects using classification

- Read the following passage from Pattie Malone's paper, "Burnout in the Healthcare Sector."
- How does the author classify the effects (symptoms) of stress? On a separate sheet of paper, make a small chart illustrating the author's method of classification.

How Can Human Resources Management Prevent Burnout?

1   In order to prevent burnout, it is important to first recognize its symptoms. Because burnout is the result of chronic stress, the symptoms of burnout are very similar to the symptoms of stress. These symptoms can be divided into individual and organizational symptoms. The individual symptoms of burnout are cynicism, physical and psychological deterioration, depression, irritability, and a

5   growing dislike of people. A person need not exhibit all of these symptoms to be experiencing burnout. The organizational symptoms of burnout are a change in work performance, such as reduced productivity, high absenteeism, low morale, high turnover, and increased worker's compensation claims for mental stress injuries (Maslach, 1982; Sweenay, 1992).

ⒹⒾⓈⒸⓄⓋⒺⓇⓎ
7.9: Ordering immediate and remote effects

What are the effects of windstorms?
- On a separate sheet of paper, list the general effects of windstorms.
- Then order them according to when they occur: as immediate effects and as remote effects.

ⒹⒾⓈⒸⓄⓋⒺⓇⓎ
7.10: Analyzing a model essay classifying effects

- Read the following model essay on tornadoes.
- Then answer the Discussion Questions that follow.

The Kinds of Tornadoes and Their Effects

1   Tornadoes are violent twisting windstorms that can accompany thunderstorms. The word "tornado" comes from two Spanish words, *tronada,* meaning "thunderstorm," and *tornar,* meaning "to turn" (Henson 26). More than 1,000 tornadoes strike the U.S. annually, killing or injuring hundreds and causing millions of dollars in property damage. Tornadoes are classified according to the

5   severity of the tornadic storm (or its rank) as defined on the Fujita Wind-Damage Scale: weak, strong, and violent.
      The weakest tornadoes, classified as F0 and F1 on the Fujita scale, cause light to moderate damage. The annual frequency of weak tornadoes is 65%. Weak tornadoes cause approximately 1% to 3% of the tornado deaths annually. F0 tornadoes, the weakest yet most common type of

10   tornado, cause light damage. Approximately 600 to 700 F0s touch down each year. Huge G. Crowther, a meteorologist with the National Severe Storms Forecast Center in Kansas City, Missouri, reports that in 1994, for instance, there were 698 F0 tornadoes (1995, 45). With wind speeds of up to 72 miles per hour, F0s can tear branches off trees and knock down billboards and chimneys, according to the Fujita scale (45). The F0 tornado that touched down in Sandflat, Texas,

15   on January 4, 1993, the first tornado of the year, only damaged a mobile home and three houses (1994, 28). Although weak, F0 tornadoes can kill. The one that hit Littlefork, Maine, on August 9, 1993, killed 2 people (33).
      The second type of weak tornado is the F1 tornado, which causes moderate damage, according to the Fujita scale. Approximately 200 to 300 (or 25%) of the tornadoes that occur annually are F1

20   tornadoes. In 1995, 263 F1 tornadoes hit various states (Crowther 45). On the average, injuries

due to F1s tend to be low. In 1993, for example, F1s caused only 4 injuries (1994, 33). According to the Fujita scale, F1 tornadoes have wind speeds of anywhere from 72 to 112 miles per hour. Such tornadoes can tear the surface off roofs of houses, demolish garages that are attached to houses, and dislodge or push around mobile homes. Crowther reports that an F1 tornado traveling down a 1½-mile path in Chester County, Pennsylvania on June 9, 1993, killed a man in Caln when a tree fell on his car (31). Another F1 that hit Marshall County, Minnesota, on June 26, 1991 caused two million dollars worth of damage (Leftwich, Wilson, Crowther 31).

Next in rank of severity on the Fujita scale are F2 and F3 (strong) tornadoes, which cause significant to severe damage. Approximately 7% of tornadoes per year are strong tornadoes, which cause approximately 33% of all tornado deaths per year. The first type of strong tornado is the F2. There are approximately 80 to 100 F2 tornadoes per year, which represents 4% of the national average. Traveling with wind speeds from 113 to 157 miles per hour, F2s can rip trees out of the ground or break them in two, tear roofs off houses, demolish mobile homes, and tip over train cars, according to the Fujita scale. To illustrate, a swarm of F2s in Kansas and Oklahoma on April 26, 1991 damaged 17 homes, a garden center, and several farm houses (Leftwich, Wilson, Crowther 26). Also, on April 30, 1994, at Pond Bank, Pennsylvania, an F2 injured 2 people and electrocuted 15 cows. According to one eyewitness, "The fence illuminated like a heating element in a toaster" (Crowther 1995, 45). Another F2 hitting Cedarville, Georgia, in 1994 sucked a man out of a closet and threw him a thousand yards. Fortunately he survived (46).

F3 tornadoes, the second kind of strong tornado, are severe storms. Their frequency is low: 3% of all tornadoes per year. More injuries in 1994 were due to F3s than F2s, 207 as opposed to 61 (49). These tornadoes have wind speeds from 158 to 206 miles per hour. Thus, F3s can tear off roofs and walls from well-built houses, turn trains over, throw cars around, and pull most trees in a forest out by the roots, according to the Fujita scale. One such tornado touched down in March, 1994 in Dawsonville, Georgia. Traveling at 44 miles per hour on a 1½-mile-wide path, it killed 3 people and injured 45. It also killed half a million chickens, uprooted hundreds of thousands of trees, and caused $17 million worth of damage (45). Another F3 at Dahlonega, Georgia traveled 23 miles on a ¾-mile-wide path, killing 3 and injuring 15. It caused $3 million worth of damage. One eyewitness reports, "I had just enough time to get my little girl, who was in her bed, and run to the interior hallway, where we all crouched on the floor." Within a few minutes, the hallway was all that remained of the house (45).

The most dangerous and frightening tornadoes are the violent F4 and F5 tornadoes, or killer tornadoes, which cause devastating to incredible damage. Although only up to 0.5% of the tornadoes recorded per year are violent, these tornadoes cause approximately 70% of the tornado fatalities per year. Fairly infrequent (5 or 6 occur annually), F4s have wind speeds of 207 to 260 miles per hour and cause devastating damage. They can completely demolish well-built homes and turn large objects (like cars) into missiles. According to Crowther, an F4 that hit Lancaster, Texas on April 25, 1994, killed 3, injured 48, and caused $50 million worth of damage. Another hit Lafayette, Indiana on April 26, 1994, killing 3, injuring 70, and causing $3 million worth of damage (1995, 49). One attack by a killer F4 occurred on Palm Sunday in 1994. The actual storm spawned 27 tornadoes in Alabama, Georgia, and the Carolinas, killing 40 and injuring more than 350. The worst of these tornadoes was an F4, which hit a church during a Palm Sunday service, killing 20 and injuring 92. It also tore the roof of the church off, collapsed brick walls, and broke a window, all within 20 seconds. One woman said that the church seemed to "fold in" and that she thought the altar saved her life (44).

F5 tornadoes are the most destructive type of killer tornadoes, causing incredible damage. They are very rare; only 1 or 2 tornadoes per year are F5s. The wind speeds are over 260 miles per hour. These black monsters can pick up large, well-built houses off their foundations, carry them away, and smash them to bits. Moreover, they can take the bark off trees and cause considerable damage to steel-reinforced structures, according to the Fujita scale. One F5 left 17 dead and 225 injured after hitting Wichita and Andover, Kansas on April 26, 1991 (Leftwich, Wilson and Crowther, 32). The worst case of an F5, and the worst recorded outbreak of tornadoes in history, is now remembered as Jumbo (or Super) Outbreak, which occurred on April 3, 1974. According to an article in <u>Weatherwise</u>, three parallel squall lines with winds over 260 miles per hour spawned 148 tornadoes with combined paths of 2,000 miles or more, extending from Mississippi to Michigan. These tornadoes lasted 18 hours on the ground, causing 309 fatalities and 5,000 injuries. The F5 swept away homes and trailers, threw a minibus over a bridge, and destroyed nearly half the town of Xenia, Ohio, leaving half of the 25,000 residents homeless (JR 58-9).

80   In conclusion, regardless of strength, all tornadoes can kill, injure, and cause property damage. Such storms are not to be taken lightly. Although fascinating to watch, even the weakest tornado can be an enemy to anything in its path. As one eyewitness said after a tornado hit his Kansas town, "We don't take anything for granted anymore, and we watch the weather like the back of our hand. We watch it day and night."

(qtd. in Weatherwise, February/March, 1992, 29, from Kansas Storms: Destruction, Tragedy, and Recovery, 1991. Diane Silver, editor. Hearth Publishing: Hillsboro, Kansas) [1,315 words] (Barbara Leonhard, American)

Bibliography

Crowther, Huge G. "Tornadoes Hit New Heights: Weather of 1992." Weatherwise Feb./Mar. 1993: 29–37.

_____. "Tornadoes: Weather of 1993." Weatherwise Feb./Mar. 1994: 28–35.

_____. "Tornadoes: Weather of 1994." Weatherwise Feb./Mar. 1995: 43–51.

Henson, Robert. "Piece by Piece." Weatherwise Apr./May 1995: 25–30.

JR. "The Jumbo Outbreak." Weatherwise Je./Jul 1995: 58–59.

Leftwich, Preston W., Larry F. Wilson, and Huge G. Crowther. "Tornadoes: Record Pace Continues." Weatherwise Feb./Mar. 1992: 23–33.

Rawlinson, Howard E. "Tornado." American Heritage Feb./Mar. 1995: 42–45.

Ⓠ Discussion Questions

Use the previous essay to answer the following questions.

1. What are the major kinds of tornadoes? What are the subclasses?
2. What is the writer's principle of classification?
3. What are the effects of each type of tornado? Why are the effects different in each category?
4. What kind of tornado is the most common?
5. Does the previous model essay focus more on immediate or remote effects? Why?

Framing the Effect Essay

Framing an essay of effect is very similar to framing an essay of cause. Special terminology is also used to state effects. In the following thesis statement patterns, notice that the terms for stating effects include nouns such as *effects* and *symptoms* and verbs such as *produce, benefit,* and *affect.* Moreover, in a thesis statement for an essay of effect, the effects are listed in a logical order as the MAP points. The cause is stated before the effects either as the subject of the sentence or as an object of a preposition.

Thesis Statement Patterns

There are several effects of _____, such as X, Y, and Z.
                                      (CAUSE)   *(EFFECTS/MAP POINTS)*

_____ benefit(s)/affect(s) (someone or something) in many ways, including X, Y, and Z.
         (CAUSE)   *(EFFECTS/MAP POINTS)*

_____ produce(s) several symptoms, including X, Y, and Z.
         (CAUSE)   *(EFFECTS/MAP POINTS)*

☞ Examples

Burnout produces several symptoms, including fatigue, irritability, and depression.
(CAUSE)   *(EFFECTS/MAP POINTS)*

Aerobic exercise benefits people physically and mentally.
    (CAUSE)   *(EFFECTS/MAP POINTS)*

Topic Sentence Patterns

With topic sentences, use a transition, a term such as *effect*, *result*, or *symptom*, and a MAP point to introduce each effect in the body of the essay. It is also possible to restate a previous MAP point as a transition to a new MAP point.

I. Thesis: Aerobic exercise benefits people in many ways. It contributes to higher muscle density, weight loss, and an increased sense of emotional well-being.
II. One effect of aerobic exercise is higher muscle density.
III. Not only does aerobic exercise lead to higher muscle density, but it also results in weight loss.
IV. Finally, aerobic exercise contributes to an increased sense of emotional well-being.

ⒹⒾⓈⒸⓄⓋⒺⓇⓎ
7.11: Determining and ordering effects

- Brainstorm on the effects of each of the following topics, using one of the approaches listed or one of your own.
- Organize the effects logically.
- Write thesis statements, MAPS, and topic sentences to demonstrate your order.

Possible Approaches
Classification of effects (kinds, types, symptoms, benefits)
Ranking of importance (least to most severe/important effects, symptoms, benefits)
Familiarity (most common/obvious effects, benefits, symptoms)
Chain reaction (one thing leads to another; cycle)

Topics
Effects of Urbanization
Effects of Forcing Children to Do Things That Do Not Interest Them
Effects of a Social Problem in Your Country

Out-Of-Class Writing Assignment

- Choose one of the following topics for an essay of effect.
- Write an outline and a first draft.
- Use Peer Review Form 13 from Appendix D to evaluate the first draft.

1. Some parents think the best way to influence their children is to negotiate and be encouraging. Other parents use pressure on their children, forcing them to do things. Which position do you prefer? Why is it better? Discuss three major effects of the approach you prefer. Provide convincing specific examples, details, and personal experience (your own or that of others).
2. The trend in most countries is to move away from rural areas into the cities. What effects does this have on either the rural areas or the urban areas? Choose one. Discuss three major effects. Provide convincing specific examples and details.
3. Using your notes from Discovery 7.8 and Journal Entry 27, apply what you have learned about the effects of stress and burnout. What are three effects of stress on college students? Provide convincing specific examples, details, and personal experience (your own or that of others).

Structures of Cause

In this section, you will learn how to form and use various structures of cause and effect. Many of the structures are complex, but if you can master a variety of them, your style will improve. The structures of cause include verbs (which describe the causal action), phrases (which contain nouns and modifiers), and clauses (which contain subjects and verbs).

Verbs of Cause

There are two types of verbs of cause. In each group, the cause is stated first as a subject, and the effect follows the verb as the object. The subjects and objects can be either singular or plural. Moreover, the sentences do not contain any inside punctuation. Note that the two verb groups have different structures.

Noun phrase (cause) + verb of cause + noun phrase (effect)

With this type of verb of cause, both the cause and effect are stated as noun phrases. Note that some of the verbs are followed by prepositions.

cause (*NOUN PHRASE*)	contributes to results in leads to produces is responsible for is the reason for	effect (*NOUN PHRASE*)

↪ Examples

It has been firmly established that smoking contributes to heart disease.
                                         (*CAUSE*)   (*VERB*)   (*EFFECT*)

Tornadoes cause a great deal of damage.
(*CAUSE*)   (*VERB*)   (*EFFECT*)

Noun phrase (cause) + *cause* + noun phrase (indirect object) + infinitive (effect)

With this type of verb of cause, the cause is stated as a noun phrase, but the effect is stated as an infinitive phrase. An indirect object follows the verb and is considered part of the result.

Noun phrase   causes   noun phrase (someone or something)   to do something.
(*CAUSE*)   (*VERB*)   (*INDIRECT OBJECT*)   (*INFINITIVE*)

↪ Examples

Poor parenting does not cause people to become mentally ill.
    (*CAUSE*)   (*VERB*)   (*INDIRECT*   (*INFINITIVE*)
                                         OBJECT)

Overwork and emotional exhaustion may cause healthcare professionals to burn out.
              (*CAUSE*)   (*VERB*)   (*INDIRECT OBJECT*)   (*INFINITIVE*)

Phrases of Cause

Causes can be stated in phrases beginning with *because of, due to, owing to, as a result of,* and *as a consequence of.* The phrases can either begin the sentence or follow the main clause. Use a comma after a phrase that begins the sentence. If the phrase follows the main clause, do not use a comma. Note that all of the following structures have prepositions.

Because of _____ , _____ .
Due to _____ , _____ .
Owing to _____ , _____ .
As a result of _____ , _____ .
As a consequence of _____ , _____ .
          (*CAUSE/NOUN PHRASE*)   (*EFFECT/MAIN CLAUSE*)

⇨ **Examples**

Because of strong winds, tornadoes <u>destroy everything in their path</u>.
    (PHRASE OF CAUSE)   *(EFFECT)*

Healthcare professionals <u>tend to burn out</u> <u>due to internal and external factors</u>.
                          (EFFECT)   *(PHRASE OF CAUSE)*

Clauses of Cause

Causes can also be stated in independent clauses beginning with *because, since, as*, and *inasmuch as*. All of these subordinators have the same meaning as because. The most formal subordinator in this group is *inasmuch as*. Other subordinators such as *if* and *when* can be used to show cause. An *if* clause (an adverb clause of condition) states a possible condition, and the main clause of the sentence states the result.

⇨ **Example**

If the river rises much higher, <u>the crops will be flooded</u>.
      (CONDITION)   *(EFFECT)*

When is a time subordinator that means "at the same time." Sentences that contain sequential actions and *when* describe a cause/effect relationship.

⇨ **Example**

When the sun radiates heat, <u>evaporation occurs</u>.
      (CAUSE)   *(EFFECT)*

Because _____ , _____ .
Since _____ , _____ .
Due to the fact that _____ , _____ .
              (CAUSE/DEPENDENT CLAUSE)   *(EFFECT/MAIN CLAUSE)*

<u>Because healthcare professionals are exposed to a number of emotionally demanding situations for long</u>
                                           (CAUSE)
<u>periods of time</u>, <u>burnout is common in the healthcare sector</u>.
                (EFFECT)

<u>Burnout is common in the healthcare sector</u> <u>because healthcare professionals are exposed to a</u>
          (EFFECT)   *(CAUSE)*
<u>number of emotionally demanding situations for long periods of time</u>.

⒟⒤⒮⒞⒪⒱⒠⒭⒴

7.12: Stating causes

Fill in each blank with a correct structure of cause. For some sentences, there is more than one acceptable answer.

⇨ **Example**

Overexposure to extremely cold temperatures can *cause* people to get hypothermia.

1. People can get hypothermia .... they are overexposed to extremely cold temperatures.

2. People can get hypothermia .... overexposure to extremely cold temperatures.

3. Overexposure to extremely cold temperatures can .... hypothermia.

4. Children develop teeth that resist decay .... the fluoridation of water.

5. Fewer children get cavities .... fluorides are added to the city water.

6. The jet streams (extremely strong winds at certain high altitudes) have great importance to aviation .... they affect the speeds of high-altitude flights.

7. .... the effects of the jet streams on the speed of high-altitude flights, these extremely strong winds have great importance to aviation.

8. .... the differences in temperature and humidity between air masses, storms develop.

9. Storms develop .... the differences in temperature and humidity between air masses.

10. Storms occur .... there are differences in temperature and humidity between air masses.

STRUCTURES OF EFFECT

The structures of effect include connectors, verbs, adjective clauses, and participial phrases. This section will also include an explanation of and an exercise on using chain reactions as a structure of effect.

Connectors

The connectors for effect are *as a result, consequently, therefore,* and *thus.* These transition words always occur between the sentences stating the cause and effect. Usually a period is used after the statement of cause, and the connector begins the next sentence. A semicolon can be used instead of a period. In this case, do not capitalize the connector. A comma follows the connector.

The word order for causal sentences with connectors is always the same.

Sentence (cause) + connector + sentence (effect)

	As a result,	
_____ .	Consequently,	_____ .
(CAUSE/SENTENCE)	Therefore,	*(EFFECT/SENTENCE)*
	Thus,	

⇨ Examples

Healthcare professionals are burned out. Consequently, they are cynical and irritable.
     (CAUSE)   *(EFFECT)*

More brain research is being conducted; thus, we know more about mental illness.
     (CAUSE)   *(EFFECT)*

Verbs of Effect

Sentences with verbs of effect are formed the same way as those for verbs of cause. Phrases precede and follow the verb of effect; however, the effect is stated as the subject, and the cause is stated as the object. Another difference is that while the verb *cause* is used in the active voice as a verb of cause, it is used in the passive voice as a verb of effect. However, *cause* is the only verb of effect that is in the passive voice. Note, also, that prepositions accompany the verbs of effect. Finally, just as with verbs of cause, verbs of effect can be singular or plural.

Noun phrase (effect) + verb of effect + noun phrase (cause)

Effect	results from	Cause
	is a/the result of	
	is a/the consequence of	
(Noun Phrase)	is caused by	(Noun Phrase)
	is an/the effect of	
	follows from	
	is due to	

⇨ Examples

<u>Death and destruction</u> <u>result from</u> <u>even the weakest tornadoes</u>.
        (Effects)   *(Verb)*   *(Cause)*

<u>The major mental illnesses</u> <u>are caused by</u> <u>biological factors</u>.
        (Effect)   *(Verb)*   *(Causes)*

ⓓⓘⓢⓒⓞⓥⓔⓡⓨ
7.13: **Stating causes and effects**

A.

- Write the noun form of each of the following verbs. (In some cases, the noun form is the same as the verb form or there is more than one noun form.)
- Then use the nouns to complete Part B. The first one is done for you.

1. evaporate ....*evaporation*............

2. form ....

3. rise ....

4. cool ....

5. condense ....

6. fall ....

7. precipitate ....

8. absorb ....

9. flow ....

10. radiate ....

B.
- Combine each of the following pairs of statements into one sentence, using the correct form of the words and phrases in parentheses. The cause is stated first.
- Make the necessary grammatical changes.
- Use correct subject-verb agreement. Only the base verbs are given.
- You will be using both cause and effect verbs, as well as other structures of cause and effect.

⇨ **Example**

The sun radiates heat; seawater evaporates.

(result from) *The evaporation of seawater results from the sun's radiation of heat.*

(as a result) *The sun radiates heat. As a result, seawater evaporates.*

(as a result of) *As a result of the sun's radiation of heat, seawater evaporates.*

1. Seawater evaporates; water vapor is formed.

   (due to) ....

   (be due to) ....

   (because) ....

2. Water vapor rises and cools; it condenses.

   (consequently) ....

   (contribute to) ....

   (result from)..

3. Vapor condenses; clouds are formed.

   (follow from) ....

   (cause) ....

   (because of) ....

4. Clouds move over high land; air temperature falls.

   (cause X to) ....

   (be the consequence of) ....

   (consequently) ....

5. Air temperature falls; rain is precipitated.

   (be due to) ....

   (cause) ....

   (due to) ....

6. Rain is precipitated, and it is absorbed by the soil; water flows back to the sea.

   (eventually lead to) ....

   (result from) ....

   (because) ....

Adjective Clauses of Effect

Nonrestrictive adjective clauses can be used to state effects. The main clause states the cause. The verb in the adjective clause is the singular form of a verb of cause, and the adjective clause is always preceded by a comma. Use *which,* not *that,* to introduce the adjective clause.

X happens, which causes/leads to/causes Y.
(CAUSE; ACTION 1)   *(EFFECT; ACTION 2)*

➱ Examples

Health professionals overwork, which results in stress.
    (CAUSE, ACTION 1)   *(EFFECT, ACTION 2)*

Some health professionals develop chronic stress, which leads to burnout.
        (CAUSE, ACTION 1)   *(EFFECT, ACTION 2)*

Ⓓ Ⓘ Ⓢ Ⓒ Ⓞ Ⓥ Ⓔ Ⓡ Ⓨ

7.14: **Stating effects with adjective clauses**

- Combine each pair of statements into one sentence, using an adjective clause that includes the correct form of the word or phrase in parentheses.
- Make the necessary grammatical changes.

➱ Example

The sun radiates heat; seawater evaporates. (lead to)

The sun radiates heat, which leads to the evaporation of seawater.

1. Seawater evaporates; water vapor is formed. (contribute to)

2. Water vapor rises and cools; it condenses. (result in)

3. Vapor condenses; clouds are formed. (cause)

4. Clouds move over high land; air temperature falls. (cause X to)

5. Air temperature falls; rain is precipitated. (produce)

6. Rain is precipitated, and it is absorbed by the soil; water flows back to the sea. (eventually lead to)

Participial Phrases of Effect

An adjective clause used to state effect can be changed to a participial phrase. Delete *which* and change the verb to the present participle.

⇨ **Examples**

Health professionals overwork, which results in stress.

<u>Health professionals overwork</u>, resulting in <u>stress</u>.
      (Cause, Action 1)   *(Effect, Action 2)*

Some health professionals develop chronic stress, which leads to burnout.

<u>Some health professionals develop chronic stress</u>, leading to <u>burnout</u>.
      (Cause, Action 1)   *(Effect, Action 2)*

⒟⒤⒮⒞⒪⒱⒠⒭⒴
7.15: Stating effects in participial phrases

- Combine each pair of statements into one sentence, using the present participle of the word or phrase in parentheses.
- Make the necessary grammatical changes.

⇨ **Example**

The sun radiates heat; seawater evaporates.

The sun radiates heat, leading to the evaporation of seawater.

1. Seawater evaporates; water vapor is formed. (contribute to)

   ....

2. Water vapor rises and cools; it condenses. (result in)

   ....

3. Vapor condenses; clouds are formed. (cause)

   ....

4. Clouds move over high land; air temperature falls. (cause X to)

   ....

5. Air temperature falls; rain is precipitated. (produce)

   ....

6. Rain is precipitated, and it is absorbed by the soil; water flows back to the sea. (eventually lead to)

   ....

   ....

Chain Reactions

A chain reaction is a string of causes and effects linked together. An event happens, which causes something else to happen. This in turn leads to another event, and either the cycle (e.g., water cycle or food chain) continues or the cycle ends. Following is part of the chain reaction involved in the greenhouse effect.

The Greenhouse Effect

➡ The atmosphere lets in the sunlight to heat the earth's surface.

➡ The sun's rays pass back through the lower atmosphere.

➡ The heat is easily absorbed by the water vapor and carbon dioxide.

➡ The heat is trapped inside the atmosphere (the greenhouse effect).

➡ The carbon dioxide traps more and more sunlight.

➡ The air temperature rises.

➡ Changes in climate patterns occur.

➡ The earth's major climate zones shift.

➡ Rainfall patterns change.

⒟ⒾⓈⒸⓄⓋⒺⓇⓎ
7.16:   Stating chain reactions

- Combine each of the following sets of statements into one sentence that describes a chain reaction, using the first word or phrase in parentheses and ending each sentence with an adjective clause.
- Then rewrite the sentence, this time ending it in a participial phrase by changing the adjective clause to a participial phrase that contains the second verb listed.

↪ Examples

The carbon dioxide traps sunlight ➡ the air temperature rises ➡ climate patterns change.
            (*CAUSE X TO*)   (*PRODUCE*)

The trapping of sunlight by carbon dioxide <u>causes</u> the air temperature <u>to rise, which produces</u> changes in climate patterns.

The trapping of sunlight by carbon dioxide <u>causes</u> the air temperature <u>to rise, producing</u> changes in climate patterns.

1. Heat is radiated by the sun ➡ seawater evaporates ➡ water vapor is formed.
          (*LEAD TO*)   (*RESULT IN*)

    ....

    ....

2. The vapor rises and cools ➡ it condenses ➡ clouds are formed.
          (*CAUSE*)   (*CONTRIBUTE TO*)

    ....

    ....

3. The vapor condenses ➡ clouds are formed and move toward high land ➡ the temperature falls when
   (CAUSE X TO ___)   (EVENTUALLY LEAD TO)

   the clouds arrive over high land.

   ....

   ....

4. The temperature falls ➡ rain is precipitated and absorbed by the soil ➡ water flows back to the sea.
   (CAUSE X TO ___)   (RESULT IN)

   ....

   ....

D I S C O V E R Y
7.17: Reviewing cause/effect structures

- Combine each pair of phrases into one sentence, using one of the following structures of cause or effect.
- The cause is stated first.
- Do not use a structure more than two times. More than one paraphrase is possible for each pair.
- Pay attention to capitalization, punctuation, verb tense, and subject-verb agreement.

<u>Structures of Cause and Effect</u>

as a result	because	result from	cause	leading to
as a result of	causing	result in	be caused by	cause X to

➯ Example

Tornadoes ➡ Death and destruction

Tornadoes cause death and destruction.

Death and destruction result from tornadoes.

1. F5 tornadoes are very dangerous windstorms ➡ People must seek shelter immediately

   ....

   ....

2. Chasing tornadoes ➡ Injury and death

   ....

   ....

3. The winds in the storm rotate ➡ A funnel cloud forms

   ....

   ....

4. Flying debris ➡ Injuries and deaths

   ....

   ....

5. The Jumbo (Super) Outbreak in 1974 ➡ 309 fatalities and 5,000 injuries

....

....

6. Lightning hit a wire fence during an F2 tornadic storm ➡ The electrocution of fifteen cows

....

....

ⒹⒾⓈⒸⓄⓋⒺⓇⓎ
7.18: Reviewing cause/effect grammar

- Read the following model essay carefully.
- Supply the necessary transitions for cause/effect.
- Pay attention to punctuation and sentence structure.

The Causes of the Increasing Divorce Rate in the U.S.
by Yungjing Hsieh

The divorce rate in the world is increasing now, especially in the U.S. In 1985, for every four marriages, a divorce occurred. However, there was almost an equal number of marriages and divorces in the early 1990s. The reasons that the number of divorces is still growing are that people get married hastily, they spend too little time with their spouses, and divorce is more socially acceptable than it used to be.

....
                                                        (1)
Since their youth, they have had beautiful and romantic dreams of marriage. ....
                                                                                                 (2)
...., they may seek and look forward to meeting the husband or wife of their dreams. When they meet the ideal partner, they will most likely fall deeply into romantic love. People say love is blind. Indeed, by the time the two have become lovers, they have learned to overlook or tolerate each other's shortcomings and eagerly plan the happy and magical wedding day. After getting married, however, what they do wrong may be seen as big defects, which .... conflicts between the husband and wife. Married life is not as
                (3)
wonderful as they had thought it would be while they were dating. ....
                                                                                       (4)
the dreams are broken, the couple may start to feel disappointed with everything, ...
                                                                                                           (5)
.... them to want to end the relationship, and they often do.

....
                                                        (6)
This problem can build a big gap between them. They may develop different interests, different friends, and different careers in different cities. .... these differences,
                                                                                    (7)
they may start to disagree on many things. ...., they do not have
                                                                                  (8)
time to discuss their family plans, solve their life problems, and be comfortable with each other. In order for the marriage to succeed, both the husband and wife should share family obligations as well

as their happiness and sadness toward life. On the other hand, if each of them is set in his or her own ways and does not accept the other's opinion, the crises in the marriage will intensify simply .... (9) the husband and wife are not spending enough time talking to and compromising with each other. In addition, getting too busy working and, ... (10) , neglecting the family life may .... (11) a decrease in the devotion of the couple for each other. This neglect of the marriage itself often .... (12) divorce.

Not only do people divorce .... (13) they .... (14) .... and .... (15) , but they also choose divorce as a solution to their problems .... (16) divorce .... (17) .... Years ago, not only the couple but also their families felt shame .... (18) the divorce. Most people looked down on the divorced couple, especially on the wife. .... (19) the embarrassment and guilt, the married couple often thought twice about using divorce as a solution to their problems. The couple might have allowed more time to think about the problems deeply and resolved them. For example, both John and Sara were idealistic about marriage, and each of them had his or her own expectations about what marriage would be like. After a five-month romance, they married full of hope and unrealistic expectations. Nevertheless, soon after their wedding, their dreams were broken by the realities of married life. Although they were disappointed and had frequent quarrels, they did not divorce .... (20) they were afraid of being ostracized by society. Instead, they talked for a long time, thought deeply about their problems, and resolved their differences. They stayed together and became happier with their marriage. If this case had happened today, however, John and Sara may have simply gotten a divorce, and people would not have been at all surprised.

In conclusion, the increasing divorce rate may be the result of hasty decisions to marry, too little devotion to a relationship, and changes in social values. People should consider their future plans patiently and realistically. .... (21) , they will not make the end of the marriage a tragedy in their lives. Helen Rowland said, "Love, the quest; marriage, the conquest; divorce, the inquest." Indeed, people should emphasize the importance of marriage and stop turning to divorce as a solution. (Used with permission, Yungjing Hsieh, Taiwanese)

CHAPTER *summary*

- The cause/effect method (causal analysis) involves examining reasons (causes) or results (effects). Use the critical-thinking process to identify logical causes and effects. Avoid the post-hoc fallacy. Do not base the analysis on coincidences. Use current theories, facts, and findings to support the causal analysis. Choose expert opinion carefully because not all sources may be current or credible. Do not become too general or simplistic in your analysis. There is usually more than one cause or effect to consider.

- Order the causes and effects logically. Factors to consider include the relevance (or importance) and immediacy of the causes or effects; whether the causes or effects are part of a chain reaction; which causes or effects are the most familiar to the audience; and if the causes or effects can be classified into categories (kinds or types, symptoms, benefits).

- The structures of cause and effect can be classified into several groups: verbs, connectors, phrases (prepositional and participial), and clauses (adverb and adjective). With verbs of cause, state the cause first. With verbs of effect, state the effect first. State the causes and effects as phrases. With connectors, state the cause first. Remember that connectors join two complete sentences. Therefore, punctuate correctly. Use noun phrases after prepositions. For adjective clauses that state effects, use a comma before it and *which* (nonessential adjective clause). The verb in this kind of clause is singular. For participial adjective phrases, use the *-ing* form of the verb. The verb is in the active voice. Remember to omit *which*, but do not omit the comma.

- A chain reaction is a string of causes and effects linked together. Chain reactions are commonly used in the science disciplines to describe cycles. In the case of chain reactions, structures of cause and effect can be expressed as adjective clauses or participial phrases.

Chapter 8

Using Sources

CHAPTER TOPICS

- ▶ PLAGIARISM
- ▶ STATING ACKNOWLEDGMENTS
- ▶ PARAPHRASING
- ▶ SUMMARIZING
- ▶ DIRECT AND INDIRECT QUOTATION

What is cheating?

One thing we are taught at a very young age is not to cheat. What is cheating? Give examples and explain why we were taught that such behavior is bad. [700-800 words, every other line]

DISCOVERY

8.1: Discussing cheating in school

- In groups, discuss the following questions.
- Take notes on a separate sheet of paper.
- Report your findings to the class.

1. Why do some students cheat? List the reasons.
2. How do students cheat? List some examples of cheating behavior.
3. What are the consequences of cheating? List them.
4. Do professionals (e.g., professors and scientists) ever cheat? Why? How?
5. Have you ever heard of plagiarism? What is it?

PLAGIARISM

Plagiarism is a form of cheating that involves borrowing or paraphrasing ideas from another person without acknowledging the source. That is, plagiarism involves stealing from other people's published or unpublished outlines, paragraphs, essays, papers, or speeches. The plagiarized portion can be anywhere from one or two characteristic words to an entire document.

For example, you may not realize it, but you actually own all of the papers that you have written this semester. Therefore, if someone uses all or part of one of your papers without giving you credit for writing it, that person has plagiarized. Likewise, if you use another student's paper or written work of any kind (even short paragraph exercises) without proper acknowledgment, you are plagiarizing.

Plagiarism is a crime in many countries because of copyright laws. A copyright is one's ownership of a created work. Plagiarism is considered a serious matter, therefore, and students who plagiarize are reported and punished. Punishment can be in the form of a failing grade on the paper in question, a failing grade in the course, and/or expulsion from school. Similarly, a professional who plagiarizes can lose his or her job. If you are ever unsure of your work or how to handle a source, speak to your professor. You do not want to inadvertently plagiarize and risk a failing grade in a course and/or expulsion from school. It is your responsibility to learn how to use sources correctly. Your professors can recommend research style manuals designed for your major that explain how to acknowledge sources and use correct bibliographic form.

🅓🅘🅢🅒🅞🅥🅔🅡🅨
8.2: Identifying examples of plagiarism

Write an X next to each action that constitutes plagiarism.

1. .... inventing (making up, creating) content for a research paper

2. .... talking to another student during an exam

3. .... submitting a composition that was copied from someone else

4. .... paraphrasing from someone else's article without acknowledging the source

5. .... taking a test for someone else

6. .... falsifying research data

7. .... writing a composition using someone else's outline, opinions, or ideas

8. .... writing information (names, dates, mathematical formulas, and the like) on pieces of paper, articles of clothing, or parts of the body to refer to while taking a test

9. .... submitting for publication an article which was already published by someone else

10. .... looking at another person's answers on a test

STATING ACKNOWLEDGMENTS

To avoid plagiarism, you need to learn how to cite sources correctly. The discussion on citing sources will be in two parts. This section will cover methods for stating acknowledgments. Later in this chapter, rules for punctuating direct and indirect quotations will be discussed.

When citing sources, it is necessary to inform the reader about the authors and texts used in the research. Such statements, called acknowledgments, help clarify where one source ends and another source begins. They also help indicate which ideas are yours and which are from sources. Acknowledge both paraphrased and directly quoted information. It is not necessary to acknowledge well-known facts or common knowledge. However, whenever you use a source to get information, you must acknowledge the source. In order to state acknowledgments clearly and correctly, follow these guidelines.

Reporting Verbs

Use reporting verbs with direct and indirect quotations whether it is the first or subsequent mention of the source. The following chart lists suggestions for the use of reporting verbs. Note that when using reporting verbs to state theory or opinion in direct quotation, it is not necessary to shift tense from present to past if the information that is being stated is still accurate.

Fact	Theory/Opinion		Demonstration
say	claim	feel	indicate
report	argue	deny	point out
state	believe	maintain	show
	contend		

⇨ Example

Direct Quotation	In 1987, Dr. Benjamin Spock stated, "Children—especially young children—will pattern themselves after violent behavior just as readily as they will imitate good behavior."
Indirect Quotation	Many experts agree with Dr. Spock's claim that young children in particular are just as likely to imitate violent actions as they are nonviolent ones.

First Reference

Use one of the following patterns to introduce an indirect quotation (paraphrasing) the first time you use a source. Note that the main clause often contains a noun clause. The noun clauses are enclosed in brackets.

Pattern 1

According to (full name), _____ .
     (PHRASE)   *(MAIN CLAUSE)*

⇨ Example

According to Huge G. Crowther, there were 316 tornadoes in June of 1993.
     (PHRASE)   *(MAIN CLAUSE)*

Pattern 2

(Full name), (source and/or credentials), _____ .
    (ADJECTIVE CLAUSE OR PHRASE)   *(MAIN CLAUSE)*

⇨ Example

Huge G. Crowther, a meteorologist with the National Severe Storms Forecast Center in Kansas
  (FULL NAME)   *(SOURCE AND/OR CREDENTIALS IN THE FORM OF AN ADJECTIVE CLAUSE OR PHRASE)*

City, reports [that the tornado that hit Petersburg on August 6, 1993 caused 246 injuries] .
               (MAIN CLAUSE)

Pattern 3

According to an article in (name of magazine, journal, or paper), _____ .
                                            (Phrase)   *(Main Clause)*

☞ **Example**

According to an article in the 1994 Feb./Mar. issue of *Weatherwise*, the most devastating
                                    (Phrase)

tornado outbreak in history occurred on April 3, 1974.
                              (Main Clause)

Pattern 4

(Name of author is unknown.)
In an article in (name of magazine, journal, paper), it is reported [that _____] .
                              (Phrase)   *(Main Clause)*

☞ **Example**

In an article in the 1995 June/July issue of *Weatherwise*, it is reported [that the most
                                  (Phrase)   *(Main Clause)*

devastating tornado outbreak in history occurred on April 3, 1974] .

Subsequent Reference

After the first reference to an author, use the author's last name only, not the full name.

Pattern 1

(Author's last name) says/goes on to say [that _____] .
                                (Main Clause)

☞ **Example**

Crowther says/goes on to say/reports [that the deadliest tornado in 1993 was an F4 that hit
                              (Main Clause)
Tulsa, Oklahoma, killing 7 and injuring 100] .

Pattern 2

According to (author's last name), _____ .
                              (Phrase)   *(Main Clause)*

☞ **Example**

According to Crowther, the deadliest tornado in 1993 was an F4 that hit Tulsa, Oklahoma,
                  (Phrase)   *(Main Clause)*
killing 7 and injuring 100.

Pattern 3

Use this pattern if your paper contains more than one source by the same author and the author was already introduced earlier in the paper. Even though the source itself is being mentioned for the first time, do not reintroduce the author by his or her full name.

In (source), (author's last name) reports [that_____] .
   (PHRASE)   *(MAIN CLAUSE)*

⇨ **Example**

In the 1994 Feb./Mar. issue of *Weatherwise*, Crowther says [that the deadliest tornado in
          (PHRASE)   *(MAIN CLAUSE)*
1993 was an F4 that hit Tulsa, Oklahoma, killing 7 and injuring 100] .

It is not always necessary to mention the author's name and the title of the source if the information is factual. However, you must show the source of the information by using in-text documentation or a footnote.

⇨ **Example**

Full Acknowledgment	In an article in the 1995 June/July issue of *Weatherwise,* it is reported that the most devastating tornado outbreak in history occurred on April 3, 1974. (JR 58-9) [source of information]
Shortened Acknowledgment	The most devastating tornado outbreak in history occurred on April 3, 1974. (JR 58-9) [source of information]

PARAPHRASING

Paraphrasing involves restating in your own words the original wording in a source. The restatement must include careful word choices that fit the context and tone of the original passage. This is not always easy.

⇨ **Example**

Original	In order to find a suitable apartment, you must follow a very systematic approach.
Correct Paraphrase	If you want to locate an appropriate apartment, you have to complete the following steps carefully.
Incorrect Paraphrase	If you want to recover a suited apartment, you need to obey an organized access.

recover:	wrong word choice. Although "locate" and "recover" can also mean "to find," "recover" means more specifically "to find something that was lost."
suited:	wrong word choice. We can say that an apartment is "well-suited" or "appropriate" to someone, but not "suited," which means "clothed."
obey:	wrong word choice. We obey laws, rules, and parents, not steps.
access:	wrong word choice. Although one synonym of "approach" is "access," "approach" means "method" in this context.

There are several kinds of changes you can make to paraphrase a source. Do not use just one, however. To avoid plagiarism, it is best to make as many changes as possible to the original text. Moreover, as you use these methods, pay close attention to accuracy and grammar.

Using Synonyms

A word that has the same or a very similar meaning as another is a synonym. When paraphrasing, use a synonym or synonymous phrase that can occur in the same context as the original word or phrase used in the source. It should also have the same tone (level of formality) and contextual meaning as the original word or phrase. The previous example of finding a good apartment illustrates the problems that can occur if the word choices do not match the tone and context of the original passage.

↪ Example

Original Passage	Paraphrasing is hard to do without good examples.
Paraphrases	Paraphrasing is difficult/challenging/an ordeal if there are no effective examples to study.

         hard = difficult, challenging, an ordeal
         without good examples = if there are no effective examples to study

Original Passage	F5 tornadoes are very dangerous windstorms; as a result, people must seek shelter immediately.
Paraphrase	F5 tornadoes are such severe windstorms that people must find a safe place right away.

         very = such   seek = find
         dangerous = severe   a shelter = a safe place

To find effective synonyms, use a thesaurus, which is a reference book in which words are organized into categories that contain specific words and phrases with similar meanings. By looking up the category, you can find a variety of synonyms to substitute for the word or phrase you are looking to paraphrase. For people for whom English is not a native language, it is helpful to use a thesaurus that provides examples of how to use synonyms in context.

Some sources that will help you to find synonyms include *Longman's Language Activator* (Longman Group UK Ltd., Essex, England, 1993), which organizes synonyms into word families, and *Longman's Lexicon of Contemporary English* (McArthur, Tom, Longman Group UK Ltd., Essex, England,1981), which organizes synonyms by content areas, such as education, health, and entertainment. Both references provide examples of the synonyms in sentences.

Changing Word Forms

In Chapter 5, you learned that content words can be repeated in different forms in a paragraph. In Chapters 6 and 7, you practiced how to restate sentences containing structures of comparison/contrast and cause/effect. These changes often involve converting verbs (and adjectives) to nouns and vice versa.

↪ Example

Original Passage	In a tornadic storm, property is destroyed.
Paraphrase	A tornado causes destruction of property.

Original Passage	In a tornadic storm, property is damaged.
Paraphrase	A tornado causes property damage.

Changing Direct Quotation to Indirect Quotation

To use direct quotation, copy the author's words exactly as they are written, and use quotation marks around all of the copied material. Acknowledge the source. Do not overuse direct quotation; use it only when the author's exact words give your argument more credibility and/or present the information more succinctly than a paraphrase would. Also, do not directly quote factual material.

To use indirect quotation, paraphrase the original direct quotation. Use more than one of the techniques for paraphrasing to restate the quotation. Do not use quotation marks. Remember to cite the source appropriately. Paraphrase whenever possible.

<u>Direct Quotation: Original Wording</u>	<u>Indirect Quotation: Paraphrase</u>
Dr. Benjamin Spock said, "It's generally accepted that on-screen violence is harmful to children."*	According to Dr. Benjamin Spock, most people believe that TV and movie violence affects children adversely.
"Children—especially young children—will pattern themselves after violent behavior just as readily as they will imitate good behavior."	He maintained that young children in particular are just as likely to imitate violent actions as they are nonviolent ones.
"Watching violence has a desensitizing and brutal affect on people—children and adults alike."	Spock also said that people who watch too much violence will become desensitized to it regardless of age.
"I mean that individuals brought up by kindly parents will at first be shocked and horrified when they see one person committing an act of violence against another. But if they continue to see violence regularly, they will gradually begin to take it for granted as standard human behavior."	As Spock explained, when people who are from good families are first exposed to violence, they react with shock and horror. However, the more violence they see, the less shock and horror they they feel. Thus, violence becomes an everyday experience.

If the original quotation is stated in such a way that paraphrasing would detract from the impact or wit of the statement, it is more effective to use direct quotation.

☞ Example

Original Passage	"Sports do not build character. They reveal it." (Heywood Hale Broun)
Paraphrase	Heywood Hale Broun maintains that participating in sports brings out the competitors' innate sportsmanship. (weakened message)

Changing Voice

In Chapter 5, you learned how to form passive verbs. This skill will help you with paraphrasing. Be careful, however. Do not convert active verbs into passive verbs unless it is appropriate to do so. In general, active voice is preferred in academic writing because the focus of most academic writing is on the agent (the doer). In the following example, the active voice is appropriate because the focus (good students) is also the agent. Using the passive voice would change the focus to the receiver (activities of good students), which creates problems with coherence in the paper.

☞ Example

Appropriate Focus (Active Voice)	Good students participate in class activities, complete their assignments on time, and do exemplary work.
	(The sentence is clearly focused on the topic of good students.)
Inappropriate Focus (Passive Voice)	Class activities are participated in, assignments are completed, and exemplary work is done by good students.
	(Changing the focus from the agent to the receiver creates problems with expression. The sentence is awkward and does not address the topic of good students directly.)

---

*Spock, Benjamin, M.D., "How On-Screen Violence Hurts Your Kids," Redbook, pp. 26-27, Nov. 1987.

Dr. Spock (1903-1998) was an American pediatrician best known for his book "Baby and Child Care," which was originally published in 1946.

However, use of the passive voice is preferred if the agent (doer) is unimportant, unknown, or understood. For example, the passive voice is often used in scientific or technical writing because assignments often require that the focus be on the receiver (object). In a technical process, the agent is unimportant, unknown, or understood. A writer reporting on a technical process such as the manufacturing of silk, for example, would have to use passive voice. Otherwise, the focus would be inappropriate, as illustrated in the following two passages.

☞ Example

Appropriate Focus (Passive Voice)	The cocoons are sorted and soaked before the silk fibers are wound onto reels. After this step, the raw silk is shipped to factories, where it is washed and dried.
	(The topic requires that the writer focus on the process of manufacturing silk rather than on the workers.)
Inappropriate Focus (Active Voice)	Workers sort and soak the cocoons before they wind the silk fibers onto reels. After this step, the workers ship the raw silk to factories to factories, where other workers wash and dry the silk.
	(In this case, changing the voice from passive to active is inappropriate because it changes the topic from how silk is manufactured to the workers. Information about the agent is not important.)

Changing Clauses and Phrases

Another technique is to convert clauses to phrases or phrases to clauses. You practiced this in Chapter 7.

Original Passage	The flow of water back to the sea *results from the precipitation of rain and its absorption by the soil.* (phrase)
Paraphrase	*Because rain is precipitated and absorbed by the soil* (adverb clause), water flows back to the sea.
Other Changes	the flow of water (noun phrase) = water flows (clause)
	the precipitation of rain and its absorption (phrase) = rain is precipitated and absorbed by (passive voice)
Original Passage	Seawater evaporates. *As a result, water vapor is formed.* (main clause)
Paraphrase(s)	Seawater evaporates, *which leads to the formation of water vapor.* (adjective clause)
	Seawater evaporates, *resulting in the formation of water vapor.* (adjective phrase)
Other Changes	as a result (connector) = leads to (verb)
	is formed (verb) = the formation (noun)
	which leads to = resulting in

Changing Word Order

To change word order, determine a different order for the information in the passage. In other words, you can move information from one part of a sentence to another. The following direct quotation is from the December 1995 issue of the "Mayo Clinic Health Letter." A number of paraphrasing techniques were used.

➾ Example

Original Passage	Situations that create stress are as unique as you are. Your personality, genes, and experiences influence how you deal with stress.
Paraphrase	Stressful situations affect people differently. How you manage stress is determined by your personality characteristics, genetic makeup, and life experiences.
Changes	situations that create stress = stressful situations (new word order and word forms)
	are as unique as you are = affect people differently (synonymous phrase, different kind of clause)
	how you deal with stress = how you manage stress (synonymous phrase, new word order)
	personality = personality characteristics (synonymous phrase)
	genes = genetic makeup (synonymous phrase)
	experiences = life experiences (synonymous phrase)

ⒹⒾⓈⒸⓄⓋⒺⓇⓎ
8.3: Identifying paraphrasing techniques

• Study each quotation (on the left) and its respective paraphrase (on the right).
• In the space provided, list the paraphrasing techniques used for the paraphrased words in italics. There may be more than one technique in each paraphrase.

➾ Example

"*It's generally accepted* that on-screen violence is harmful to children."	*Most people agree* that TV and movie violence affects children adversely.

Technique(s): _passive to active voice, synonymous phrase_

1. "It's generally accepted that *on-screen violence is harmful to children.*"   Most people believe that *TV and movie violence affects children adversely.*

Technique(s): ....

2. "It's generally accepted that on-screen violence *is harmful to children.*"   Most people believe that TV and movie violence *affects children adversely.*

Technique(s): ....

3. "*Children—especially young children—will* pattern themselves after violent behavior just as readily as they will imitate good behavior."   He maintained that *young children in particular* are just as likely to imitate violent actions as they are nonviolent ones.

Technique(s): ....

4. "Children—especially young children—*will pattern themselves after violent behavior just as readily as they will imitate good behavior.*"

   He maintained that young children in particular *are just as likely to imitate violent actions as they are nonviolent ones.*

   Technique(s): ....

5. "*Watching violence* has a desensitizing affect and brutal effect on *people—children and adults alike.*"

   Spock also said that *people who watch too much violence* will become desensitized to it regardless of age.

   Technique(s): ....

6. "Watching violence *has a desensitizing and brutal effect* on people—*children and adults alike.*"

   Spock also said that people who watch too much violence *will become desensitized* to it *regardless of age.*

   Technique(s): ....

7. "I mean that individuals brought up by kindly parents *will at first be shocked and horrified when they see one person committing an act of violence against another.* But if they continue to see violence regularly, they will gradually begin to take it for granted as standard human behavior."

   As Spock explained, when people who are from good families are *first exposed to violence, they react with shock and horror.* However, the more violence they see, the less shock and horror they feel. Thus, violence becomes an everyday experience.

   Technique(s): ....

8. "I mean that *individuals brought up by kindly parents* will at first be shocked and horrified when they see one person committing an act of violence against another. But if they continue to see violence regularly, they will gradually begin to take it for granted as standard human behavior."

   As Spock explained, when *people who are from good families* are first exposed to violence, they react with shock and horror. However, the more violence they see, the less shock and horror they feel. Thus, violence becomes an everyday experience.

   Technique(s): ....

ⓓⓘⓢⓒⓞⓥⓔⓡⓨ

8.4: Practicing structured paraphrasing

Following are some direct quotations by the well-known anthropologist Margaret Mead.
- In pairs, paraphrase each sentence, replacing each word or phrase in brackets ([ ]) with a synonymous word or phrase from the list. Report on other appropriate paraphrasing techniques as well.

Synonyms

the environment	continue	wars do not result in
both available and obligatory	experience a way of life	maintain
world's rebellious young people	Earth	know
unable to sustain life	ability	permitted
young people	total destruction	diminish
provide food for all people in the world	birth control	

1. "The [young people who are rebelling all around the world] will never [know a world] in which [war does not mean] [annihilation]."

   According to Margaret Mead,* ....

   ....

   ....

2. "[The young] [believe] that [contraception] is [possible and necessary] and that our [capacity] to [feed the world] will [not last]."

   Mead continues to say that ....

   ....

   ....

3. "They [realize] that if the pollution of [air and land and water] is [allowed] to [go on], [this planet] will become [uninhabitable]."

   Mead also maintains that ....

   ....

   ....

As you can see, paraphrases should be grammatically correct and should include logical word choices that retain the author's meaning and tone. The ideas do not have to be in the same word order; in fact, successful paraphrases may reflect a number of changes. So far, you have had structured practice with paraphrasing. Because paraphrasing is a thinking process, not a substitution drill in which words are replaced only to fill in slots, you need less structured practice. As you practice, follow these rules.

Rules for Effective Paraphrasing

1. Refer to the author and text whenever you paraphrase from a source. (*According to* + author's name + *in* + name of source/text + main clause.)

2. Do not say "I think . . ." or use other wording to imply that an idea that came from a specific source is your own opinion. Do not claim the author's ideas as your own even if you agree with the author.

3. Research and take notes carefully; do not misuse the sources. Take notes in your own words (e.g., outlines), summarize, and keep accurate records of each source (author[s], title of publication, and page numbers).

4. If you copy anything word for word, use quotation marks, copy accurately, and acknowledge the source accurately.

5. Maintain the original meaning of the passage. (Be accurate.)

6. Keep the same tone (e.g., serious, humorous, sarcastic).

7. Do not add your own ideas, examples, details, or other forms of support to a paraphrase (or summary).

8. Do not try to follow the original text word for word. Get the general idea and put it in your own words. Put the text out of sight! That may help prevent you from copying or paraphrasing too closely. The point is that if you truly understand the text, you will have less trouble paraphrasing than if you do not understand the text.

---

* "Opinion: Margaret Mead on Youth," The New York Times Company, 1969. From a lecture Mead gave at New York City's American Museum of Natural History. Also qtd. in Hirasawa, Louise and Linda Markstein, "Developing Reading Skills," 1774: 11-12, Newbury House Publishers, Inc., Rowley, Mass. Margaret Mead (1901-1978) was a famous American anthropologist known for her book "Coming of Age in Samoa," first published in 1928.

DISCOVERY

8.5: Practicing unstructured paraphrasing with short quotations

- Using the space provided, complete the paraphrase for each of the following quotations.
- Experiment with wording. You do not need (nor is it always desirable) to follow the same word order.
- Remember to acknowledge sources.

⇨ Example

Original	My roommate says, "Stress almost always causes me to lose sleep."
Paraphrase	My roommate says that because of stress, she often cannot sleep. My roommate says she often has insomnia due to feeling stressed. My roommate claims that her loss of sleep is often the result of stress.

1. "Our reaction to stress has an impact on our physical health and mental health." (Karima A. Haynes, *Ebony* magazine)

   According to .... in .... ,

   ....

   ....

2. "Stressed persons tend to sleep less, exercise less, have poorer diets, smoke more, and use alcohol and other drugs more often than unstressed people." (Dr. Tracy B. Herbert, Department of Psychology, Carnegie Mellon University)

   ...., who is ...., says that

   ....

   ....

3. "Reducing stress improves both physical and mental well-being." (Ithaca Gateways, "Stressed Out: Effects of Stress")

   In ...., Ithaca Gateways reports that

   ....

   ....

4. "When your body is under a tremendous amount of stress you accumulate a lot of hormones that weaken the body's resistance to disease." (Dr. Juanity Doss, quoted in *Ebony* magazine, July 1994)

   ....

   ....

   ....

D I S C O V E R Y

8.6: Paraphrasing longer passages

- On a separate sheet of paper, paraphrase the following quote by Dr. Benjamin Spock.
- Use a variety of techniques, following the rules for effective paraphrasing.
- Limit your paraphrase to approximately 100 words.
- Use Peer Review Form 14 from Appendix D to evaluate your work.

"What, then, can parents do? I think that they must first resolve that programs dealing in any kind of violence or brutality are off-limits. This means, of course, that parents must keep a sharp eye on what their children are watching. Secondly, parents must really mean it when they forbid a certain program. Their efforts won't work if they forbid a program on Monday or Wednesday, but fail to notice what their children are watching on other days of the week—or notice but feel too tired to enforce the rule. I'm firmly convinced that if parents feel strongly that something is bad for their children, they can make a rule stick. But when parents vacillate, children get the message that persistent arguments or sneakiness may work often enough to be well worth trying." [134 words]

Source: Spock, Benjamin, M.D. "How On-Screen Violence Hurts Your Kids." *Redbook* (Nov. 1987), 26-27.

Journal ENTRY 29

Do you think that on-screen violence is harmful to children?

Write an essay in which you agree or disagree with Dr. Spock that children become desensitized to violence if they see it portrayed too often on TV and in movies. Discuss at least two reasons with examples and details. Use your own words. [700-800 words, every other line.]

SUMMARIZING

Most of the paraphrasing you will do will be in the form of summaries. It is unlikely that you will ever paraphrase an entire article. However, it is possible that you will paraphrase the main points of an article. That is, you will summarize the main points in your own words to support your writing. Reporting on the findings of experts is considered to be strong support in writing.

A summary contains the main ideas of the original document. Depending on the method of development used by the writer, it might include major examples. Sometimes a summary contains indirect quotation, but it usually does not contain direct quotation. Therefore, do not use direct quotation of the original wording.

A summary should be written in your own words. You should not use the original wording. Instead, you should read the original article, book, report, and so on carefully in order to understand the author's ideas. Make an outline of the text in your own words. Use phrases in the outline. Then use your own words to say what the author wrote.

A summary contains the attitude and opinion of the author, so do not let your opinion interfere with the ideas you are summarizing. Also, do not add any ideas to the summary that are not in the text being summarized. Do not elaborate with details not used in the original passage.

A summary should be concise, accurate, clearly written, complete, and well organized. It should also reflect your ability to understand the meanings of words, the author's attitude, and any implied meanings.

In a summary, never criticize or judge the writer in any way. A summary is not a critique, response, or editorial.

Following is a summary of "The Kinds of Tornadoes and Their Effects" from Chapter 7. Note that the summary is a clearly organized and complete synopsis of the characteristics of each major kind of tornado. Furthermore, only the major details and examples are included.

Summary

"The Kinds of Tornadoes and Their Effects"

1   There are three major kinds of tornadoes: weak, strong, and violent. These rankings are based on the Fujita Wind-Damage Scale. The most common tornadoes, F0 and F1, are classified as weak. Of the tornadoes reported annually, 65% are F1s, and 25% are F2s. The wind speeds of F0 and F1 tornadoes are from 40 to 112 miles per hour, causing light to moderate damage, such as
5   ripping branches off trees, knocking billboards and chimneys over, pulling the surfaces off roofs of houses, destroying attached garages, and dislodging mobile homes. Although these tornadoes are weak, they account for 1% to 3% of tornado deaths per year. The second type of tornado is classified as strong. Approximately 4% of tornadoes occurring annually are F2s, and 3% are F3s. F2 and F3 tornadoes have wind speeds from 113 to 206 miles per hour, which causes considerable
10   to severe damage. The damage of strong tornadoes ranges from uprooting trees and breaking them in two, ripping roofs off houses, destroying mobile homes, and pushing over train cars to destroying entire forests and throwing cars around. These tornadoes are responsible for 33% of tornado deaths per year. The most dangerous kind of tornado is classified as violent. Although only approximately 0.5% of tornadoes per year fall into this category (F4 and F5), they cause nearly 70%
15   of tornado fatalities per year. The wind speeds of violent tornadoes can exceed 260 miles per hour. Due to their intensity, violent tornadoes cause devastating to incredible damage, including carrying away and completely demolishing homes, turning cars into missiles, and stripping bark off trees. No matter how strong the wind speeds are, all tornadoes are dangerous. (276 words)

In-Class Writing Assignment

Using the study guide you completed on the contrast of the Irish and the Americans in Chapter 6, write a summary of the model essay in your own words. Use Peer Review Form 15 in Appendix D to evaluate the summaries. [250-300 words, every other line]

DIRECT AND INDIRECT QUOTATION

In the sections on stating acknowledgments and paraphrasing, you learned the differences between direct and indirect quotation. A direct quotation includes the writer's original wording copied directly from the original source and punctuation that sets off the original passage from the rest of the paper. An indirect quotation includes paraphrases of the writer's original wording in the source. Because the original wording is paraphrased, no additional punctuation is necessary in indirect quotation.

Direct Quotation

The purpose of using direct quotation is to show the writer's exact words. Therefore, you must copy the passage word for word. Do not make any changes to the text. To indicate that the passage is a direct quotation, use the following punctuation rules. Pay close attention to the use of capitalization and the placement of punctuation marks.

Rules for Direct Quotation

1. If a main clause precedes the quoted passage, use a comma after the reporting verb. Place quotation marks at the beginning and at the end of the quoted passage. If the quotation consists of two or more sentences, do not put quotation marks around each sentence. New quotation marks indicate a new source.

↪ **Example**

> Dr. Benjamin Spock stated, "I'm firmly convinced that if parents feel strongly that something is bad for their children, they can make a rule stick. But when parents vacillate, children get the message that persistent arguments or sneakiness may work often enough to be well worth trying."

2. If the direct quotation ends with a period, comma, question mark, or exclamation point, the punctuation is placed inside the quotation marks. However, if the question mark or exclamation point is not part of the direct quotation, place it outside of the quotation marks.

↪ **Examples**

> One parent demanded, "What are we to do about the violence on that show?"
> Who asked about the violence on "Robo Police"?
> The angry father exclaimed, "We demand that the show be censored!"
> I cannot believe you used the word "censored"!

3. If the acknowledgment comes at the end of a direct quotation of a statement, place a comma inside the quotation marks and put a period at the end of the sentence. If the direct quotation is a question or an exclamation, put the appropriate mark inside the quotation marks and a period at the end of the sentence.

↪ **Example**

> "I'm firmly convinced that if parents feel strongly that something is bad for their children,
> they can make a rule stick," Dr. Spock said.
> "What are we to do?" the angry parents asked.
> "We demand some answers!" the angry father yelled.

4. If the acknowledgment interrupts (comes in the middle of) the quotation, place the quotation marks at each end and beginning point. Keep periods and commas inside the quotation marks. If the second part of the quotation is a new sentence, capitalize the first word. However, if the acknowledgment is in the middle of one sentence, do not capitalize the first word in the second part of the quotation.

↪ **Example**

> "What, then, can parents do? I think that they must first resolve that programs dealing in
> any kind of violence or brutality are off-limits," Dr. Spock said. "This means, of course,
> that parents must keep a sharp eye on what their children are watching." (more than one
> sentence)

> "I'm firmly convinced that if parents feel strongly that something is bad for their children,"
> Dr. Spock said, "they can make the rule stick." (one sentence)

5. If the direct quotation is a fragment, put quotation marks around the fragment and do not capitalize it.

↪ **Example**

> Spock maintained that parents who strongly believe that something is bad for a child "can
> make a rule stick."

7. Use single quotation marks for quotations within quotations.

➥ **Example**

> "I wonder about unemployed blacksmiths," said comedian Jerry Seinfeld. "Do they stand around talking about possible jobs, saying, 'Yeah, I got a few irons in the fire'?"

Once you have learned how to correctly punctuate direct quotations, it may become tempting to use them a great deal. However, direct quotations are used sparingly (not often) in academic writing. For an example of the correct balance of direct and indirect quotations, look at one of the model essays in previous chapters, such as "The Life Cycle of Tornadoes" in Chapter 5 or the essay contrasting the Irish immigrants and Americans in Chapter 6. Note that these essays contain very few direct quotations and those that were used were especially descriptive and would have been weakened by paraphrasing.

ⅅ ⅈ ⓈⒸⓄⓋⒺⓇⓎ

8.7: **Punctuating direct quotations**

On a separate sheet of paper, rewrite each of the following quotations, using correct punctuation and capitalization for direct quotation.

➥ **Example**

> What, then, can parents do I think that they must first resolve that programs dealing in any kind of violence or brutality are off-limits Dr. Spock said this means of course that parents must keep a sharp eye on what their children are watching

> *"What, then, can parents do? I think that they must first resolve that programs dealing in any kind of violence or brutality are off-limits," Dr. Spock said. "This means, of course, that parents must keep a sharp eye on what their children are watching."*

1. television is something by our times, out of our times, for our times it reflects the virtues and faults of our times Aubrey Singer stated
2. my fellow citizens of the world President John F. Kennedy said ask not what America will do for you, but what together we can do for the freedom of man
3. Dr. Martin Luther King, Jr. said we all know through painful experience that freedom is never voluntarily given by the oppressor; it must be demanded by the oppressed
4. Robert Kasanoff maintains there does, and ought to, exist a right to lie he contends the state must recognize and protect the right to lie
5. if you can't convince them Harry S. Truman said confuse them
6. if we are a country committed to free speech asked comedian Steven Wright then why do we have phone bills

Indirect Quotation

Indirect quotation is more common in academic writing than direct quotation. In fact, your professors will expect you to synthesize information from a number of sources and summarize it in your own words. It is unlikely that you will have only one source. For example, the writer of "The Life Cycle of Tornadoes" from Chapter 5 used multiple sources of information, sometimes in the same paragraph. In addition, the writer did not depend too much on one source in any one section of the paper.

Rules for Indirect Quotation

To use indirect quotation correctly, you need to employ the paraphrasing techniques and follow the rules for effective paraphrasing and summarizing taught earlier in this chapter. Although indirect quotation does not require additional punctuation in the paraphrased information, it does require other specific changes that are not necessary in direct quotation. In addition to paraphrasing, if the reporting verb is in the past tense, make the following changes.

1. Shift the tense of each verb and modal one tense backward.

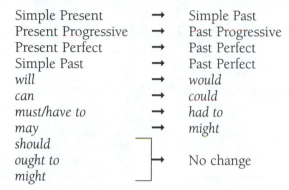

Simple Present	→	Simple Past
Present Progressive	→	Past Progressive
Present Perfect	→	Past Perfect
Simple Past	→	Past Perfect
will	→	*would*
can	→	*could*
must/have to	→	*had to*
may	→	*might*
should		
ought to	→	No change
might		

2. Change the pronouns.

↪ Example

Direct Quotation	"*I* can't talk now. *I* have to go to the doctor," Vicky said.
Indirect Quotation	Vicky told *me* (that) *she* couldn't talk because *she* had to go to the doctor.

3. Change the time expressions, especially for remote (not immediate) reports.

today	→	that day
tomorrow	→	the next/following day
next year/week/month	→	the next/following year/week/month
ago	→	before
last night/week/year	→	the night/week/year before
this	→	that
these	→	those
now	→	then
soon	→	later
here	→	there

↪ Example

Remote Report	On Monday, Mother said, "I went shopping today."
	On Monday, Mother told me (that) she had gone shopping that day.
Immediate Report	Mother: I went shopping today.
	Sam: What did Mom just say?
	Mary: She said (that) she went shopping today.

ⒹⒾⓈⒸⓄⓋⒺⓇⓎ
8.8:   Changing direct quotation to indirect quotation

Using the rules for indirect quotation, change the following direct quotations to indirect quotations. For those quotations containing modals, the change in tense has been provided for you.

↪ **Example**

Direct Quotation	"We farm the same way our fathers and fathers before us did," the Irish immigrant said.
Indirect Quotation	The Irish immigrant said (that) they farmed the same way their fathers and grandfathers had.

1. Direct Quotation   "We are moving to America to better our lives," the Irish farmer told his children.

   Indirect Quotation   ....

   ....

2. Direct Quotation   "I have never seen so many job opportunities!" exclaimed the farmer's son.

   Indirect Quotation   ....

   ....

3. Direct Quotation   The Irish lad reported to his family, "I tried to find a job in town."

   Indirect Quotation   ....

   ....

4. Direct Quotation   "I'll look again tomorrow," he promised.
   will   →   *would*

   Indirect Quotation   ....

   ....

5. Direct Quotation   "I can't conceive of a future here," said the Irish lad.
   can   →   *could*

   Indirect Quotation   ....

   ....

6. Direct Quotation   "We must work together if we want to make it in our new country," the farmer told his son.
   have to   →   *had to*

   Indirect Quotation   ....

   ....

CHAPTER *summary*

- Academic honesty is important in school and in a career. Both students and professionals must follow the same standards. Although it may be tempting to cheat and/or plagiarize, academic dishonesty has serious consequences, ranging from getting a failing grade on the assignment (or a severe reprimand) to expulsion from school (or loss of a job).

- Plagiarism is the act of stealing part or all of someone else's outline, draft, essay, article, or book. In U.S. culture, it is wrong to copy verbatim (word for word) from someone else's published or unpublished writing without correct documentation. Because of copyright laws, you must document your sources by using in-text acknowledgments (such as *"According to . . .,"*) and citations (or footnotes), and list the sources in a bibliography (references or works cited list). Consult with a professor in your major about which of the various style manuals to use. You must also learn the difference between direct and indirect quotation and master the skills of paraphrasing and summarizing.

- Direct quotation is the original wording of a source. Use quotation marks around any characteristic phrases, sentences, or passages copied verbatim from the source. Do not change anything in the passage you are directly quoting, and do not overuse direct quotation. Use direct quotation when the original words lend more credibility or emphasis to your argument. Most of the time, you will paraphrase and summarize.

- Indirect quotation is a report of what the source said. In indirect quotation, do not use quotation marks. Also, paraphrase (use your own words and sentence structures) to restate the information from the source. You may also have to change the tense, pronouns, and time expressions. Be careful to maintain the original meaning and tone of the passage. Do not include your own opinions as part of the paraphrase.

- A summary is a paraphrase of the main points (and possibly major examples) in the source and is, thus, shorter than the original passage(s). To summarize, use your own words (indirect quotation) and be accurate, well organized, and concise. Do not critique the source or add your own opinions in other ways.

- Whether you are paraphrasing or summarizing, make it clear where one source ends and another source begins by using reporting verbs and other strategies for acknowledging the sources.

Chapter 9

Essay Tests

CHAPTER TOPICS

▶ WHAT IS AN ESSAY TEST?

▶ STUDYING FOR AN ESSAY TEST

▶ ADJECTIVE CLAUSES

▶ FORMAL DEFINITIONS

▶ INFORMAL DEFINITIONS

WHAT IS AN ESSAY TEST?

If you are taking courses in the humanities or social sciences, you will probably have to take essay tests. Although some essay tests are take-home exams, many essay tests are formal in-class writings for which you are given a specific amount of time to complete. Rather than choose the correct answer from a list of options (a multiple-choice test) or fill in the blanks with the correct answer, you will be required on an essay test to write complete sentences, paragraphs, short essays, and long essays. An essay test may contain more than one part and, thus, require you to write more than one essay answer in the time allotted, which will vary according to the test conditions. For example, a take-home essay test will have a specific due date (the date it is due back to the professor), but will not specify how much time to spend on the test. However, an in-class essay test will specify a time limit, which can range from one class period to six or more hours (comprehensive exams).

Because of the time limit and the number of essays you may have to write, it is important for you to understand the test questions (assignments) and to organize the answers quickly and effectively. What you have learned so far in this textbook will help you with focus and organization on essay tests. Some of the models in these chapters, in fact, were written under test conditions.

STUDYING FOR AN ESSAY TEST

⒟⒤⒮⒞⒪⒱⒠⒭⒴
9.1:   Discussing study skills

• In groups, discuss the following questions. Take notes on a separate sheet of paper.
• Report to the class.
   1. Test anxiety is the stress one feels before and/or during a test. Do you ever experience test anxiety? Why?
   2. What is the difference between doing homework and studying?
   3. What is the difference between reviewing class notes and revising class notes?
   4. What are the best ways to prepare for a multiple-choice test and an essay test? Compare the methods you would use for each.

Essay Tests and the Process of Writing

Studying for an essay test involves more than just memorizing names and dates. An essay test requires you to use critical-thinking skills. In other words, since an essay test is not a multiple-choice test in which you can recognize the correct answer, it is important for you to be able to use all the critical-thinking skills that you have learned in this course.

Prewriting Activities

Active Learning

The prewriting stage of the essay test begins in the classroom as you are learning the course materials. Your success on an essay test will depend on your involvement in the class, your study methods, and your ability to organize class materials effectively.

The first step is to become fully involved in the class. Studies show that students who attend class regularly, take notes, and participate in class discussions perform better on tests than students who take a passive approach to learning. Class attendance is important because essay tests do not cover only what is in the textbook or outside readings. Professors often lecture about related topics that are not in the readings, and they often expand on (add to) the concepts that were covered in the assigned readings. Moreover, professors often give out outlines and other handouts in class that may be referred to in the tests. Therefore, regular attendance is important. If you miss class, it is easy to fall behind. The more classes you miss, the harder it is to keep up with the pace of the course. Second, while you are in class, do not assume a passive attitude, even if the course seems boring to you. Professors appreciate stimulating discussions because a lot of learning takes place with the exchange of ideas. They expect you to ask questions and explore ideas to show that you are thinking about the topics and that you are interested in the course. Therefore, do not hesitate to raise your hand; your questions will help everyone in class. In addition, if you frequently participate in class, you will be better prepared to answer those essay test questions about topics that were addressed in class discussions. The professor, in fact, might use the class discussion as a review for the test.

The second step in this stage is to learn effective study methods, which will contribute to your success on an essay test. Do not just do the homework, which may consist of reading a chapter and answering questions. Save time for studying, which involves thinking about what you have learned (reviewing) and looking ahead (previewing). When studying, first review and then preview. These activities will help you with both note-taking and class discussion. Reviewing will help you clarify information and see relationships among the ideas. When reviewing, carefully read the professor's comments on materials handed back, recopy and improve the class notes, and look over previous notes, outlines, and study charts based on assigned readings. Students who revise and review their notes often do better on exams than students who do not.

Let's examine in more detail the benefits of previewing. First, previewing will help you keep up with the required reading. It is important to keep up with, if not ahead of, the syllabus (schedule of assigned readings for the course). That is, do all of the assigned readings before the actual day the readings and related topics will be discussed in class. While you are reading, underline or highlight the important points, and make marginal notes. It might even be of more help to outline the chapter(s) and/or design study charts. These outlines and charts will enable you to review more efficiently. To help you remember ideas, you could also color-code key vocabulary or arrange the information on the page in an interesting way. Whether you choose to outline or to design study charts, make sure the information is accurate and complete.

Previewing will also help you with class participation. Actively previewing lecture material will make class more interesting for you. If you are familiar with the background material, you will have less trouble understanding the vocabulary in the lectures, and you will be better able to answer the professor's questions. You will also be able to ask questions and participate in class discussions if you feel confident about the material. The fact that you are well prepared will make a good impression on the professor.

Another prewriting skill that is essential to success on essay tests is organization. Revising notes, writing outlines, and designing study charts will benefit you only if the material is easy to find. Have a separate place in a loose-leaf notebook for each aspect of the class: class notes and handouts; notes, outlines, and study charts based on the assigned readings; past tests, quizzes, and papers; and vocabulary review. Always date and label your class notes, and as you receive handouts, date and file them with the appropriate class notes. It is easier to file recopied (and thus refined) notes in chronological order in a loose-leaf notebook. The notes, outlines, and study charts based on the assigned readings, moreover, could be kept in a separate part of the notebook. Be sure to clearly label these notes with the complete bibliographic information needed to identify the source: the author's name, title of work, publisher, date of publication, page numbers, and so on. You may be required to cite the source on an essay test (and definitely on a term paper). Although you may not need to give page numbers on an essay test, you will probably need to use the author's name and title of work. Another section of your notebook could contain homework assignments and tests and papers that have been graded. Study and learn from the professor's corrections and comments so that you do not repeat your errors in future assignments and tests. Finally, it would benefit you to reserve a section in your notebook for vocabulary review. It is important to know what each vocabulary word means, how to use it in a sentence, and how to spell it. Otherwise, you might get a lower grade for using a vocabulary word incorrectly, even though you mastered the course material.

Synthesizing

Once you follow the suggestions for active learning, you will be ready for the next prewriting activity, synthesis. Synthesis is an important critical-thinking skill that involves finding relationships among ideas. In other words, you might need to bring together ideas from the lecture notes, discussions, and readings to answer a question on an essay test. All of the sources will contribute to the thesis. This level of critical thinking is very hard to achieve if you have not been studying. In fact, it is unlikely that you could cram this type of information into your head the night before an in-class essay test, especially if you have not done much of the reading, note-taking, charting, or outlining. Also, if you do not have an organized notebook, it will be harder to assemble effective essays on a take-home exam, in which you are allowed to use the notes, outlines, and study charts.

One valuable exercise to help you synthesize is to actually predict (anticipate) the essay questions. Predicting is an effective study skill. First, review the notes, outlines, and study charts. What topics did the professor spend the most time on or seem the most interested in? What topics came up frequently in the readings? After predicting the topics, consider the methods the professor may require you to use in the essay test answers. For example, can theories or authors be compared/contrasted? Could the professor ask you to trace the history of the development of a theory or invention? Is it likely you will be asked to examine causes or effects? Finally, consider the scope of the question because that will determine the length of the answer. Will you need only a few sentences? One paragraph? A five-paragraph essay? Will you be asked to identify or define an item (two or three sentences) or discuss an idea (one or more paragraphs)?

Organizing Predicted Essay Answers

After predicting the topics that might be asked and methods that might be required, use your notes, outlines, and charts to brainstorm on support for the questions you have predicted. You may even write informal outlines or charts as practice for developing the essay answers. However, if the essay test is to be given in class, you should not actually write the essay outside of class. If you assume too much while preparing for an essay test, you might misread the assignment and do poorly on the test. It is just as bad to change a question to suit yourself; never change the assignment to slant it toward an area that interests you more or in which you feel better prepared to write about. Another reason not to prewrite essays outside of class is that it takes too much time to write out the entire essays to study for essay test questions. Making informal outlines or charts as review is more time efficient. It takes less time to list the major points in the order you would discuss them than to write 500 words on the topic. If you plan effectively before the test, you will cut down considerably on the time it will take you to complete it.

Finally, when studying for the essay test, you must not memorize passages from the readings to copy word for word as your essay test answer. This action is plagiarism and, as you learned in Chapter 8, plagiarism has serious consequences. Again, write notes, summaries, outlines, and study charts in your own words so that you will not plagiarize. If you are copying word for word, use direct quotes and acknowledge the sources. Likewise, for take-home essay tests, use the sources correctly and accurately to avoid accusations of academic dishonesty.

ⓓⓘⓢⓒⓞⓥⓔⓡⓨ
9.2: Predicting essay test questions

- Imagine that you have to take an essay test on tornadoes.
- Select one of the following essays: "The Life Cycle of Tornadoes," "Tornado Safety" (both in Chapter 5), or "The Kinds of Tornadoes and Their Effects" (Chapter 7).
- Brainstorm on predicting possible essay test questions for the essay you have selected.
- Then select three of those questions and write them on a separate sheet of paper.
- Make informal outlines or charts showing how you would answer each question.
- Compare your questions, outlines, and charts in groups.
- Then hand your materials in as your assignment.

Strategies for Writing Essay Test Answers

Once you have mastered the previous prewriting skills, you are ready to take the essay test. When you receive the essay test, the first thing you should do is to read the test over carefully and analyze it. Do not start writing right away. Instead, ask yourself these questions:

- How many parts are there on the test?
- How many points is each part worth?
- What is required on each part?
- How much time is there for the whole test?
- What is the best way to proceed? Which part should be done first? How much time should be allotted for each part?

Analyzing the Parts of the Essay Test

An essay test usually contains more than one part. The three most common parts are identification, paragraph answer, and essay answer. The instructions, scope of the questions, and point values will indicate how long an answer should be. The following are some possible strategies for each part of the test.

Identification (Short-Answer) Questions

The easiest (and usually first) part of the test is usually comprised of identification (short-answer) questions. These types of questions will require you to name and identify or briefly define persons, places, things, or theories. It is possible you would have several identifications to make in the time given. You will probably be given choices; do not write about all of them just to demonstrate your knowledge. Also, do not write more for each item than you have to, because you need to watch the time and save your energy for the most difficult parts of the test.

For identification questions:
• Write a phrase, a sentence, or several phrases or sentences.
• Be concise and specific.
• Show breadth of thought and be accurate.
• Be organized and complete.
• Answer the exact number of questions assigned.
• Stay within the time limit (3 minutes or less per item).

⇨ **Example**

> Part I: Briefly name and identify or define five of the following. (15 points)
>
> a. The Parthenon   d. The Acropolis
> b. The Peloponnesian War   e. Phidias
> c. The Greek Kouros   f. The temple of the Athena Nike

Paragraph Answer

Another part that might be on an essay test requires answers of one paragraph. It is possible for one essay test to contain several questions that require answers of this length. Again, if you have a choice of topics, write only on the number of topics assigned; do not write on all of the topics. Finally, watch the time.

For a one-paragraph answer:
• Write one organized paragraph of several sentences.
• Present the topic sentence right away. Address the assignment. Do not change the focus of the assignment.
• Present accurate, concise, informative support that is on the topic. Avoid general or shallow support. The professor wants substance.
• Follow the rules for paragraph unity and coherence; include logical, relevant, and well-organized support. Use transitions and coherence devices effectively.
• Use correct grammar and effective word choices; be clear, concise, and formal.
• Include a short summary if necessary.
• Do only the number of topics assigned.
• Stay within the time limit (15 minutes per topic).

⇨ **Example**

> Part II: Choose two of the following topics and write one well-developed paragraph for each. (20 points)
>
> a. The Doric Order
> b. The Ionic Order
> c. The Corinthian Order

Short and Long Essay Answers

Although this part of the test will be worth the most points, it is often placed at the end of the test. Do not underestimate its importance simply because it is at the end or because you feel fatigued. In fact, it might be a good idea to do this part first, when you have the most energy. This type of question requires the most development (five or more paragraphs); therefore, be informative and well organized.

For essay answers:
• Write more than one paragraph for each question.
• Follow the rules for effective essay development and paragraph development.
• Begin with a thesis that has a precise opinion and a MAP. Use the essay question to help you form the thesis, and write on the topic assigned. Do not write an elaborate introduction. Keep the hook brief and informative.
• Use the MAP to determine the topics of each paragraph in the body of the essay. Each paragraph topic should follow a task in the assignment.
• Develop each paragraph using the same method you did for paragraph answers. Give as much information as possible.

- Include a short summary.
- Do only the number of essays assigned.
- Stay within the time limit (30 to 60 minutes per essay answer, depending on the scope of the questions).

↪ **Example**

> Part III: Write a fully developed essay to answer the following question. Be complete and address all parts of the question.(65 points)
>
> Trace the elements and sources of Greek temple architecture sacred to the ancient Greeks. Be sure to discuss the kind of material (the kind of stone and its qualities) as well as the architectural order of each.

The most important thing to remember when taking an essay test is to be as informative as possible. Do not assume that you do not have to state certain facts just because the professor knows the answers. The professor expects you to state as much information as possible to show that you have mastered the material taught. In fact, the number of points you receive for each will be based on how many pieces of specific information you include in the answer. Points will be deducted if the answer is incomplete, superficial, repetitive, and/or unclear.

D I S C O V E R Y
9.3: Analyzing an essay test

- Read the following model essay test about TV and American society.
- Then answer the Discussion Questions that follow.

Model Essay Test

Part I: Name and identify or briefly define three of the following. (15 points)

   a. Dr. Benjamin Spock   d. censorship
   b. the "boob tube"   e. imitation
   c. acceptable aggression

Part II: Choose two of the following items. For each item, write one well-developed paragraph that fully answers the question. (40 points)

   1. Define desensitization. What causes desensitization in TV viewers and what are some of the results of it?
   2. What is meant by media interchangeability? With which other media is TV the most interchangeable? Why?
   3. Discuss general TV viewing habits of Americans. Consider age, sex, ethnicity, income, and education of viewers.

Part III: Select one of the following questions and write a fully developed essay that answers the question. Use information from your reading and the class lectures to support the ideas that you present. (45 points)

   1. Many people—psychologists and sociologists included—believe that the television industry is irresponsible. They believe that the industry should consider the good of the people and should attempt to educate and inform the public with its programming. What three statements does the television industry make in response to this? Show how these statements are false.

   2. It is generally accepted today that television has a large influence on life in American society. Discuss and evaluate the effects of TV on viewers.

❷ Discussion Questions

Use the previous model essay test to answer the following questions.
1. How many parts are there on the test?
2. How many points is each part worth?
3. What is the total number of points possible on the test?
4. How many items are required in Part I? How many points is each item worth in Part I?
5. How many items are required in Part II? How many points is each item worth in Part II?
6. How many items are required in Part III? How many points is Part III worth?
7. Let's say you have 110 minutes to complete this test. How much time will you spend on each part? Why?
8. Which part of the test will you do first? Why?
9. What are the assignment tasks in each question in Parts II and III? How would you organize your answers?

Revising, Proofreading, and Editing the Essay Test Answers

The last two steps in the writing process are revising (making major changes) and proofreading and editing (making minor changes). If the essay test is a take-home exam, you might have time to revise, proofread, and edit your answers. In fact, the professor expects you to do these things. However, if the test is in class, you might not have much time for these activities, especially revision. Again, the key is to organize your materials before the test so that you can devote more time to writing the answers and possibly proofreading and editing what you have written. If you discover a place to add more sentences, however, write out the sentences neatly in an available space and draw arrows (or use a numbering code) to indicate where the professor can insert the information while reading the answer. Finally, check for neatness; illegible words and messy revisions distract from the content and can affect your score.

How will effective time management help you before and during an essay test?

Review the previous discussion of the process of studying for and taking essay tests. Write a summary of this process in your own words. Then discuss the benefits of effective time management of essay tests. [700-800 words, every other line]

In-Class Writing Assignment

- Your instructor will give you an essay test on a familiar topic, along with some materials to study before the test day.
- On the day of the test, bring two #2 pencils and an eraser to class.
- You will not be allowed to use dictionaries or other materials.

ADJECTIVE CLAUSES

In this chapter, you will learn more about adjective (relative) clauses, especially with regard to formal and informal definitions. You will need to use these definition patterns on essay tests.

Formation and Placement of Adjective Clauses

Adjective clauses are dependent clauses that modify (describe, limit, and give information about) nouns. There are different patterns for adjective clauses. By using these patterns, you will be able to cut down on unnecessary repetition and develop sentence variety. The two patterns covered in this section are the subject and object pronoun patterns.

Pattern 1: Subject Pronoun

In the subject pattern, the pronoun *who, which,* or *that* is the subject of the adjective clause. In other words, the pronoun replaces the subject of the sentence. The following examples show how to combine two sentences to create a complex sentence with a subject pattern adjective clause without creating unnecessary repetition. Follow these rules:

1. Replace repeated information with the appropriate subject pronoun: *who* for people, *which* for things, and *that* for both people and things.

2. Place the adjective clause after the noun it describes.

In the following example, note that the adjective clause is placed after the noun that the subject pronoun replaces. The adjective clause defines the kind of public official a senator is.

⇨ **Example**

U.S. senators are <u>public officials</u>. <u>These public officials</u> are elected to serve in the Senate.

U.S. senators are <u>public officials</u> [<u>who/that</u> are elected to serve in the Senate].

In the following example, note the placement of the two adjective clauses. The adjective clauses define the kind of precipitation snow is.

⇨ **Example**

Snow is <u>precipitation</u>. <u>This kind of precipitation</u> appears in the shape of ice crystals. <u>This kind of precipitation</u> is formed directly from the freezing of water vapor in the air.

Snow is <u>precipitation</u> [<u>that/which</u> appears in the shape of ice crystals] and [<u>that/which</u> is formed directly from the freezing of water vapor in the air].

3. In subject adjective clauses, the verb agrees with the noun antecedent.

⇨ **Example**

Snow is *precipitation* that *appears* in the shape of ice crystals.

U.S. senators are *public officials* who *are* elected to serve in the Senate.

4. Do not omit the relative pronoun if it is the subject of the adjective clause, and do not repeat the subject.

⇨ **Examples**

<u>Problem:</u>
Missing subject   U.S. senators are public officials [(?) are elected to serve in the Senate].

<u>Problem:</u>
Double subject   Snow is precipitation [which ~~it~~ appears in the shape of ice crystals].

ⓄⓊⓈⒸⓄⓋⒺⓇⓎ

9.4: Using subject pattern adjective clauses

On a separate piece of paper, combine each of the following pairs of sentences.
• Change the second sentence in each pair to an adjective clause.
• Then combine it correctly with the first sentence and write the new sentence.

1. A fact is a specific piece of information. This information has been verified.
2. A folk dance is a traditional dance. This traditional dance originated among the common people of a nation or a region.
3. A monocrat is a person. This kind of person favors autocracy.
4. A monk is a man. This kind of man lives in a monastery. Also, this man belongs to a brotherhood. The brotherhood requires a life of devotion and strict discipline. (This item requires a sentence with three adjective clauses.)

Pattern 2: Object Pronoun

Adjective pronouns can replace the objects of verbs and prepositions. For this pattern, use *whom* or *that* for people, *which* for things, and *that* for both people and things. Follow these rules:

1. Replace the object of the verb with the appropriate object pronoun.
2. Move the object pronoun to the beginning of the adjective clause.
3. Place the adjective clause after the noun it describes.

➮ Examples

The scientist is not well known. You nominated the scientist for the award.

The scientist is not well known. [whom/that you nominated for the award]

The scientist [whom/that you nominated for the award] is not well known.

The experiment failed to produce the desired results. We did the experiment last week.

The experiment failed to produce the desired results. [which/that we did last week]

The experiment [which/that we did last week] failed to produce the desired results.

Remember to delete the original object to avoid unnecessary repetition.

➮ Example

Problem:
Repeated object   The scientist [whom/that you nominated the scientist for the award] is not well known.

4. If the repeated information is the object of a preposition, retain the preposition. The preposition may come at the beginning or the end of the adjective clause. If the preposition comes at the beginning of the adjective clause, use the pronoun *whom* or *which* (not *that*). Do not delete the preposition.

➮ Examples

The physicist had been nominated before. The Nobel Prize was awarded to the physicist.

The physicist had been nominated before. [to whom the Nobel Prize was awarded]

Formal pattern   The physicist [to whom the Nobel Prize was awarded] had been nominated before.

Informal pattern   The physicist [whom/that the Nobel Prize was awarded to] had been nominated before.

5. Whereas subject adjective pronouns cannot be omitted from a complete clause, object pronouns may be omitted without changing the meaning of the sentence.

⇨ **Examples**

The scientist [whom/that you nominated for the award] is not well known.
The scientist [you nominated for the award] is not well known.

The experiment [which/that we did last week] failed to produce the desired results.
The experiment [we did last week] failed to produce the desired results.

Although the object pronoun of the adjective clause can be omitted, never delete the preposition from the adjective clause.

⇨ **Example**

Problem:
Missing preposition   The physicist [the Nobel Prize was awarded (?)] had been nominated before.

ⓓⓘⓢⓒⓞⓥⓔⓡⓨ
9.5: **Using object pattern adjective clauses**

A. On a separate sheet of paper, combine each of the following pairs of sentences.
• Change the second sentence in each pair to an adjective clause.
• Then combine it correctly with the first sentence and write the new sentence.
• Pay attention to the use of prepositions.

1. A kowtow is a Chinese greeting. A person touches the forehead to the ground as a sign of respect in this greeting.
2. A binnacle is a nonmagnetic stand. The ship's compass case is set on this stand.
3. Henry Watson Fowler is a person. Scholars are indebted to him for writing *The Dictionary of Modern Usage* (1926).
4. Biological warfare is a type of military operation. Disease-producing microorganisms or organic biocides are used in this a type of military operation to kill humans and destroy livestock and crops.

B. Correct the error in object pattern for each sentence. If there is no error, write "correct" in the space provided.

1. A guest is one to who hospitality is extended at someone's home.

....

2. Judaism is the monotheistic religion to which Jews adhere.

....

3. A jukebox is an enclosed phonograph that people put coins to select records to play.

....

4. Hearing is the sense by which sound is perceived by this sense.

....

ⓓⓘⓢⓒⓞⓥⓔⓡⓨ
9.6: Reviewing subject and object adjective clause patterns

- On a separate sheet of paper, combine each of the following sets of sentences into one sentence, using subject and object adjective clause patterns.
- Use formal patterns.

↬ **Examples**

A juju is an object. The object is used as a charm in West Africa. Also, supernatural power is attributed to the object.

A juju is an object that is used as a charm in West Africa and to which supernatural power is attributed.

A confessional is a room. The room is a small, enclosed stall. A priest hears confessions in this stall.

A confessional is a room that is a small, enclosed stall in which a priest hears confessions.

1. An ant cow is an aphid. This aphid produces a thick, sweet substance. Ants feed on this substance.
2. A culch is an oyster bed. The bed is made of crushed shells and gravel. Oyster spawn may stick to the crushed shells and gravel.
3. A doormat is a mat. This mat is placed in front of a doorway. People wipe their shoes on this mat before they enter a house.
4. A safety island is an area for pedestrians. This area for pedestrians is marked off within a roadway. Traffic is banned from the area.

FORMAL DEFINITIONS

Adjective Clauses

There are two major types of adjective clauses: essential (restrictive), which are not enclosed in commas, and nonessential (nonrestrictive), which are enclosed in commas. Essential adjective clauses are generally used in formal definitions, and nonessential adjective clauses are usually used in informal definitions and appositives.

In the previous section, you practiced forming essential adjective clauses. Essential adjective clauses are essential (important or necessary) to limit (restrict) the nouns they modify, so they are not set off with commas. Essential adjective clauses answer the questions "What kind or type?", "Which one?", etc. In the following sentences, the word "plants" is not limited. Therefore, the difference between perennials and annuals is not clear.

↬ **Examples**

Perennials are plants.   (What kind of plants are perennials?)
Annuals are plants.   (What kind of plants are annuals?)

Essential adjective clauses can be used to distinguish between perennials and annuals. Notice that there are no commas because the adjective clauses provide necessary information to differentiate these kinds of plants. The adjective clauses can begin with the relative pronoun *which* or *that.*

↬ **Examples**

Perennials are plants which/that return every growing season.
Annuals are plants which/that last only one growing season.

The previous sentences are examples of formal definitions. Formal definitions consist of three parts: the term being defined, the class (group, category) the term belongs to, and the information that differentiates terms that belong to the same class (differentia). Formal definitions are stated two ways. Note that there are no commas in either Pattern or B, and that the relative pronouns *that* and *which* can both be used. Also, note that the verb is active in Pattern A and passive in Pattern B.

Pattern A

Term	+	Verb	+	Class	+	Differentia
Perennials		are		plants		which/that return every growing season.
Annuals		are		plants		which/that last only one growing season

Pattern B

Class	+	Differentia	+	Verb	+	Term
Plants		*which/that return every growing season*		are called		perennials.
Plants		*which/that last only one growing season*		are called		annuals.

ⓓⓘⓢⓒⓞⓥⓔⓡⓨ

9.7: Identifying the parts of formal definitions

In each of the following sentences, label the three parts of formal definitions: a) the term being defined, b) the class (group, category) to which the term belongs, and c) the information which differentiates terms that belong to the same class (differentia).

⇨ **Examples**

Facts are specific pieces of information that have been verified.

  (a)   (b)   (c)

Plants that last only one growing season are called annuals.

  (b)   (c)   (a)

1. A kowtow is a Chinese greeting in which a person touches the forehead to the ground as a sign of respect.
2. A nonmagnetic stand on which the ship's compass case is set is called a binnacle.
3. Henry Watson Fowler is the person to whom scholars are indebted for writing *The Dictionary of Modern Usage* (1926).
4. Biological warfare is a type of military operation in which disease-producing microorganisms or organic biocides are used to kill humans and destroy livestock and crops.

ⓓⓘⓢⓒⓞⓥⓔⓡⓨ

9.8: Paraphrasing formal definitions

On a separate sheet of paper, paraphrase the following statements, using Pattern B for formal definitions.

⇨ **Example**

Perennials are plants that return every growing season.

Plants that return every growing season are called perennials.

1. Bees are stinging insects that suck nectar and gather pollen from flowers.
2. Hornets are stinging wasps that build large papery nests.
3. Facts are specific pieces of information that have been verified as true.

4. Folk dances are traditional dances that originated among the common people of a nation or region.
5. Monocrats are people that favor autocracy.
6. Monks are men who live in monasteries and who belong to brotherhoods that require a life of devotion and strict discipline.

Adjective Phrases

You might have noticed that some of the sentences you wrote in the previous Discovery exercises were lengthy. To be concise and to save time writing, you can change subject adjective clauses to adjective phrases. In Chapter 5, you learned how to change time clauses to time phrases.

⇨ Examples

<u>Time Clauses</u>

When rosebushes are given the proper amount of sunlight and water (passive voice), they produce beautiful blooms in the summertime.

When Professor Miller was writing the class lecture (active voice), she needed to refer to a dictionary several times.

<u>Participial Phrases of Time</u>

When given the proper amount of sunlight and water (passive voice), rosebushes produce beautiful blooms in the summertime.

When writing the class lecture (active voice), Professor Miller needed to refer to a dictionary several times.

To change adjective clauses to adjective phrases, the rules are the same.
1. Make sure both clauses refer to the same subject.

2. Delete the subject + *be*. Either the past participle (signifying passive voice) or the present participle (signifying active voice) will remain. Do not change the voice.

3. If the clause does not contain the verb *be*, change the verb to an *-ing* form.

Passive Voice

Delete subject + *be*   U.S. senators are public officials [~~who are~~ elected to serve in the Senate].
                                                        (FULL ADJECTIVE CLAUSE)

Keep *-ed*   U.S. senators are public officials [elected to serve in the Senate].
                                                        (ADJECTIVE PHRASE)

Active Voice

<u>With *be*</u>

Delete subject + *be*   A person [~~who is~~ running for public office] is called a candidate.
                                                        (FULL ADJECTIVE CLAUSE)

Keep *-ing*   A person [running for public office] is called a candidate.
                                                        (ADJECTIVE PHRASE)

<u>Without *be*</u>

Delete subject   Plants [~~which~~ last ^*ing* only one growing season] are called annuals.
                                                        (FULL ADJECTIVE CLAUSE)

Use *-ing* form   Plants [lasting only one growing season] are called annuals.
                                                        (ADJECTIVE PHRASE)

ⓓⓘⓢⓒⓞⓥⓔⓡⓨ
9.9:   Forming adjective phrases

- On a separate sheet of paper, change each of the following adjective clauses to an adjective phrase. Refer to the previous rules and examples.
- If no change is possible, write "not possible" below the adjective clause. Only subject adjective clauses can be changed to phrases.

↬ Examples

> The process <u>in which liquid is vaporized by the application of heat</u> is called boiling.
> *not possible*

> A folk dance is a traditional dance that originated among the common people of a nation or a region.

> *A folk dance is a traditional dance originating among the common people of a nation or a region.*

1. A monocrat is a person who favors autocracy.
2. A monk is a man who lives in a monastery. A monk also belongs to a brotherhood that requires a life of devotion and strict discipline.
3. Shatter cones are conical rock fragments that are formed from the high pressure of volcanic activity and that have striations that radiate from the apex.
4. Ant cows are aphids that produce a thick, sweet substance on which ants feed.
5. A culch is an oyster bed that is made of crushed shells and gravel to which oyster spawn may stick.
6. A dunlin is a brown and white sandpiper that lives in the northern regions.
7. A safety island is an area that is provided for the safety of pedestrians. It is marked off within a roadway from which traffic is banned.
8. Antechambers are small rooms that serve as entryways into larger rooms.

INFORMAL DEFINITIONS

To state informal definitions, use nonessential adjective clauses. Adjective clauses are nonessential if they are not needed to limit, restrict, or define the noun. Whereas essential adjective clauses are needed to define which one or what kind, nonessential adjective clauses simply supply additional information about the noun. Therefore, commas are used to set off a nonessential clause in the following cases.

1. The nonessential clause is a proper noun (the name of a specific person, place, or thing). Proper nouns are capitalized.

↬ Examples

> AIDS, which is the acronym for "acquired immune deficiency syndrome," is a disease that is caused by HIV.

> HIV, which is a virus that attacks the body's immune system, is the abbreviation for "human immunodeficiency virus."

> Scholars are indebted to Henry Watson Fowler, who is the author of *The Dictionary of Modern Usage* (1926).

Note: The pronouns *which* and *who* (not *that*) are used in nonessential adjective clauses.

2. The information in the clause applies to all members of the class to which the noun antecedent belongs.

➥ **Examples**

> Kangaroos, which are herbivorous marsupials, have short forelimbs, large hind limbs, and sharp cutting teeth.
>
> (All kangaroos are marsupials, and all kangaroos have the physical features listed.)

<u>Compare</u>

Adjective clauses are essential if the information applies to only some of the class. In this case, commas are not used.

➥ **Examples**

> Kangaroos that are three months old are called joeys.
>
> (Not all kangaroos are three months old, and not all kangaroos are called joeys.)

Moreover, in informal definitions, the class and/or differentia are stated in nonessential adjective clauses that modify the term.

Formal definition Kangaroos are herbivorous marsupials which have short forelimbs, large hind limbs, and sharp cutting teeth.

<u>Word Order</u>

1. Term: kangaroo
2. Class: herbivorous marsupials
3. Differentia: short forelimbs, large hind limbs, and sharp cutting teeth

Informal definition Kangaroos, which are herbivorous marsupials, have short fore-limbs, large hind limbs, and sharp cutting teeth.

<u>Word Order</u>

1. Term: kangaroo
2. Class: herbivorous marsupials
3. Differentia: short forelimbs, large hind limbs, and sharp cutting teeth

3. There is only one noun antecedent.

➥ **Examples**

> The urgent matter was brought to the attention of the president of the United States, who had just returned from Camp David.

4. The context has limited the noun because of subsequent reference. In other words, when a noun is initially introduced into the context (first reference), it is indefinite (general). To signify this, use *a* or *an*. When that noun is used again in the same context (subsequent reference), it becomes definite (specific), so use *the*. In addition, an adjective clause modifying a definite noun is nonessential because the context has limited the noun.

➥ **Examples**

> On April 3, 1974, *a* tornado struck in Northern Alabama. *The* tornado, *which* had wind speeds of 260 mph, cut a 51-mile-long path. (JR, "The Jumbo Outbreak." *Weatherwise*, Je./Jul. 1995, pp. 58-59.)

🄳🄸🅂🄲🄾🅅🄴🅁🅈
9.10: Punctuating adjective clauses

- Read the following study chart on migraine headaches.
- In the sentences that follow the chart, add commas to set off the nonessential adjective clauses.
- Indicate where the pronoun *that* could be used instead of *which*.

Migraines

	<u>Classic Migraines</u>	<u>Common Migraines</u>
Warning signs:	Aura, muscle tension	No aura or muscle tension
Head pain:	On one side or both sides of the head	On only one side of the head
Onset:	Fast	Slow
Duration:	15 to 20 minutes	Longer than that of classic migraines
Major causes:	Changes in the levels of serotonin	
	Changes in the blood vessels in the brain	
Some triggers:	Foods with phenylalanine, tyramine, and sodium nitrite	
	Depression, stress, exhaustion	
	Changes in weather or altitude	
	Loud noises, strong odors, bright lights	
	Missing meals or fasting	
Treatments:	Aspirin, acetaminophen, ibuprofen, naproxen, ergotamine, sumatriptan, Stadol NS	

This chart is based on information from the pamphlet "Migraine Headaches: Ways to Deal With Pain," (#1533), © 1993 AAFP, revised September 1997. AAFP, 8880 Ward Parkway, Kansas City, MO 64114. See also "Family Medicine Online" at [http:www.aafp.org] and "Health Answers" at [http://www.healthanswers.com].

1. The AAFP which is a large medical specialty group publishes several materials on health information.

2. Migraines which are severe headaches can last up to 24 hours.

3. Common migraines are severe headaches which are not characterized by an aura at the onset and which are not caused by muscle tension.

4. Classic migraines which are characterized by an aura at the onset last 15 to 20 minutes.

5. Foods which contain sodium nitrite, tyramine, and phenylalanine can trigger migraines.

6. Ergotamine which is a drug which is used to treat migraines must not be used every day.

7. Narcotics are drugs which are classified as addictive. Stadol NS which is a nasal spray prescribed to treat persistent and painful migraines must be used cautiously because it is addictive.

8. Some of the drugs which are used to treat migraines are given as shots.

9. Some things which trigger migraines include stress, fasting, depression, and changes in the weather.

10. Changes in serotonin which is a chemical in the brain can cause migraines.

Nonessential Adjective Phrases

To form adjective phrases from nonessential adjective clauses, follow the same rules as for essential adjective phrases that you read about earlier in this chapter. Notice that sometimes a noun phrase remains when you omit the pronoun and the verb *be*. Also, notice that some sentences in which clauses have been replaced with phrases sound much less awkward.

Clauses	AIDS, which is the acronym for "acquired immune deficiency syndrome," is a disease that is caused by HIV, which is a virus that attacks the body's immune system. HIV is the acronym for "human immunodeficiency virus."
Phrases	AIDS, the acronym for "acquired immune deficiency syndrome," is a disease caused by HIV, a virus that attacks the body's immune system. HIV is the acronym for "human immunodeficiency virus."
Clauses	Scholars are indebted to Henry Watson Fowler, who is the author of *The Dictionary of Modern Usage* (1926), which is an indispensable reference book.
Phrases	Scholars are indebted to Henry Watson Fowler, the author of *The Dictionary of Modern Usage* (1926), an indispensable reference book.

DISCOVERY
9.11: Changing adjective clauses to phrases

On a separate sheet of paper, change all of the adjective clauses in Discovery 9.10 to adjective phrases.

CHAPTER *summary*

- Essay tests are exams that require answers in complete sentences, paragraphs, or essays. Essay tests are usually given in class and have a specified time limit. Sometimes essay tests are given as take-home exams for which you are given a specific due date, but no specific number of minutes or hours in which to complete it. In either case, you need to finish the test within the time limit and not ask for more time.

- Studying for and taking an essay test involves following the writing process. During the first stage (prewriting), be an active participant in class, preview and review often, and stay organized. In the next stage (organizing), predict essay test questions, synthesize your notes, and practice organizing possible answers to the test questions. During the actual test, read the test carefully before beginning, plan your strategy, and watch your time. While writing, use correct grammar and effective paragraph and/or essay organization. Above all, be informative. Revising, the next step, might be more difficult to do on an in-class test. You might have time to make additions neatly in an available space. However, if the essay test is a take-home exam, you can revise as much as possible to perfect the answers, as long as you submit the test by the due date. Finally, proofread and edit take-home tests effectively. On in-class tests, allow time for proofreading and editing.

- An essay test may consist of some or all of the following parts: a short answer (name, identify, and define), a single-paragraph answer, and an essay answer (short or long). Always read through the test before you begin. Analyze the parts and point values, plan your strategy, and keep track of time. Do not spend too much time on parts of lesser value at the expense of the major parts of the test.

- Also, make sure that you fully respond to all of the required questions. Do not do more than you are required to do, and do not change the questions. Address each part of the essay question. Convert each assignment task into a thesis or topic sentence (as you would do for any essay assignment).

- Use effective sentence organization. Adjective clauses and phrases are used for stating formal and informal definitions. Adjective phrases are more concise than adjective clauses. Essential adjective clauses and phrases are used with formal definitions. Commas are not used with essential adjective clauses and phrases because the clauses and phrases are needed to limit (define and restrict) the noun antecedent. Also, the information may be about some (not all) of the members of the class or be a first reference.

- Nonessential adjective clauses and phrases are used with informal definitions. Nonessential adjective clauses and phrases are set off by commas because these structures are not needed to specify or limit the noun antecedent. The information in the adjective clause or phrase describes all of the members of the class, or the noun antecedent is one of a kind, a proper noun, or subsequent reference.

Appendix

A   *Format Guidelines for Academic Writing Assignments*

B   *Correction Symbols*

C   *Subject-Verb Agreement*

Appendix A

Format Guidelines for Academic Writing Assignments

The following format guidelines for academic writing assignments are standard requirements at most universities in the U.S. and Canada. You will be graded on the format of your paper because its appearance affects the paper's content and readability. Because you put a lot of time and effort into writing the paper, you want to make sure that it shows in the final product.

Some professors accept handwritten papers, but most prefer typed papers. Before submitting an assignment, double-check with your professor on his or her preference.

1. **Paper Type.** If handwriting, use only 8 1/2″ x 11″ white 3-hole loose-leaf paper. Paper torn out of a spiral notebook is unacceptable. If typing, use standard blank typing paper.

2. **Use of Paper.** Write or type on only one side of the paper.

3. **Characters.** If handwriting the paper, use ink, not pencil, and write neatly. If typing, use font size 12, and do not put the entire text in bold. As for font style, choose any clear printed style, not script.

4. **Label.** In the upper right-hand corner (or on a separate cover page), write or type your full name, ID number, the course and section number, the assignment, and the date (label).

   ➾ **Example**

   Jane Doe
   008976
   ELSP 003, Section 1
   C1D1
   January 19, 1999

5. **Title.** Write the title in the center of the top line of page 1 or centered on the cover page. Use the following rules for titles.
   - Follow the assignment focus.
   - Use phrases, not sentences, for the title. Write a short phrase indicating the topic of the paper. Do not use the topic sentence or thesis as a title.
   - Capitalize the first and last words in the title. Capitalize all other words except for any articles, coordinating conjunctions (*and, but, or, for, nor*), and prepositions of four or fewer letters.
   - Do not underline the title or enclose it in quotation marks.
   - Do not use a period at the end of the title.

   ➾ **Example**

   How to Write a Title
   The Characteristics of a Good Teacher
   The Benefits of Travel

6. **Indentations.** Indent the first line of every new paragraph in the paper. The indentation should be no longer than 1 inch, or 5 spaces.

7. **Lines.** Write on every other line (skip lines), or double-space if typing. When you start a new paragraph, skip only one line.

8. **Margins.** Do not write in the margins. Leave 1-inch margins on the top, sides, and bottom of the paper. Also, if you are handwriting the paper, make sure the holes are on the left side of the paper.

9. **Pagination.** The number of the first page should be either omitted or centered at the bottom of the page. Number the rest of the pages in the upper right-hand corner and submit the paper with the pages in the correct order. Most word-processing programs offer the option to paginate automatically.

10. **Spelling.** Proofread the paper carefully for misspellings and errors in mechanics. If typing on a computer or word processor, use the spelling-check feature. If you are unsure of the spelling of a word, check an American English dictionary. Spell out numbers under 10 and any number that begins a sentence. Avoid using contractions in academic writing.

11. **Punctuation**
    - Do not leave extra spaces after abbreviations such as a.m. and p.m., after beginning parentheses, or before (or after) dashes.
    - Leave one space after final parentheses, commas (,), semicolons (;), and colons (:).
    - Leave two spaces after the final punctuation in a sentence, such as periods (.), exclamation points (!), and question marks (?).
    - If you need a symbol that is not on your keyboard, add it in black ink.

12. **Stapling.** Staple all the pages together in the upper left-hand corner in the correct order.

Writing Process for Computer-typed Papers

Typed papers are easier to read and look more professional than handwritten papers. Thus, professors usually require that papers be typed. Learning to use a word-processing program on a computer is the most efficient way to compose a paper, even though it might take longer at first while you are learning. But in the long run it will save you time because you can revise more easily.

Follow this process for typing your papers on the computer.

1. After you have planned and organized your composition, type your draft on the computer. Some people like to write out the first draft by hand and then type it on the computer. Choose whichever method works best for you.

2. Print out the first draft and make revision notes directly on the hard copy (the printed-out copy of your composition). Studies show that most people revise more effectively on the hard copy than on the computer screen. Write the draft number and the date of the revision on the first page of the hard copy (e.g., "First Draft, January 5, 1998") so that you have a chronological record of the changes made before the final draft.

3. Type your revisions on the computer. Save frequently so that you do not lose your hard work. Print out another copy. Then revise again as you proofread the hard copy.

4. Type your final revisions and proofreading corrections on the computer. After that, make sure that the format follows the appropriate guidelines. Use the spelling-check feature to catch any new spelling errors.

5. Print the final draft (and save the document on disk because you may need it again for revision). Use a laser or laser-quality printer and check that the print is dark enough to read. Make sure the pages are numbered and in order before handing in the paper.

6. Save all the hard copies that you have proofread and made revision notes on because you may need to hand these drafts in, especially if you are required to submit all of your materials. It is also a good idea to make a couple of copies of the final draft and make a back-up disk in case something should happen to the hard drive.

Appendix B

Correction Symbols

The following symbols will be used to help you make corrections to your written work. Insert the appropriate symbol near the error. You should become familiar with them to make editing your work easier.

SYMBOL	MEANING, CORRECTION ADVICE, AND EXAMPLES
FRAG	**fragment**; complete the sentence

> **Example**

| Original Sentence | I went to the doctor. Because I was sick. |
| Revised Sentence | I went to the doctor because I was sick. |

R-O   **run-on**; divide the sentences with a period or semicolon, or use a conjunction

> **Example**

| Original Sentence | He will go to school he will make good grades. |
| Revised Sentence | He will go to school, and he will make good grades. |

P   **punctuation**; add, omit, or change it

> **Example**

| Original Sentence | I'll call you, after I get home. |
| Revised Sentence | I'll call you after I get home. |

Δ   **article**; use *a, an, the,* or no article

> **Example**

| Original Sentence | Learn about the culture as well as language. |
| Revised Sentence | Learn about the culture as well as the language. |

∧   **missing text**; add a word or group of words

> **Example**

| Original Sentence | Please speak to me before leave. |
| Revised Sentence | Please speak to me before you leave. |

Ø   **omit**; take out this unnecessary word or phrase

> **Example**

| Original Sentence | I like the my teacher. |
| Revised Sentence | I like my teacher. |

F **form**; use another form of the same word or verb

➩ **Example**

Original Sentence	The U.S. and Japan used to be very difference.
Revised Sentence	The U.S. and Japan used to be very different.

W **word choice**; use a different word or phrase

➩ **Example**

Original Sentence	I have been knowing English for two years.
Revised Sentence	I have been studying English for two years.

S **spelling**; check spelling, using a spelling-check feature or a dictionary; divide words correctly

➩ **Example**

Original Sentence	I dicided to study at MU.
Revised Sentence	I decided to study at MU.

WO **word order**; use English word order; switch or move words or groups of words

➩ **Example**

Original Sentence	Hot and spicy food Korean is delicious, such as kimchi.
Revised Sentence	Hot and spicy Korean food, such as kimchi, is delicious.

C **capitalization**; change to capital or lowercase letter

➩ **Example**

Original Sentence	The united states is a big country.
Revised Sentence	The United States is a big country.

**number agreement**; use countable/noncountable and singular/plural nouns correctly

➩ **Example**

Original Sentence	The equipments in the lab will help me do my researches.
Revised Sentence	The equipment in the lab will help me do my research.

AGR **agreement**; use correct subject-verb or pronoun-antecedent agreement

➩ **Example**

Original Sentence	John do not like sports because it is boring.
Revised Sentence	John does not like sports because they are boring.

T **verb tense**; change the verb tense

➩ **Example**

Original Sentence	When I come to the U.S., I was surprised by many things.
Revised Sentence	When I came to the U.S., I was surprised by many things.

REF **reference**; change the sentence to clarify what word this word refers to

➩ **Example**

Original Sentence	John called Bill when he finished eating.
Revised Sentence	When John finished eating, he called Bill.

∪ **join**; combine these two words into one

    ↪ **Example**

        Original Sentence   Does any one know the answer to this question?
        Revised Sentence   Does anyone know the answer to this question?

COMBINE **combine**; join these sentences or phrases

    ↪ **Example**

        Original Sentence   I have a brother. He lives in Ohio. He has two children. They are cute.
        Revised Sentence   My brother, who lives in Ohio, has two cute children.

DIVIDE **divide**; this sentence is too long; divide or shorten it

    ↪ **Example**

        Original Sentence   My brother, who lives in Ohio, has two cute children, who like to go swimming in the city pool even though one of them almost drowned last summer, a very frightening experience.
        Revised Sentence   My brother, who lives in Ohio, has two cute children. They all like to go swimming in the city pool even though one of the children almost drowned last summer. It was a very frightening experience.

/ **separate**; separate into two words

    ↪ **Example**

        Original Sentence   Joe was injured in the accident, and he maybe in the hospital for a while.
        Revised Sentence   Joe was injured in the accident, and he may be in the hospital for a while.

// **parallelism**; make these structures parallel

    ↪ **Example**

        Original Sentence   I like to cook, sleeping late, and when I work out.
        Revised Sentence   I like to cook, sleep late, and work out.

¶ **paragraphing**; combine or separate the paragraphs

? **unclear, unreadable, doubtful, awkward**; reword this part so that it is clear and effective

Appendix C

Subject-Verb Agreement

1. When the following words are used as subjects, they are always singular. Some of these words are plural in meaning, but they always require a singular verb, even if a plural phrase follows.

everyone	everybody	everything	neither
someone	somebody	something	either
anyone	anybody	anything	each
no one	nobody	nothing	one

   ⇨ **Examples**

   Everyone is sick with the flu, so school is canceled.
   Nobody has time to help me.
   Either of the recipes *is* good, so it does not matter which one you give me.
   Every cup and saucer *is* broken.
   One of the best books written *is Joy Luck Club,* by Amy Tan.

2. Some nouns ending in *-s,* including proper names, academic subjects, and diseases, take singular verbs. Pronouns and modifiers used with these nouns should also be singular.

   ⇨ **Examples**

mathematics	measles	news	physics
economics	mumps	ethics	politics

   Economics is an important field to study.
   The *news* about your award *was* exciting.

   Some words, such as *species* and *series,* are the same in the plural and singular forms.

   ⇨ **Examples**

   The *series* about dolphins *was* very interesting.
   Eight *series* of tests *were* performed on that new product.

   When statistics refers to facts and figures, it is plural; when it refers to the course of study, it is singular.

   ⇨ **Examples**

   The *statistics* in this article *are* misleading.
   Statistics is a challenging course.

3. Plural titles of books, magazines, movies, and plays take singular verbs.

⇨ **Examples**

> **Mermaids** *is* a film starring Cher.
> **Cats** *is* the longest-running play on Broadway.

4. Expressions stating one amount (a unit) of time, money, weight, distance, volume, and so on are plural in form but take singular verbs.

⇨ **Examples**

> *Two weeks is* not enough time for me to finish this paper.
> *Ten pounds is* too much weight to gain during the semester break.

5. As subjects, gerunds are singular. Compound gerunds are plural.

⇨ **Examples**

> *Consuming too much caffeine is* bad for the nerves.
> *Getting regular exercise and taking a warm bath are* two good ways to relieve stress.

6. Noncountable nouns are singular and take singular modifiers. The following nouns may be countable in other languages or in specific fields of study, but they are noncountable in standard American English.

⇨ **Examples**

Noncountable Nouns	Modifiers
entertainment	much (in negatives and questions)
fun	little (not much)
research	a little (some)
luck	a great deal of
equipment	quite a bit of
homework, work	amount of
advice	piece/bit of

The new lab **equipment is** expensive.
The **homework** for today **was** time-consuming.

7. Subjects that are joined by *and* or *both . . . and* take a plural verb.

⇨ **Examples**

> *Both cats and dogs make* good pets, but I prefer cats.
> *Baseball, football, and soccer are* outdoor sports.

8. Plural modifiers used as subjects take plural verbs.

> **Examples**

<u>Plural Modifiers</u>

few (not many)	both
a few (some)	a lot of
many	two, three, four . . .
several	a (great) number of

Several (people) *have* signed up for the trip so far.
Only *a few* (students) *are* absent today.

9. Sometimes adjectives preceded by the article *the* are used as subjects of sentences. These subjects are always plural because the understood subject is plural.

> **Examples**

the rich	the living	the injured
the poor	the dead	the physically challenged

The rich get richer; *the poor get* poorer.
The injured have been taken to St. Vincent's Medical Center.

10. Nouns that indicate sets take plural verbs, except when preceded by a singular modifier that is the subject with which the verb must agree.

> **Examples**

<u>Clothes</u>	<u>Tools</u>
jeans	scissors
pants	pliers
trousers	tweezers
sunglasses	
eyeglasses	

The *scissors are* over there. Will you get them for me?
My new *pair* of scissors *is* over there. Will you get it for me?
Your new *jeans are* torn! What happened to them?
Your new *pair* of jeans *is* torn. What happened to it?

11. The plural form of some irregular countable nouns do not end in -s and can take either a singular or plural verb, depending on the number of the subject.

> **Examples**

That *deer is* beautiful.   (There is only one.)
Those *sheep need* shearing.   (There are two or more.)

12. Phrases and clauses that come between the subject and verb do not change the number of the subject.

> **Examples**

My *mother* together/along with my aunts *is* going to Europe in the spring.
A *teacher* who has 30 students *spends* a lot of time grading.

13. For sentences with certain correlative conjunctions (*not only . . . but also, neither . . . nor, either . . . or*), the verb agrees with the noun closest to it (the proximity principle).

> ➾ **Examples**

> Neither the surgeon nor the **nurses have done** anything wrong.
> Neither the nurses nor the **surgeon has done** anything wrong.
> Either my brothers or my **sister has** your books.
> Either my sister or my **brothers have** your books.

14. In sentences that begin with *there, here,* or question words (*who, what, when, where, why,* and *how*), the noun immediately following the verb is the subject of the sentence.

> ➾ **Examples**

> There **are** three **assignments** due on Monday.
> Where **are** my new **gloves**? I put **them** on the table a few minutes ago, and now
>   **they are** missing.
> Here **is** the **newspaper** you asked for.

15. In a sentence beginning with a quantity expression, the verb form is singular or plural, depending on the noun following the quantity expression. In the case of *minority* and *majority*, these quantity expressions are similar to collectives and can be either singular or plural.

> ➾ **Examples**

> <u>Quantity Expressions</u>

> | | |
> |---|---|
> | all | majority |
> | half | minority |
> | most | percent |
> | none | some |

> All of the **book is** ruined.
> All of my **books were** soaked in the flood.
> Fifty percent of our **students oppose** the issue
> Half of the **cookies are** gone! Who ate them?
> Half of the **cake is** gone! Who ate it?
> The **majority rules;** the bill is vetoed.
> A majority of **teachers work** in the summer.

16. The expression *a number* is plural when it is modifying a plural noun that is the subject of the sentence; *the number* is singular when it is the subject of the sentence.

> ➾ **Examples**

> A number of **items were** missing from the store.
> The number of **applicants** for this position **is** 50.

17. Nouns for nationality that end in *-ese, -ch,* or *-sh* can be singular or plural, depending on their meaning. When the word refers to the language, it takes a singular verb. When it refers to the people of the country, it takes a plural verb and is preceded by the article *the*.

⇨ **Examples**

> *French is* a romance language.
> *The French are* famous for their fine wines and excellent cuisine.

18. Collective nouns are usually singular if the members of the group are functioning as a unit. However, they can be plural if the members of the group are functioning as individuals.

⇨ **Examples**

> Collective Nouns
>
> | | |
> |---|---|
> | class | faculty |
> | committee | team |
> | audience | jury |
> | army | the staff |
>
> The *class has* an exam on Wednesday.
> The *faculty disagree* on the referendum. *They are* voting next week.

19. English has borrowed some words from Greek and Latin, some of which have irregular singular and plural forms.

Origin	Singular	Plural	Singular (Plural) Examples
Greek	-is	-es	basis (bases), crisis (crises)
Greek	-on	-a	phenomenon (phenomena)
Latin (masculine)	-us	-i	radius (radii), alumnus (alumni)
Latin (feminine)	-a	-ae	alga (algae), vita (vitae)
Latin (neuter)	-um	-a	datum (data), medium (media)
Latin	-ix	-ixes/-ices	appendix (appendixes/appendices)
Latin	-ex	-exes/-ices	index (indexes/indices)

Note: Current usage of *data* (the plural form of *datum*) to describe facts, information, or statistics can be either singular or plural form.

⇨ **Examples**

> These *data represent* our current findings.
> The *data* you requested *is* now available from the accounting department.

Appendix

D *Peer Review Forms*

Appendix D

Peer Review Forms

INSTRUCTIONS

1. You will be exchanging each peer review form with at least two other students in your peer review group, so you will need a minimum of two copies. Your instructor will advise you in advance how many copies to make. Some peer review forms are two pages long, so make sure that you tear out and photocopy both pages and staple each photocopied set together. File the original forms in your binder in the event you need to make another copy.

2. Prior to each peer review activity, clearly print your name on the line provided above "Writer" on each page of the form.

3. Trade one of these peer review forms and your assignment with another person in the peer review group. When you receive your classmate's peer review form, clearly print your name on the line provided above "Peer Reviewer."

4. Read the questions on the peer review form. Ask the instructor for assistance if you do not understand any of the questions on the form. Read the assignment carefully one time. Then read it again and answer the questions on the form. Be honest and helpful. Explain the answers in complete sentences.

5. Do not make marks or comments (correct the grammar or mechanics) directly on the assignment. Make all of your comments on the peer review form. Complete the form before discussing the assignment with your classmate.

6. When all the students in your group have finished, return the assignment and your completed peer review form to the student whom you exchanged forms with. Repeat the process with another student by exchanging a second copy of the peer review form and your assignment with another student. When your classmates are finished reviewing, study the comments they made about your assignment. If you do not understand a comment, ask for clarification.

7. During the discussion, refer to "Ground Rules for Peer-Reviewing" and "Strategies for Clarification" on pages 45–46 in Chapter 2. Also, stay focused on the task of peer reviewing.

8. Before revising your assignment, study your instructor's and classmates' comments. Note the major areas that need work. Replan the content, organization, and expressions accordingly. Do not be discouraged if the readers disagree. Each reader notices different things, and that is why you need more than one reader. If you have questions about strategies for revising, ask your instructor.

....

Writer   Peer Reviewer

Peer Review Form 1
COMPOSITION PEER REVIEW

1. Does the composition follow the assignment?

   ....

   ....

2. Is the topic of the composition clearly introduced? Is it effectively focused?

   ....

   ....

3. Are the main points clearly stated?

   ....

   ....

4. Is the content informative and convincing? Why or why not?

   ....

   ....

5. Is the composition clear?

   ....

   ....

6. Is the composition unified (no irrelevant support)?

   ....

   ....

7. Is the composition well organized?

   ....

   ....

Writer ....   Peer Reviewer ....

Peer Review Form 1

COMPOSITION PEER REVIEW (continued)

8. Is the tone formal and objective?

   ....

   ....

9. Is the use of language effective?

   ....

   ....

10. Is the conclusion logical?

    ....

    ....

11. What does the writer do especially well?

    ....

    ....

12. Make three suggestions to the writer.

    ....

    ....

    ....

Writer .... Peer Reviewer

Peer Review Form 2
PEER REVIEW FOR REVISION

1. Did the writer successfully follow your suggestions in your original peer review? What did the writer do especially well in the revision?

2. How and where did the writer make the content more convincing?

3. What new things did you learn about the topic assigned?

4. How and where did the organization improve?

5. How and where did the language (grammar and vocabulary) improve?

6. What did you learn from this writer about writing? What changes will you make to how you revise in the future?

Harcourt Brace & Company

Writer   Peer Reviewer

Peer Review Form 3
PROBLEM-SOLVING PEER REVIEW

1. Does the composition follow the assignment?

   ....

2. Is the topic of the composition clearly stated? Is it effectively focused?

   ....

   ....

3. Are the subtopics clearly stated?

   ....

4. Are the subtopics explained?

   ....

5. Are there general examples? Are they effective?

   ....

   ....

6. Are there specific examples? Are they explained?

   ....

   ....

7. What does the writer do especially well?

   ....

   ....

8. Do you have any relevant personal experience that could be included in this writer's composition?

   ....

   ....

Writer ....   Peer Reviewer ....

Peer Review Form 4

PARAGRAPH OUTLINE PEER REVIEW

1. Is the outline in the correct format (e.g., letters and numbers are in the right places, properly indented)?

....

....

2. Is the topic clearly introduced and focused correctly? (Does it follow the assignment?)

....

....

3. Are there at least two major subtopics (A, B, C)?

....

....

4. Are the subtopics clearly stated and distinct from one another (no overlap)?

....

....

5. Are the subtopics relevant to the topic sentence? Are they ordered logically and equal in value?

....

....

6. Are there at least two supporting points for each subtopic (1, 2, 3)?

....

....

7. Are there relevant and informative examples and details for each supporting point (a, b, c)?

....

....

Harcourt Brace & Company

Writer   Peer Reviewer

Peer Review Form 4

PARAGRAPH OUTLINE PEER REVIEW (continued)

8. Are the supporting points ordered logically and equal in value (no overlap)?

   ....

   ....

9. Are there logical concluding remarks (no new topics)?

   ....

   ....

10. What is the best part of the outline?

   ....

   ....

11. Make three suggestions to the writer.

   ....

   ....

   ....

Writer .... Peer Reviewer ....

Peer Review Form 5
ESSAY INTRODUCTION PEER REVIEW

1. Does the introduction follow the assignment?

   ....

   ....

2. What is the writer's hook? Is the hook effective?

   ....

   ....

3. What is the writer's thesis? Is the thesis clearly written?

   ....

   ....

4. What are the writer's purpose and method?

   ....

   ....

5. What is the writer's MAP? Is the MAP parallel and logical?

   ....

   ....

6. What does the writer do especially well?

   ....

   ....

7. Make three suggestions to the writer.

   ....

   ....

Harcourt Brace & Company

....
Writer   Peer Reviewer

Peer Review Form 6
ESSAY OUTLINE PEER REVIEW

1. Does the essay outline follow the assignment?

   ....

   ....

2. What is the writer's hook? Is the hook effective?

   ....

   ....

3. What is the writer's thesis? Is the thesis clearly written?

   ....

   ....

4. What are the writer's purpose and method?

   ....

   ....

5. What is the writer's MAP? Is the MAP parallel and logical?

   ....

   ....

6. Are the essay paragraphs labeled appropriately (I, II, III)?

   ....

   ....

7. Are the body paragraphs logically ordered?

   ....

   ....

Harcourt Brace & Company

Writer ....   Peer Reviewer ....

Peer Review Form 6

ESSAY OUTLINE PEER REVIEW (continued)

8. Are there clear topic sentences for each body paragraph?

9. Does each paragraph have at least two main points?

10. Do the subtopics (A, B, C) in any of the paragraphs overlap?

11. Does each main point have at least two logical supporting points (1, 2, 3)?

12. Are there specific levels in the outline (a, b, c)?

13. Is the support effective (convincing, unified, balanced)?

14. What does the writer do especially well?

15. Make three suggestions to the writer.

Writer ....   Peer Reviewer ....

Peer Review Form 7

ESSAY CONCLUSION PEER REVIEW

1. Does the conclusion begin with a signal (*In conclusion, Indeed, To conclude*)?

2. Does the conclusion recall the limited topic and opinion in the thesis?

3. Are the MAP points summarized (paraphrased, if possible)?

4. Are all the MAP points recognized in the summary?

5. Are any new MAP points brought up?

6. Does the conclusion contain a final comment (opinion)?

7. Does the conclusion follow the essay logically?

Writer   Peer Reviewer

Peer Review Form 7

ESSAY CONCLUSION PEER REVIEW (continued)

8. What does the writer do especially well?

    ....

    ....

9. Make three suggestions to the writer.

    ....

    ....

    ....

Writer .... Peer Reviewer ....

Peer Review Form 8

ESSAY PEER REVIEW

1. Does the essay follow the assignment?

   ....

   ....

2. What is the writer's hook? Is the hook effective?

   ....

   ....

3. What is the writer's thesis? Is the thesis clearly written and complete?

   ....

   ....

4. What are the writer's purpose and method?

   ....

   ....

5. What is the writer's MAP? Is the MAP parallel and logical?

   ....

   ....

6. How many body paragraphs are there? Are they logically ordered?

   ....

   ....

7. Are the topic sentences for each body paragraph clearly written?

   ....

   ....

Writer ....   Peer Reviewer ....

Peer Review Form 8

ESSAY PEER REVIEW (continued)

8. Does each paragraph have at least two main points?

   ....

   ....

9. Do the MAP points or support overlap in any of the paragraphs?

   ....

   ....

10. What kinds of support are used? Is the support convincing and substantial?

    ....

    ....

11. Is the conclusion logical and complete?

    ....

    ....

12. What does the writer do especially well?

    ....

    ....

13. Make three suggestions to the writer.

    ....

    ....

    ....

....
Writer   Peer Reviewer

Peer Review Form 9
CHRONOLOGICAL DEVELOPMENT PEER REVIEW

1. Does the essay follow the assignment?

   ....

   ....

2. What is the writer's hook? Is the hook effective?

   ....

   ....

3. Is the purpose of the past narration/process description clear?

   ....

   ....

4. Is the thesis complete and clear? Does it contain words appropriate to the method?

   ....

   ....

5. Is the content complete, interesting, and informative? How can the writer improve the content?

   ....

   ....

6. Are there any supporting points that do not relate to the thesis or subtopics?

   ....

   ....

7. Are the events/stages/steps/ways ordered logically?

   ....

   ....

Writer   Peer Reviewer

Peer Review Form 9

CHRONOLOGICAL DEVELOPMENT PEER REVIEW (continued)

8. Are sequential/nonsequential transitions used correctly?

9. Does the writer use a variety of time phrases, clauses, and connectors to provide coherence?

10. Are old ideas used to provide coherence?

11. Are the content words concise, specific, and accurate?

12. Are the verb tenses used correctly?

13. Is the conclusion complete and logical?

14. What does the writer do especially well?

15. Make three suggestions to the writer.

Writer .... Peer Reviewer

Peer Review Form 10
ANALOGY PEER REVIEW

1. What are the topics being compared?

   ....

   ....

2. Are the topics logical choices for the analogy?

   ....

   ....

3. Is the analogy clear?

   ....

   ....

4. Is it complete? Are there enough details and examples?

   ....

   ....

5. Does the vocabulary contribute to the development of the analogy?

   ....

   ....

6. Is the analogy well organized?

   ....

   ....

7. Are structures of comparison used effectively?

   ....

   ....

Writer ....   Peer Reviewer

Peer Review Form 10

ANALOGY PEER REVIEW (continued)

8. What does the writer do especially well?

   ....

   ....

9. How can the analogy be improved? Give the writer three suggestions.

   ....

   ....

   ....

Writer ....

Peer Reviewer ....

Peer Review Form 11

COMPARISON/CONTRAST OUTLINE PEER REVIEW

1. Does the outline follow the assignment?

   ....

   ....

2. Is the introduction complete, with a hook, a complete thesis, and a parallel MAP?

   ....

   ....

3. What is the purpose of the comparison/contrast?

   ....

   ....

4. Do the paragraph topics follow the order of the MAP?

   ....

   ....

5. Are complete topic sentences (not phrases) supplied for each paragraph? If so, are they labeled (II, III, IV)?

   ....

   ....

6. Do the thesis statement and topic sentences repeat words from the assignment? Do they contain vocabulary for comparison/contrast?

   ....

   ....

7. Is the outline clearly in either block or alternating form?

   ....

   ....

Harcourt Brace & Company

Writer ....   Peer Reviewer ....

Peer Review Form 11

8. Does each paragraph have the appropriate numbers of divisions (A, B, C)?

9. Do the subdivisions have a sufficient number of informative supporting points (1, 2, 3, a, b, c)?

10. Is the support unified at all levels and logically ordered according to the method?

11. Does the writer give equal attention to both topics being compared/contrasted?

12. Is the conclusion logical and complete?

13. What does the writer do especially well?

14. Make three suggestions to the writer.

Writer _____   Peer Reviewer _____

Peer Review Form 12

COMPARISON/CONTRAST ESSAY PEER REVIEW

1. Does the essay follow the assignment?

   ....

   ....

2. Is the introduction complete, with a hook, a complete thesis, and a parallel MAP?

   ....

   ....

3. What is the purpose of the comparison/contrast?

   ....

   ....

4. Do the paragraph topics follow the order of the MAP?

   ....

   ....

5. Are complete topic sentences supplied for each paragraph? Do they have transitions?

   ....

   ....

6. Do the thesis statements, topic sentences, and subtopic sentences repeat words from the assignment? Do they contain vocabulary for comparison/contrast?

   ....

   ....

7. Is the essay clearly in either block or alternating form?

   ....

   ....

....
Writer   Peer Reviewer

Peer Review Form 12

COMPARISON/CONTRAST ESSAY PEER REVIEW (continued)

8. Does each paragraph have the appropriate number of subtopics? Are the subtopics clearly introduced?

....

9. Is the support convincing, unified at all levels, and logically ordered according to the method?

....

....

10. Does the writer give equal attention to both topics being compared/contrasted?

....

....

11. Is the conclusion logical and complete?

....

....

12. Is the use of comparison/contrast grammar effective throughout the essay? Are old ideas used effectively?

....

....

13. What does the writer do especially well?

....

....

14. Make three suggestions to the writer.

....

....

....

....
Writer

....
Peer Reviewer

Peer Review Form 13

CAUSE/EFFECT ESSAY PEER REVIEW

1. Does the essay follow the assignment?

   ....

   ....

2. Does the introduction have an effective hook? What kind of hook is it?

   ....

   ....

3. Is there a thesis with a precise opinion and vocabulary from the assignment?

   ....

   ....

4. Does the thesis include cause/effect grammar? Does it include a MAP with three different MAP points in parallel form?

   ....

   ....

5. Are there complete topic sentences that have transitions? Do they include cause/effect grammar, recall the thesis, and state the topic clearly?

   ....

   ....

6. Is the body effectively ordered (familiarity, importance, classification, chain reaction)?

   ....

   ....

7. Is the support logical, substantial, and specific?

   ....

   ....

Writer   Peer Reviewer

Peer Review Form 13

CAUSE/EFFECT ESSAY PEER REVIEW (continued)

8. Where can the support improve?

9. Is the support effectively ordered (no overlap)?

10. Likewise, is the support in each paragraph relevant?

11. Is the essay coherent (does it effectively use cause/effect grammar)?

12. Is the conclusion complete and logical?

13. What does the writer do well?

14. Make three suggestions to the writer.

Writer .... Peer Reviewer ....

Peer Review Form 14

PARAPHRASE PEER REVIEW

1. Did the writer refer to the author and text as required?

   ....

   ....

2. Did the writer use terms that indicate opinion ("I think . . .") or claim the author's ideas as his/her own? If so, show where to change such references.

   ....

   ....

3. Did the writer misuse the source? If so, explain where.

   ....

   ....

4. Did the writer maintain the original meaning of the passage (accuracy)? If not, show where the wording should be revised.

   ....

   ....

5. Did the writer keep the same tone (serious, humorous, sarcastic) throughout? If not, show where the tone should be revised.

   ....

   ....

6. Did the writer add his/her own ideas, examples, details, or other forms of support to the paraphrase? If so, show where to change such references.

   ....

   ....

Writer .... Peer Reviewer ....

Peer Review Form 14

PARAPHRASE PEER REVIEW (continued)

7. Did the writer use techniques of paraphrasing effectively? Where?

....

....

8. Did the writer use correct capitalization and punctuation (no quotations for paraphrases)?

....

....

9. What did the writer do especially well?

....

....

10. Make three suggestions to the writer.

....

....

....

Writer _____   Peer Reviewer _____

Peer Review Form 15
SUMMARY PEER REVIEW

1. Does the summary contain the main ideas of the original text?

   ....

   ....

2. Does it contain indirect quotation?

   ....

   ....

3. Does it contain direct quotation? If so, was the direct quotation necessary?

   ....

   ....

4. Was the direct quotation stated and punctuated correctly?

   ....

   ....

5. Did the writer use his or her own words?

   ....

   ....

6. Did the writer let his or her own opinions interfere with the ideas in the text?

   ....

   ....

Writer ....   Peer Reviewer ....

Peer Review Form 15

SUMMARY PEER REVIEW (continued)

7. Did the writer add any ideas to the summary that are not in the original text?

....

....

8. Is the summary concise, accurate, clearly written, complete, and well organized? Discuss where there are problems.

....

....

9. Does the summary reflect the writer's ability to understand the meanings of words, the original author's attitude, and any implied meanings?

....

....

10. Did the writer criticize or judge the author in any way?

....

....

11. What did the writer do especially well?

....

....

12. Make three suggestions to the writer.

....

....

....

Index

academic honesty, 221–239
   cheating, 200, 221–222
   consequences of, 221–222
   plagiarism, 222–223, 244
academic writing
   characteristics of, 2–3, 29, 98–99 (labeled model)
   cultural differences, 2, 7–8
academic writing assignments, 32–36, 40, 66, 73, 106
   design of, 35–36
   instructions in, 35–36
   taking essay tests, 241–246, 258
   terms in, 33–34, 107
acknowledgments, stating, 223–225, 239
   direct vs. indirect quotations, 223, 226–227, 234–237
active voice (see *voice, active*)
adjectives, singular demonstrative, 19
adjective clauses (see *clauses, adjective*)
agreement, 19–20 (chart), 29
   adjective-noun, 20
   number, 19–20 (chart), 29
   pronoun-antecedent, 20, 29
   subject-verb, 20, 29, 248
alternating method (see *comparison/contrast, alternating method*)
analogies (see *comparisons; analogies*)
analysis (analyze), 33, 244–246, 258
argumentation (argue), 33 (see also *hooks, refutation; logical thinking*)
articles, 19
ascending order (best–last), 109–110
assignment task, 35–36
audience, 2, 4–5, 9, 12, 29, 56, 73, 102, 138
   (see also *formality, levels of*)

best first/last/no best (see *order, importance*)
bibliographic form, 222, 238
block method (see *comparison/contrast, block method*)
body paragraphs, 105–110, 130 (see also *order; outlining; topic sentences*)
brainstorming methods, 33, 40, 42–44, 73, 66
   charting, 44
   clustering, 43

   listing, 42–43
"by the way" statements (see *unity*)

capitalization, 254 (see also *quotations; sentences, types of; transitions*)
categories (see *classification; methods*)
causes, analysis of, 33–34, 190–202, 219
   critical thinking (see *logical thinking, post-hoc fallacy*)
   identifying causes, 194–198
causes, essays of, 192–194, 217–218 (model)
   framing, 200–201
   thesis statements, 201
   topic sentences, 201
causes, order of, 199–200, 219
   chain reaction, 200
   classification, 199
   familiarity, 200
   importance, 199
causes, structures of, 207–209, 219
   adverb clauses, 209
   adverb phrases, 208
   verbs, 208
chain reactions, 199–200, 215, 219
charting, 31, 40, 66
   study charts, 31, 166, 177, 194, 242
cheating (see *academic honesty*)
chronological development, 131–159
   narration, 131–137, 145, 146–147 (models)
   narration vs. process development, 145
   process description, 137–145 (model)
   time expressions in, 132, 151–156
   time lines, 134–135
citations, 239
clarification, strategies for, 46
classical rhetorical patterns (see *methods*)
classification (classify), 33–34
   combined with cause, 192–194 (model), 200, 219
   combined with effect analysis, 203–206 (models), 219
   combined with time order, 176–177 (model)
   outlines, 109–110
clause markers (see *subordinators*)
clauses, adjective (see also *definitions*)
   effect, 213, 219

essential, 88, 248–252, 258
    nonessential, 213, 254–258,
    object pattern, 249–250
    subject pattern, 213, 248
clauses, adverb, 88 (chart)
    cause/effect, 88, 209, 213, 219
    comparison, 88, 181
    concession, 88
    conditional, 88, 209
    contrast, 88, 184
    time, 88, 122–123 (see also *tenses*)
clauses, dependent, 181, 184, 223–225
    (see also *sentences, types of*)
    types of (chart), 88
clauses, independent (main), 87–93, 181, 184, 223–225
clauses, noun, 88, 223–225
closing remarks (see *conclusions*)
coherence, 10–12 (see also *old idea–new idea; transitions*)
colloquial discourse (see *formality, levels of*)
colons, 102, 138
commas, 61–64
    in adjective clauses, 61, 88, 213, 219, 248–252,
      254–255, 258
    in adverb clauses, 87–90, 122–123, 208–209
    in direct quotations, 234–236
    in enumeration patterns, 106, 180, 183, 201, 207
    in indirect quotations, 226–227, 236–237
    in MAP lists, 102, 138, 180, 183, 201, 206
    in parallel lists, 57–58
    in participial phrases, 214, 219, 253
    in phrases, 119, 152–154, 208–209
    in run-on sentences, 64, 66
    with connectors, 85–87, 120, 155, 210, 219
    with coordinating conjunctions, 85–86
comma splices (see *run-on sentences*)
comparison/contrast, alternating method, 163–165,
    187–188 (models)
    internal transitions, 183–184
    outline form, 162, 167–168, 170
    thesis statements, 162, 183
    topic sentences, 183
    vs. block form, 170, 174, 189
comparison/contrast analysis, 33–34, 161–189
    methods of (chart), 162, 166–170, 189
    points of, 162, 166–170, 189
    reasons for (chart), 162, 189
    time order, 174–177 (model)
comparison/contrast, block method
    old idea–new idea, 185–186, 189
    outline form, 162, 169–170
    thesis statements, 162, 169, 180, 183
    time order, 174

topic sentences, 162, 169
    vs. alternating, 170, 174, 189
comparison/contrast, structures of
    comparison, 179–180, 189
    contrast, 182–184, 189
comparison/contrast, time order, 174–177, 189
    outline form, past vs. present, 174
    tracing events, 175–177 (model)
comparisons, analogies, 63, 162, 171–173, 188
    examples of, 63, 68, 69, 76, 91, 101–102, 171–173
    internal transitions, 180–181
    thesis statements, 162, 171–173, 179
    topic sentence patterns, 179
concluding remarks (see *conclusions*)
conclusions, 82–83, 93, 105, 111
    in process development, 139
conjunctions, coordinating, 3
    compound sentences, 85–86
    compound-complex sentences, 90
    in assignments, 35–36
    meanings of (charts), 86–87
    parallel lists, 57
    punctuation of, 57
    run-on sentences, correction of, 64
conjunctions, correlative, 58
connectors
    addition, 106, 159
    chronological order, 156
    comparison, 180
    contrast, 183
    effect, 210, 219
    exemplification, 120
    meanings of (chart), 86–87
content words, 12
    descriptive use of, 146–148
    old idea–new idea, 12, 148–151, 185–186
    repetition of, 12, 106, 148
    synonyms, 148, 226
    unnecessary/excessive repetition of, 10–12,
      24–25, 248–258
contractions, 9
convincing, 2, 5 (see also *logical thinking; support*)
    on essay tests, 244–246
critical-thinking skills, 2, 32, 40, 66, 242–247, 258
    (see also *logical thinking*)

deductive pattern (see *linear logic*)
definitions (define), 33, 244–245, 258 (see also *clauses,
    adjective*)
    formal, 251–253
    informal, 254–255

depth of thought, 68 (see also *shallow [sophomoric] thinking*)
descending order (see *order, importance*)
description (describe), 33, 146–147
digression (see *unity*)
direct quotations (see *quotations, direct*)
discourse (see *formality, levels of*)
discussion skills (discuss), 45–46
dramatic hooks, 33 (see *hooks*)

editing, 33, 40, 66, 247, 258
effects, analysis of, 33–34, 202–207 (models), 219
    framing essays of, 206–207
    thesis statements, 206
    topic sentences, 207
effects, order of, 203–204, 219
    chain reaction, 199, 203, 215
    classification, 203–206 (model)
    familiarity, 203
    immediate vs. remote, 203–204
    importance, 203
effects, structures of, 210–215, 219
    adjective clauses, 210, 213
    chain reactions, 215
    connectors, 210
    participial adjective phrases, 214
    verbs, 211
English rhetorical system (see *methods*)
enumeration (enumerate), 34
enumeration signals, 106, 138, 156–157, 159
    addition, 106, 157, 180, 183, 199–202
    nonsequential process, 138, 157–158
    patterns, 106, 201, 203
    sequential process, 138, 156, 159
equal order (see *order, importance*)
essays, 95–118, 130
    essay test answers, 244–247, 258
    labeled model, 98–99
    parts of (overview of), 97
essay tests, 33–36, 99, 241–258
    parts of, 244–247
    studying for, 242–244
    time management of in-class writing assignments, 40–41, 44, 244–247
evaluations (evaluate), 34
examples, 33–36, 76–77, 125–126, 130 (see also *exemplification, structures of*)
exemplification, structures of, 118–120, 130
    active verbs, 120
    connectors, 120
    nouns, 119

passive verbs, 120
phrase markers, 119
explanation (explain), 34 (see also *support*)
expository writing, 67–68, 130
    (see also *support; tenses*)

familiarity, order of (see *order, familiarity*)
focus (see *academic writing assignments; thesis statements; topic sentences*)
formal discourse (see *formality, levels of*)
formality, levels of 4–5 (chart), 9, 29
    audience, 2–5, 10, 29, 56, 73, 102, 138
    colloquial discourse, 5, 9
    colloquial vs. formal (chart), 9
    examples of, 7–8
    formal discourse, 5, 9
    informal discourse, 5
    technical discourse, 5
    tone, 4–5
fragments, sentence 91–93 (see also *topic sentences*)
funnel hooks (see *hooks*)
fused sentences (see *run-on sentences*)

hooks, 99–101, 130
    dramatic, 100
    funnel, 101
    question, 100
    quotation, 100
    refutation, 101

identifications, 244–245, 258 (see also *definitions*)
idioms, 9
illustrations (illustrate), 33–34 (see *examples; exemplification, structures of*)
imperatives
    in assignment tasks, 35, 42
    in main clauses, 122
importance, order of (see *order, importance*)
inclusive language (see *point of view, problems with*)
indirect quotations (see *quotations*)
inductive pattern (see *linear logic*)
informal discourse (see *formality, levels of*)
introductions, essay, 99–102, 130 (see also *hooks; MAPS*)

levels of formality (see *formality, levels of*)
levels of generality (see *support*)
limited topic, 69, 106 (see also *academic writing assignments*)

linear logic, 2
  deductive, 2–3
  inductive, 3
logical thinking, 191, 194, 196, (see also *critical-thinking skills; support, problems with*)
  determining logical causes/effects, 191–196, 202–203
  post-hoc fallacy, 196
  simplistic (weak) thinking, 194, 199, 202–203

main clauses (see *clauses, independent*)
MAPS, 99, 102, 105–106, 108, 125, 130
mechanics, 106 (see also *capitalization; punctuation*)
message, 4, 102
methods, 3, 99, 101–102, 107 (see also *topic sentences*)
modals
  meanings of (chart), 143
  will vs. may, 142

narration, 132–147, 159 (see also *chronological development*)
  framing of, time lines, 134–135
  narration vs. process development, 137, 145 (chart)
  time expressions in, 132, 151–155
  time-order outline, 108, 174
  verbs for chronological order, 155
nonsequential process, 138, 157–159
nouns, 19–20, 29
  countable, 19–20
  noncountable, 19–20

objectivity, 5, 14, 29, 32
occasions, 5
old idea–new idea
  content words, 148–151
  paragraph-to-paragraph, 157, 169, 201, 207
  passive voice, 150
  time clauses, 149
  time phrases, 152–154
order, chronological, 34 (see also *order, process; order, time*)
order, familiarity, 110, 130, 200, 219
order, importance, 108–110, 130, 199, 201, 219
  ascending (best last), 109–110
  descending (best first), 109
  equal (no best), 109
order, process, 107–108, 130–131, 159
  nonsequential, 138, 157–158
  sequential, 138, 156

order, time, 108, 131–137, 174
  immediate vs. remote, 203–206 (model), 219
outline/trace, 34, 133–134 (model), 135–136 (model), 176–177 (model)
  past vs. present, 174
organizing, 33, 40, 66, 243–244, 258 (see also *outlining*)
outlining
  alternating form, 167–168, 170
  block form, 169–170
  cause/effect, 199–201, 206–207
  classification, 109–110, 200
  essay-level, 105–110, 130
  essay tests, 243–244, 258
  narration, 108, 132–136
  paragraph-level, 79–81, 93
  process description, 107–108, 138–139
  rules for, 79–81, 105
overlap, 77, 102 (see also *support*)

paragraphs, 67–85, 93
  essay test answers, 245, 258
  paragraph to essay, 97
parallelism, 57–58, 66 (see also *conjunctions, coordinating; MAPS; outlining; subtopics*)
  conjunctions, correlative, 58
paraphrases, 106, 111, 231, 239
  problems with, 225
  rules for effective, 231
  techniques, 225–229
participial phrases (see *phrases, participial*)
passive voice (see *voice, passive*)
peer review, 45–46, 48, 50, 66, 115–118
  benefits of, 45
  ground rules for, 45
  model, 48, 50
  related to revision, 45–56, 115–118
  strategies for clarification, 46
periods, 61–64
persuasive (persuade), 5 (see also **support**)
phrase markers
  addition, 157
  alternatives, 157
  cause, 208–209
  comparison, 181
  contrast, 183
  exemplification, 119
  time, 132
phrases, participial
  effect, 214, 219
  essential, 248–249, 258
  nonessential, 214, 219, 254–255, 258

Index

time, 153–154
plagiarism (see *academic honesty*)
point of view, 10, 12–17, 29
   first person, 12–13, 29
   second person, 13–14, 29
   summary chart, 14
   third person, 14–17, 29
point of view, problems with, 15–17, 29
   awkward pronoun use, 15–16
   consistency, 17
   sexism (inclusive language), 15–16
possessives, 19
post-hoc fallacy, 196 (see also *logical thinking*)
precise opinion, 69, 97, 99, 106
predicting, 243–244, 258
prepositions (see also *phrase markers; transitions*)
   in adjective clauses, 249–250
   verbs of cause and effect, 208, 211
previewing, 242–243, 258
process description, 33–34, 137–145 (models),
    159 (see also *order, process*)
   Four C's of (chart), 139
   framing essays of, 138–139
   modals in, 142–143 (chart)
   nonsequential vs. sequential transitions, 138,
    156–159
   present perfect in, 153
   verbs for chronological order, 155
   vs. narration, 137, 145 (chart)
process of writing (see *writing process, activities*)
pronouns
   adjective clauses, 213, 219, 248–252, 254–255, 258
   reference and use, 22–25 (chart), 29, 107 (see also
    point of view; point of view, problems with)
proofreading, 33, 40, 66, 247, 258
punctuation (see also *sentences, types of*)
   colon, 102
   commas (see *commas*)
   necessity for, 61–63, 66
   power of the (.), (;), (,) (chart), 63
   quotation marks, 231, 234–237
   run-on sentences, 64, 66
   semicolons, 61–64, 86
purpose, 2, 5, 33–36, 69, 101–102, 135–136

quantity words, 19
question hooks (see *hooks*)
quotation hooks (see *hooks*)
quotations, 223–225, 226–227, 231, 234–239
   direct, 234, 236
   indirect, 236–239

noun clauses, 88, 223–225

references
   first, 223–224, 255, 258
   subsequent, 224–225, 255, 258
refutation hooks (see *hooks*)
relevance (see *unity*)
repetition, 29 (see also *content words; pronouns,
   reference and use*)
responses (respond), 34, 233
restatements (see *paraphrases*)
revising, 33, 40, 66, 242, 247, 258
   related to peer-reviewing, 45–56, 115–118
rhetorical terms, 35–36 (see also *methods*)
run-on sentences, 64, 66

sequential process, 138, 156–157, 159
semicolons, 61–64, 86
sentences, types of, 3, 85–90, 93
   complex, 87–88 (see also *clauses*)
   compound, 85–86
   compound-complex, 90
   simple, 85
sexism (see *point of view, problems with*)
shallow (sophomoric) thinking, 2–3, 77, 80 (see also
   depth of thought)
simplistic (weak) thinking (see *logical thinking*)
situations (see *occasions*)
slang (see *formality, levels of*)
sources, using, 221–239
statement of purpose, 4, 135–136 (model)
study skills
   essay tests, 241–247, 258
   study charts, 31, 166, 177, 194, 242
   time management, 31–32, 66
   writing process, suggested time management,
    40–42, 44, 66
subordinators (clause markers)
   cause, 209
   comparison, 181
   contrast, 184
   effect, 213
   meanings of (chart), 87
   time, 122–123
subtopics (see also *support*)
   essay, 105, 107
   paragraph, 74, 76–78, 93
summaries (summarize), 34, 233–234,
   236, 239
support, 2–3, 35, 93

essay body, 105
essay test answers, 244–247, 258
evaluating subtopics, 74
levels of generality, 75–78, 125
problems with, 77 (chart), 78
pyramid of (chart), 76
sources of, 2–3
time-shifting, past vs. present, 125 (chart), 126
(transitions)
topic limitation, 77–79
synonyms (see *content words*)
synthesis (synthesize), 52, 243, 258

technical discourse (see *formality, levels of*)
tenses
choosing in time clauses, 122–123
modals, 142–143
present perfect in process description, 153
sequence of, indirect quotation, 237
simple past, 123, 125–126
simple present, 122–123, 125–126
time-shifting, 125–126, 237
thesis statements, 2, 101–102
cause, 201
chronological order, 107–108, 138, 156–157
comparison, 162, 180
contrast, 162, 183
effect, 206
enumeration (see *order, familiarity; order, importance*)
focus of (see *academic writing assignments*)
rules for, 101–102
time expressions
chronological order, 132, 151–155
indirect quotation, 237
time-shifting, 126, 237
time lines, 134–135
time management
weekly, 31–32, 66
writing process, suggested time management,
40–42, 44, 66
time shifting (see *support; tenses*)
tone (see *formality, levels of*)
topic limitation, 77–79
topic sentences 2, 69–70, 93, 106–110
cause, 201
chronological order, 107–108, 156–157
comparison, 179
contrast, 183
effect, 207
enumeration, 106, 156–157
essay body, 105–110

focus of (see *academic writing assignments*)
paragraphs, 69–70
transitions, 12
addition, 106, 157
cause/effect, 208–219
chronological development, 132, 137, 151–159
comparison/contrast, 180–181, 183–184
conclusions, 83, 111
enumeration, 106, 157–158 (model)
exemplification, 119–120
paragraph-to-paragraph, 157, 168, 201, 207
spoken vs. formal, 9
time-shifting, 126, 237

unity, 2, 73–83, 101–102

verbs
assignment terms, 33–34
cause, 208
chronological order, 155
contrast, 183
effect, 211
exemplification, 120
modals, 142–143, 237
reporting, 223
vocabulary, 3 (see also *content words*)
voice, active (see also *verbs*)
assignment terms, 33–34
focus in process description, 138
paraphrasing, 227–228, 239
participial phrases, 152–153, 214, 253
tenses, 122–123, 125–126, 137, 145
voice, passive (see also *verbs*)
focus in process description, 138
formation, 150
old idea–new idea, 150
paraphrasing, 227–228
participial phrases, 153–154, 253
Western rhetorical patterns (see *methods*)

writing process, activities 33, 40, 66
essay tests, 242–247, 258
revision and peer-reviewing, 45–56, 115–118